SPECTROSCOPY

SPECTROSCOPY

By

Dr. Shardendu Kislaya

M.Sc., Ph.D., B.Ed.

DISCOVERY PUBLISHING HOUSE PVT. LTD.

NEW DELHI-110 002

Published by:
Tilak Wasan
DISCOVERY PUBLISHING HOUSE PVT. LTD.
4383/4B, Ansari Road, Darya Ganj
New Delhi-110 002 (India)
Phone : +91-11-23279245, 43596064-65
Fax : +91-11-23253475
E-mail : discoverypublishinghouse@gmail.com
sales@discoverypublishinggroup.com
parul.wasan@gmail.com
web : www.discoverypublishinggroup.com

***First Edition:* 2014**

ISBN: 978-93-5056-435-6

Spectroscopy

Printed at:
Dynamic Printers
Delhi

Preface

Spectroscopy was originally the study of the interaction between radiation and matter as a function of wavelength [(λ) lamda). Spectroscopic techniques form the largest and most important single group of techniques used in chemistry. This book takes a tutorial approach to the use of spectroscopic measurement techniques in analytical science, providing immediate guidance and advice to individuals in the course of their work. In fact, historically, spectroscopy referred to the use of visible light dispersed according to its wavelength, e.g. by a prism. Spectrometry is the spectroscopic technique used to assess the concentration or amount of a given chemical (atomic, molecular, or ionic) species. In this case, the instrument that performs such measurements is a spectrometer, spectrophotometer, or spectrograph. Spectroscopy/spectrometry is often used in physical and analytical chemistry for the identification of substances through the spectrum emitted from or absorbed by them.

Atomic spectroscopy is the determination of elemental composition by its electromagnetic or mass spectrum. The study of the electromagnetic spectrum of elements is called Optical Atomic Spectroscopy. Electrons exist in energy levels within an atom. These levels have well defined energies and electrons moving between them must absorb or emit energy equal to the difference between them. In optical spectroscopy, the energy absorbed to move an electron to a more energetic level and/or the energy emitted as the electron moves to a less energetic energy level is in the form of a photon.

Electrons exist in energy levels within an atom. These levels have well defined energies and electrons moving between them must absorb or emit an energy equal to the difference between them. In optical spectroscopy, the energy absorbed to move an electron to a more energetic level and/or the energy emitted as the electron moves to a lower energy level is in the form of a photon (a particle of light). Because this energy is well-defined, an atom's identity can be found by the energy of this transition. The wavelength of light can be related to its energy. It is usually easier to measure the wavelength of light than to directly measure its energy.

Spectroscopy is the use of the absorption, emission, or scattering of electromagnetic radiation by atoms or molecules (or atomic or molecular ions) to qualitatively or quantitatively study the atoms or molecules, or to study physical processes. The interaction of radiation with matter can cause redirection of the radiation and/or transitions between the energy levels of the atoms or molecules. A transition from a lower level to a higher level with transfer of energy from the radiation field to the atom or molecule is called absorption. A transition from a higher level to a lower level is called emission if energy is transfered to the radiation field, or nonradiative decay if no radiation is emitted. Redirection of light due to its interaction with matter is called scattering, and may or may not occur with transfer of energy, i.e., the scattered radiation has a slightly different or the same wavelength.

The formulae for hydrogenic spectrum including the account of Lamb shift are written in simple analytical form. The book is of interest to specialists, graduate and postgraduate students, who are involved into the experimental and theoretical research in the field of modern atomic spectroscopy.

—Author

Contents

1

Introduction

Spectroscopy is a technique that uses the interaction of energy with a sample to perform an analysis.

SPECTRUM

The data that are obtained from spectroscopy are called a spectrum. A spectrum is a plot of the intensity of energy detected versus the wavelength (or mass or momentum or frequency, etc.) of the energy.

SPECTRUM OBTAINED

A spectrum can be used to obtain information about atomic and molecular energy levels, molecular geometries, chemical bonds, interactions of molecules, and related processes. Often, spectra are used to identify the components of a sample (qualitative analysis). Spectra may also be used to measure the amount of material in a sample (quantitative analysis).

Instruments

There are several instruments that are used to perform a spectroscopic analysis. In simplest terms, spectroscopy requires an energy source (commonly a laser, but this could be an ion source or radiation source) and a device for measuring the change in the energy source after it has interacted with the sample (often a spectrophotometer or interferometer).

SOME TYPES OF SPECTROSCOPY

There are as many different types of spectroscopy as there are energy sources. Here are some examples:

Astronomical Spectroscopy

Energy from celestial objects is used to analyse their chemical composition, density, pressure, temperature, magnetic fields, velocity, and other characteristics. There are many energy types (spectroscopies) that may be used in astronomical spectroscopy.

Atomic Absorption Spectroscopy

Energy absorbed by the sample is used to assess its characteristics. Sometimes absorbed energy causes light to be released from the sample, which may be measured by a technique such as fluorescence spectroscopy.

Attenuated Total Reflectance Spectroscopy

This is the study of substances in thin films or on surfaces. The sample is penetrated by an energy beam one or more times and the reflected energy is analysed. Attenuated total reflectance spectroscopy and the related technique called frustrated multiple internal reflection spectroscopy are used to analyse coatings and opaque liquids.

Electron Paramagnetic Spectroscopy

This is a microwave technique based on splitting electronic energy fields in a magnetic field. It is used to determine structures of samples containing unpaired electrons.

Electron Spectroscopy

There are several types of electron spectroscopy, all associated with measuring changes in electronic energy levels.

Fourier Transform Spectrosopy

This is a family of spectroscopic techniques in which the sample is irradiated by all relevant wavelengths simultaneously for a short period of time. The absorption spectrum is obtained by applying a mathematical analysis to the resulting energy pattern.

Gamma-ray Spectroscopy

Gamma radiation is the energy source in this type of spectroscopy, which includes activation analysis and Mossbauer spectroscopy.

Infrared Spectroscopy

The infrared absorption spectrum of a substance is sometimes called its molecular fingerprint. Although frequently used to identify materials, infrared spectroscopy also may be used to quantify the number of absorbing molecules.

Laser Spectroscopy

Absorption spectroscopy, fluorescence spectroscopy, Raman spectroscopy, and surface-enhanced Raman spectroscopy commonly use laser light as an energy source. Laser spectroscopies provide information about the interaction of coherent light with matter. Laser spectrocopy generally has high resolution and sensitivity.

Mass Spectrometry

A mass spectrometer source produces ions. Information about a sample may be obtained by analysing the dispersion of ions when they interact with the sample, generally using the mass-to-charge ratio.

Multiplex or Frequency-Modulated Spectroscopy

In this type of spectroscopy, each optical wavelength that is recorded is encoded with an audio frequency containing the original wavelength information. A wavelength analyser can then reconstruct the original spectrum.

Raman Spectroscopy

Raman scattering of light by molecules may be used to provide information on a sample's chemical composition and molecular structure.

X-ray Spectroscopy

This technique involves excitation of inner electrons of atoms, which may be seen as x-ray absorption. An x-ray fluorescence emission spectrum may be produced when an electron falls from a higher energy state into the vacancy created by the absorbed energy.

SPECTROSCOPY PERTAINS

Spectroscopy pertains to the dispersion of an object's light into its component colours (*i.e.,* energies). By performing this dissection and analysis of an object's light, astronomers can infer the physical properties of that object (such as temperature, mass, luminosity and composition).

But before we hurtle headlong into the wild and woolly field of spectroscopy, we need to try to answer some seemingly simple questions, such as *what is light*? And *how does it behave*? These questions may seem simple to you, but they have presented some of the most difficult conceptual challenges in the long history of physics. It has only been in this century, with the creation of quantum mechanics that we have gained a quantitative understanding of how light and atoms work. The questions we pose are not always easy, but to understand and solve them will unlock a new way of looking at our Universe.

THE NATURE OF LIGHT

To understand the processes in astronomy that generate light, we must realise first that *light acts like a wave*. Light has particle-like properties too, so it's actually quite a twisted beast (which is why it took so many years to figure out). But right now, let's just explore light as a wave.

Picture yourself wading around on an ocean beach for a moment, and watch the many water waves sweeping past you. Waves are disturbances, ripples on the water, and they possess a certain height (*amplitude*), with a certain number of waves rushing past you every minute (the *frequency*) and all moving at a characteristic speed across the water (the *wave speed*).

Notice the distance between successive waves? That's called the wavelength.

Keeping this analogy in mind, let's leave the ocean beach for a while and think about light like a wave. The wave speed of a light wave is simply the speed of light, and different wavelengths of light manifest themselves as different colours! The energy of a light wave is inversely-proportional to its wavelength; in other words, low-energy waves have long wavelengths, and high-energy light waves have short wavelengths.

THE ELECTROMAGNETIC SPECTRUM

Physicists classify light waves by their energies (wavelengths). Labeled in increasing energy, we might draw the entire electromagnetic spectrum as shown in the figure below:

THE ELECTROMAGNETIC SPECTRUM

Notice how small the visible region of the spectrum is, compared to the entire range of wavelengths. Notice that radio, TV, and microwave signals are all light waves, they simply lie at wavelengths (energies) that your eye doesn't respond to. On the other end of the scale, beware the high energy UV, x-ray, and gamma-ray photons! Each one carries a lot of energy compared to their visible- and radio-wave brethren. They're the reasons you should wear sunblock, for example.

When we look at the Universe in a different "light", *i.e.*, at "non-visible" wavelengths, we probe different kinds of physical conditions — and we can see new kinds of objects! For example, high-energy gamma-ray and X-ray telescopes tend to see the most energetic dynamos in the cosmos, such as active galaxies, the remnants from massive dying stars, accretion of matter around black holes, and so forth. Visible light telescopes best probe light produced by stars. Longer-wavelength telescopes best probe dark, cool, obscured structures in the Universe: dusty star-forming regions, dark cold molecular clouds, the primordial radiation emitted by the formation of the Universe shortly after the Big Bang. Only through studying astronomical objects at many different wavelengths are astronomers able to piece together a coherent, comprehensive picture of how the Universe works!

GENERAL TYPES OF SPECTRA

Typically one can observe two distinctive classes of spectra: continous and discrete. For a continuous spectrum, the light is composed of a wide, continuous range of colours (energies). With discrete spectra, one sees only bright or dark lines at very distinct and sharply-defined colours (energies). As we'll discover shortly, discrete spectra with bright lines are called *emission* spectra, those with dark lines are termed *absorption* spectra.

CONTINUOUS SPECTRA

Continuous spectra arise from dense gases or solid objects which radiate their heat away through the production of light. Such objects emit light over a broad range of wavelengths, thus the apparent spectrum seems smooth and continuous. Stars emit light in a *predominantly* (but not completely!) continuous spectrum.

Other examples of such objects are incandescent light bulbs, electric cooking stove burners, flames, cooling fire embers. Yes, you, right this minute, are emitting a continuous spectrum — but the light waves you're emitting are not visible — they lie at infrared wavelengths (*i.e.*, lower energies, and longer wavelengths than even red light). If you had infrared-sensitive eyes, you could see people by the continuous radiation they emit!

DISCRETE SPECTRA

Discrete spectra are the observable result of the physics of atoms. There are two types of discrete spectra, emission (bright line spectra) and absorption (dark line spectra). Let's try to understand where these two types of discrete spectra.

Emission Line Spectra

Unlike a continuous spectrum source, which can have any energy it wants (all you have to do is change the temperature), the electron clouds surrounding the nuclei of atoms can have only very specific energies dictated by quantum mechanics. Each element on the periodic table has its own set of possible energy levels, and with few exceptions the levels are distinct and identifiable.

Atoms will also tend to settle to the lowest energy level (in spectroscopist's lingo, this is called the *ground state*). This means that an excited atom in a higher energy level must 'dump' some energy. The way an atom 'dumps' that energy is by emitting a wave of light with that *exact* energy.

A hydrogen atom drops from the 2nd energy level to the 1st, giving off a wave of light with an energy equal to the difference of energy between levels 2 and 1. This energy corresponds to a specific colour, or wavelength of light — and thus we see a bright line at that exact wavelength an emission spectrum is born.

Tiny changes of energy in an atom generate photons with small energies and long wavelengths, such as radio waves! Similarly, large changes of energy in an atom will mean that high-energy, short-wavelength photons (UV, X-ray, gamma-rays) are emitted.

Absorption Line Spectra

On the other hand, what would happen if we tried to reverse this process? That is, what would happen if we fired this special photon back into a ground state atom? That's right, the atom could absorb that 'specially-energetic' photon and would become excited, jumping from the ground state to a higher energy level. If a star with a 'continuous' spectrum is shining upon an atom, the wavelengths corresponding to possible energy transitions within that atom will be absorbed and therefore an observer will not see them.

SPECTROMETER WORK

Many people know how a telescope works, but relatively few have much experience with the innards of a spectrometer. So let's take apart the Astronomy Camp spectrometer to see how it works! Keep in mind that there are as many optical designs for spectrometers as there are optical designs for telescopes, and that this is but one example. Nevertheless, it points out the salient features of most optical spectrometers.

It all starts with the telescope light beam entering the spectrometer. The focal point of the telescope beam is brought to the *slit* of the spectrometer. This slit is what is ultimately imaged on the detector. In the case of the Camp spectrometer, the slit is arranged at an angle and the slit surroundings are silvered so that the portion of the telescope beam not passing through the slit can be routed instead to an eyepiece for easy telescope guiding.

The light passing through the slit then is reflected off a collimating mirror, which parallelises the beam of light, before sending it off to the diffraction grating! This optical element disperses the parallel beams of light into their component colours/wavelengths/energies. Each different wavelength comes off of the grating at a slightly different angle. So now, we have an image of the slit that is spread out like a rainbow by colour.

This new colour-dispersed beam of light is then focused and imaged on the detector by the *camera lens*. A 35 mm camera is the detector in this diagram, but at Camp, we typically use an eyepiece or a CCD array.

There is something interesting to note here — in spectroscopy, we are not looking at ALL of the light from an object, just a certain "band" of wavelengths or colours. Furthermore, even that band is dispersed ("smeared out") over the entire detector. This means that the effective brightness, or surface brightness of an object on the detector is much lower than when simply taking images of an object. This means that it takes a bigger telescope and/or more integration time to get a good spectrum of a given object than an image.

The broader you disperse the light and the narrower you make the slit, the better your spectral resolution; you can see finer and more subtle features in the spectrum. However, there is a stiff price to pay: the emergent spectrum becomes much dimmer and more diffuse. High resolution spectroscopy therefore requires large telescopes and fairly bright objects. For very faint objects, some spectral resolution often must be compromised to even see the object.

PROBING THE FORMATION OF STARS IN COLLIDING GALAXIES

Billions of years ago, when our galaxy took form, it is thought that there must have been an epoch of rapid star-forming activity that has since subsided. We can get clues to how this may have looked by observing galaxies currently exhibiting violent, extreme star-formation. Such "starburst" galaxies are studied best in the infrared and at radio wavelengths, since star-forming galaxies often harbour so much dust and gas that visible light cannot penetrate to the centers where the majority of the star formation is taking place. Below is an infrared (2.0–2.5 microns wavelength, or 20,000 - 25,000 Angstroms) spectrum of two such starburst galaxies. Most of the features you see are from molecular hydrogen, H_2, the stuff from which stars are made! These molecular hydrogen emission lines tell us that the molecular gas we see is very warm; in the top galaxy, the gas is excited by shock-heated gas. The bottom galaxy has molecular hydrogen excited by ultraviolet light emitted from recently-formed young, hot stars.

Uncovering the Mystery of Quasars

The distant nature of quasars were discovered in the early 1960's, when spectral lines were noted to be substantially-shifted *redder* than they should normally be. This *redshift* can be attributed to the recession (speeding away) of quasars from us. In the standard Big Bang model of cosmology (the faster it's speeding away from you, the more distant it is), this rapid motion implies that quasars are the most distant objects known.

The wavelength scale has been rescaled to the "appropriate" rest wavelengths for the spectral lines. The most noticeable feature is the broad emission line at 1216 Angstroms due to hydrogen atoms making the transition from the first excited state to the ground state. Although 1216 Angstroms lies deep in the ultraviolet, where the Earth's atmosphere is opaque, many quasars are receding from us so fast, this line is redshifted into the visible part of the spectrum (4000-7000 Angstroms).

Spectroscopy at Astronomy Camp

Spectroscopy at Astronomy Camp is done with a spectrograph from Optomechanics Research Inc, coupled with the Mount Lemmon 40" or 60" telescopes and the Camp's SBIG ST6 CCD detector array. With relatively short exposure times, good quality spectra can be taken of most catalogued stars and high surface-brightness deep-sky objects.

Light Pollution Filters Work

Astronomy Camp's spectrograph was mounted on the Mount Lemmon 60" telescope with the same ST6 CCD. The slit length is about 8 arcminutes long and 1 arcsecond wide; the representation of the slit width in the diagram is exaggerated.

We combined four 5-minute exposures on the Ring Nebula using the 60" and the ST6 camera. We subtracted an appropriate 5 minute dark frame from each image and then combined the images using IRAF. The resulting ST6 image follows: the dispersion (wavelength) axis is horizontal, and the spatial axis (along the Ring Nebula) is vertical. The central lines are M57, the upper and lower spikes are the calibration lamp spectra (Hg+He).

We make a 1-D spectrum from the 2-D image by summing over the aperture of the slit covering M57. Using the well-characterised wavelengths of the calibration lamps, we can use IRAF to register our spectrum to provide a nice wavelength scale. Here's what our spectrum looks like once plotted as intensity versus wavelength.

The emission line at 4861 Angstroms comes from hot, excited atomic hydrogen. Highly-excited hydrogen atoms in M57's gaseous shell, starting in energy level 4, may eventually de-excite to level 2, giving up the energy difference in waves of light at that particular energy (and... they have a wavelength of 4861 Angstroms!).

The brightest two lines at 4959 and 5007 Angstroms come from twice-ionised oxygen (labeled O^{++}, or O III in spectroscopic notation). This means that two of oxygen's eight electrons have been ripped away. This is a also clue that conditions in this nebula must be harsh. In fact, these lines can only be excited to emit light in temperatures of several thousand Kelvins and rather thin densities of 1-100 atoms per cubic centimeter.

There is no continuous spectrum here – this points out the important fact that planetary nebulae are hot rarified gases. This also points out how astronomers can get valuable information about the physical conditions and important processes in distant astronomical objects.

This spectrum also demonstrates why you can use light-pollution filters (like those made by Lumicon or Orion) to get great contrast from reflection/emission nebulae! These filters pass light waves that lie at wavelengths covered by these three lines, but block light at all other wavelengths. For nebulae, this is very beneficial since they only emit visible light in this wavelength range.

You can remove all that ugly skyglow and light pollution without reducing the brighness of the nebula you're looking for. Would such a narrow-band filter be good for looking at stars or galaxies? Hmm?

STELLAR SPECTROSCOPY

A Look at Sirius

Now, onto stellar spectroscopy. This ½ second exposure of Sirius is centered near 4000 Angstroms (blue, near-ultraviolet) and clearly shows a series of deep absorption lines. These lines are due to the hydrogen atom. Let's explore how.

In the cooler outer "atmosphere" around Sirius, mildly excited hydrogen atoms in the 2nd energy level (the 1st excited state) are 'zapped' by photons (light waves) with just the right energy to send them to even higher excited states. We match the dark absorption line that results from each transition upward in the hydrogen atom.

Notice that the higher-energy transitions on the left result in higher energy absorption lines out in the ultraviolet. This series of lines, starting from level 2, is called the Balmer series after their discoverer.

Stars are classified by their temperatures, which can be determined by the star's spectral features. The hottest stars are termed O-stars, the next cooler are B stars, then A, F, G, K, and finally M-stars. Sirius is a relatively hot A-type star at about 10,000 degrees Kelvin. Such stars have the strongest hydrogen-features (simply due to temperature — cooler stars can't 'zap' the hydrogen atoms as effectively, and hotter stars will destroy/ionise the hydrogen atoms that create the spectral lines!).

Molecules in Cool Stars!

On the other end of the scale - here is Delta Virgo; a cool M3-type giant star at about 3,500 K and viewed at about 6000 Angstroms (in red light). Note a bright continuum at far left, which suddenly dims into a series of striations (bands). These don't look like the sharp absorption lines of the hydrogen atom, do they? In fact, these bands are due to Molecules that can live in the atmospheres of these cool stars! This particular molecule is TiO (titanium oxide). Molecules have a dizzying number of lines because they not only have the electron energy levels like atoms, but also have energy sublevels due to the rotation and vibration of the molecule! At the modest resolution of our spectrometer, these hundreds of lines are blended into absorption bands.

Stars Like Our Sun

Somewhere between hotter A-type stars and cool M-class stars are stars like our sun, around 5500 degrees Kelvin. Here's Beta-Bootes, a G8 giant star (roughly what our sun will be when it begins dying in about 5 billion years). The first spectrum is at 5500 Angstroms (yellow light), just like the M-star spectrum above. Notice that molecules don't form here (it's too hot for molecules to readily form without being quickly destroyed), but there are still an awful lot of lines around. Most of these features are due to heavy elements - things like carbon (in several ionisation stages), iron, oxygen, magnesium, calcium, etc.

This is a spectrum of the same star, but now taken at 4000 Angstroms (deep blue-violet light). The deep absorption lines at left are due to the ion Calcium II (the difference between this and normal, neutral calcium is that one electron has been stripped off here). The small dip in the middle is due to a blend of metallic features and hydrogen. Notice that the hydrogen lines are very weak here - nothing at all like Sirius (a hotter A-class star).

CLASSIFICATION OF METHODS

Spectroscopy is a sufficiently broad field that many sub-disciplines exist, each with numerous implementations of specific spectroscopic techniques. The various implementations and techniques can be classified in several ways.

TYPE OF RADIATIVE ENERGY

Types of spectroscopy are distinguished by the type of radiative energy involved in the interaction. In many applications, the spectrum is determined by measuring changes in the intensity or frequency of this energy.

The types of radiative energy studied include:

- Electromagnetic radiation was the first source of energy used for spectroscopic studies. Techniques that employ electromagnetic radiation are typically classified by the wavelength region of the spectrum and include microwave, terahertz, infrared, near infrared, visible and ultraviolet, x-ray and gamma spectroscopy.
- Particles, due to their de Broglie wavelength, can also be a source of radiative energy and both electrons and neutrons are commonly used. For a particle, its kinetic energy determines its wavelength.
- Acoustic spectroscopy involves radiated pressure waves.
- Mechanical methods can be employed to impart radiating energy, similar to acoustic waves, to solid materials.

Nature of the Interaction

Types of spectroscopy can also be distinguished by the nature of the interaction between the energy and the material.

These interactions include:

- Absorption occurs when energy from the radiative source is absorbed by the material. Absorption is often determined by measuring the fraction of energy transmitted through the material; absorption will decrease the transmitted portion.
- Emission indicates that radiative energy is released by the material. A material's blackbody spectrum is a spontaneous emission spectrum determined by its temperature. Emission can also be induced by other sources of energy such as flames or sparks or electromagnetic radiation in the case of fluorescence.
- Elastic scattering and reflection spectroscopy determine how incident radiation is reflected or scattered by a material. Crystallography employs the scattering of high energy radiation, such as x-rays and electrons, to examine the arrangement of atoms in proteins and solid crystals.
- Impedance spectroscopy studies the ability of a medium to impede or slow the transmittance of energy. For optical applications, this is characterised by the index of refraction.
- Inelastic scattering phenomena involve an exchange of energy between the radiation and the matter that shifts the wavelength of the scattered radiation. These include Raman and Compton scattering.
- Coherent or resonance spectroscopy are techniques where the radiative energy couples two quantum states of the material in a coherent interaction that is sustained by the radiating field. The coherence can be disrupted by other interactions, such as particle collisions and energy transfer, and so often require high intensity radiation to be sustained. Nuclear magnetic resonance (NMR) spectroscopy is a widely

used resonance method and ultrafast laser methods are also now possible in the infrared and visible spectral regions.

TYPE OF MATERIAL

Spectroscopic studies are designed so that the radiant energy interacts with specific types of matter.

Atoms

Atomic spectroscopy was the first application of spectroscopy developed. Atomic absorption spectroscopy (AAS) and atomic emission spectroscopy (AES) involve visible and ultraviolet light. These absorptions and emissions, often referred to as atomic spectral lines, are due to electronic transitions of an outer shell electron to an excited state. Atoms also have distinct x-ray spectra that are attributable to the excitation of inner shell electrons to excited states.

Atoms of different elements have distinct spectra and therefore atomic spectroscopy allows for the identification and quantitation of a sample's elemental composition. Robert Bunsen, developer of the Bunsen burner, and Gustav Kirchhoff discovered new elements by observing their emission spectra. Atomic absorption lines are observed in the solar spectrum and referred to as Fraunhofer lines after their discoverer. A comprehensive explanation of the hydrogen spectrum was an early success of quantum mechanics and explaining the Lamb shift observed in the hydrogen spectrum led to the development of quantum electrodynamics.

Modern implementations of atomic spectroscopy for studying visible and ultraviolet transitions include flame emission spectroscopy, inductively coupled plasma atomic emission spectroscopy, glow discharge spectroscopy, microwave induced plasma spectroscopy, and spark or arc emission spectroscopy. Techniques for studying x-ray spectra include X-ray spectroscopy and X-ray fluorescence (XRF).

Molecules

The combination of atoms into molecules leads to the creation of unique types of energetic states and therefore unique spectra of the transitions between these states. Molecular spectra can be obtained due to electron spin states (electron paramagnetic resonance), molecular rotations, molecular vibration and electronic states. Rotations are collective motions of the atomic nuclei and typically lead to spectra in the microwave and millimeter-wave spectral regions; rotational spectroscopy and microwave spectroscopy are synonymous. Vibrations are relative motions of the atomic nuclei and are studied by both infrared and Raman spectroscopy. Electronic excitations are studied using visible and ultraviolet spectroscopy as well as fluorescence spectroscopy.

Studies in molecular spectroscopy led to the development of the first maser and contributed to the subsequent development of the laser.

Crystals and Extended Materials

The combination of atoms or molecules into crystals or other extended forms leads to the creation of additional energetic states. These states are numerous and therefore have a high density of states. This high density often makes the spectra weaker and less distinct, *i.e.,* broader. For instance, blackbody radiation is due to the thermal motions of atoms and molecules within a material. Acoustic and mechanical responses are due to collective motions as well.

Pure crystals, though, can have distinct spectral transitions and the crystal arrangement also has an effect on the observed molecular spectra. The regular lattice structure of crystals also scatters X-rays, electrons or neutrons allowing for crystallographic studies.

Nuclei

Nuclei also have distinct energy states that are widely separated and lead to gamma ray spectra. Distinct nuclear spin states can have their energy separated by a magnetic field, and this allows for NMR spectroscopy.

2

Electromagnetic Spectrum

The electromagnetic spectrum covers a wide range of wavelengths and photon energies. Light used to "see" an object must have a wavelength about the same size as or smaller than the object. The ALS generates light in the far ultraviolet and soft x-ray regions, which span the wavelengths suited to studying molecules and atoms.

MEASURING THE ELECTROMAGNETIC SPECTRUM

You actually know more about it than you may think! The electromagnetic (EM) spectrum is just a name that scientists give a bunch of types of radiation when they want to talk about them as a group. Radiation is energy that travels and spreads out as it goes— visible light that comes from a lamp in your house and radio waves that come from a radio station are two types of electromagnetic radiation. Other examples of EM radiation are microwaves, infrared and ultraviolet light, X-rays and gamma-rays. Hotter, more energetic objects and events create higher energy radiation than cool objects. Only extremely hot objects or particles moving at very high velocities can create high-energy radiation like X-rays and gamma-rays.

Here are the different types of radiation in the EM spectrum, in order from lowest energy to highest:

- *Radio:* This is the same kind of energy that radio stations emit into the air for your boom box to capture and turn into your favourite Mozart, Madonna, or Justin Timberlake tunes. But radio waves are also emitted by other things such as stars and gases in space. You may not be able to dance to what these objects emit, but you can use it to learn what they are made of.

- *Microwaves:* They will cook your popcorn in just a few minutes! Microwaves in space are used by astronomers to learn about the structure of nearby galaxies, and our own Milky Way!
- *Infrared:* Our skin emits infrared light, which is why we can be seen in the dark by someone using night vision goggles. In space, IR light maps the dust between stars.
- *Visible:* Yes, this is the part that our eyes see. Visible radiation is emitted by everything from fireflies to light bulbs to stars... also by fast-moving particles hitting other particles.
- *Ultraviolet:* We know that the Sun is a source of ultraviolet (or UV) radiation, because it is the UV rays that cause our skin to burn! Stars and other "hot" objects in space emit UV radiation.
- X-rays: Your doctor uses them to look at your bones and your dentist to look at your teeth. Hot gases in the Universe also emit X-rays.
- *Gamma-rays:* Radioactive materials (some natural and others made by man in things like nuclear power plants) can emit gamma-rays. Big particle accelerators that scientists use to help them understand what matter is made of can sometimes generate gamma-rays. But the biggest gamma-ray generator of all is the Universe! It makes gamma radiation in all kinds of ways.

A RADIO WAVE IS NOT A GAMMA-RAY

We may think that radio waves are completely different physical objects or events than gamma-rays. They are produced in very different ways, and we detect them in different ways. But are they really different things? The answer is 'no'. Radio waves, visible light, X-rays, and all the other parts of the electromagnetic spectrum are fundamentally the same thing. They are all electromagnetic radiation.

Electromagnetic radiation can be described in terms of a stream of photons, which are massless particles each traveling in a wave-like pattern and moving at the speed of light. Each photon contains a certain amount (or bundle) of energy, and all electromagnetic radiation consists of these photons. The only difference between the various types of electromagnetic radiation is the amount of energy found in the photons. Radio waves have photons with low energies, microwaves have a little more energy than radio waves, infrared has still more, then visible, ultraviolet, X-rays, and the most energetic of all gamma-rays.

Actually, the electromagnetic spectrum can be expressed in terms of energy, wavelength, or frequency. Each way of thinking about the EM spectrum is related to the others in a precise mathematical way. So why do we have three ways of describing things, each with a different set of physical units? After all, frequency is measured in cycles per second (which is called a Hertz), wavelength is measured in meters, and energy is measured in electron volts.

The answer is that scientists don't like to use big numbers when they don't have to. It is much easier to say or write "two kilometers or 2 km" than "two thousand meters or 2,000 m". So generally, scientists use whatever units are easiest for whatever they are working with.

In radio astronomy, astronomers tend to use wavelengths or frequencies. This is because most of the radio part of the EM spectrum falls in the range from about 1 cm to 1 km (30 gigahertz (GHz) to 100 kilohertz (kHz)). The radio is a very broad part of the EM spectrum. Infrared astronomers also use wavelength to describe their part of the EM spectrum. They tend to use microns (or millionths of meters) for wavelengths, so that they can say their part of the EM spectrum falls in the range 1 to 100 microns.

Optical astronomers use wavelengths as well. Scientists use both angstroms (0.00000001 cm, or 10^{-8} cm in scientific notation) and nanometers (0.0000001, or 10^{-7}, cm). In the newer "SI" version of the metric system, we think of visible light in units of nanometers or 0.000000001 meters (10^{-9} m). In this system, the violet, blue, green, yellow, orange, and red light we know so well has wavelengths between 400 and 700 nanometers.

This range is only a small part of the entire EM spectrum, so you can tell that the light we see is just a little fraction of all the EM radiation around us! By the time you get to the ultraviolet, X-ray, and gamma-ray regions of the EM spectrum, lengths have become too tiny to think about any more. So scientists usually refer to these photons by their energies, which are measured in electron volts. Ultraviolet radiation falls in the range from a few electron volts (eV) to about 100 eV. X-ray photons have energies in the range 100 eV to 100,000 eV (or 100 keV). Gamma-rays then are all the photons with energies greater than 100 keV.

ELECTROMAGNETIC SPECTRUM DISCOVERY

For most of history, light was the only known part of the electromagnetic spectrum. The ancient Greeks recognised that light travelled in straight lines and studied some of the properties of it, including reflection and refraction. Over the years the study of light continued and during the 16th and 17th centuries there were conflicting theories which regarded light as either a wave or a particle.

The first discovery of electromagnetic waves other than light came in 1800, when William Herschel discovered infrared light. He was studying the temperature of different colours by moving a thermometer through light split by a prism. He noticed that the hottest temperature was beyond red. He theorised that there was 'light' that you could not see. The next year, Johann Ritter worked at the other end of the spectrum and noticed that there were 'chemical rays' that behaved similar to, but were beyond, visible violet light rays. They were later renamed ultraviolet radiation.

Electromagnetic radiation had been first linked to electromagnetism in 1845, when Michael Faraday noticed that the polarisation of light traveling through a transparent material responded to a magnetic field. During the 1860s James Maxwell developed four partial differential equations for the electromagnetic field. Two of these equations predicted the possibility of, and behavior of, waves in the field. Analising the speed of these theoretical waves, Maxwell realised that they must travel at a speed that was about the known speed of light.

Maxwell's equations predicted many frequencies of electromagnetic waves traveling at the speed of light. Attempting to prove Maxwell's equations, in 1886 Heinrich Hertz built an apparatus to generate and detect what we now call radio waves. He was able to observe that they traveled at the speed of light and could be both reflected and refracted. In a later experiment he similarly produced and measured microwaves. These new waves paved the way for inventions such as the wireless telegraph and the radio.

In 1895 Wilhelm Röntgen noticed a new type of radiation emitted during an experiment. He called these X-rays and found they were able to travel through parts of the human body but were reflected or stopped by denser matter such as bones. Before long, many uses were found for them in the field of medicine.

The last portion of the electromagnetic spectrum was filled in with the discovery of gamma rays. In 1900 Paul Villard was studying radioactivity from radium. He found a new type of radiation that he first thought consisted of particles similar to alpha and beta particles, but far more penetrating. However, in 1910 British physicist William Henry Bragg demonstrated that gamma rays are electromagnetic radiation, not particles, and in 1914, Ernest Rutherford (who had named them gamma rays) and Edward Andrade measured their wavelengths, and found that they were similar to X-rays but with shorter wavelengths and higher frequency, and thus more energy per photon.

RANGE OF THE SPECTRUM

Electromagnetic waves are typically described by any of the following three physical properties: the frequency f, wavelength λ, or photon energy E. Frequencies range from 2.4×10^{23} Hz (1 GeV gamma rays) down to the local plasma frequency of the ionised interstellar medium (~1 kHz).

Wavelength is inversely proportional to the wave frequency, so gamma rays have very short wavelengths that are fractions of the size of atoms, whereas wavelengths can be as long as the universe. Photon energy is directly proportional to the wave frequency, so gamma rays have the highest energy (around a billion electron volts) and radio waves have very low energy (around a femtoelectronvolt). These relations are illustrated by the following equations:

$$f=\frac{c}{\lambda}, \text{or } f=\frac{E}{h}, \text{or } E=\frac{hc}{\lambda},$$

where:

- c = 299, 792, 458 m/s is the speed of light in vacuum and
- $h = 6.62606896(33) \times 10^{-34}$ J s $= 4.13566733(10)\times10^{-15}$ eV s is Planck's constant.

Whenever electromagnetic waves exist in a medium with matter, their wavelength is decreased. Wavelengths of electromagnetic radiation, no matter what medium they are traveling through, are usually quoted in terms of the vacuum wavelength, although this is not always explicitly stated.

Generally, electromagnetic radiation is classified by wavelength into radio wave, microwave, terahertz (or sub-millimeter) radiation, infrared, the visible region we perceive as light, ultraviolet, X-rays and gamma rays. The behavior of EM radiation depends on its wavelength. When EM radiation interacts with single atoms and molecules, its behavior also depends on the amount of energy per quantum (photon) it carries.

Spectroscopy can detect a much wider region of the EM spectrum than the visible range of 400 nm to 700 nm. A common laboratory spectroscope can detect wavelengths from 2 nm to 2500 nm. Spectroscopes are widely used in astrophysics. For example, many hydrogen atoms emit a radio wave photon that has a wavelength of 21.12 cm. Also, frequencies of 30 Hz and below can be produced by and are important in the study of certain stellar nebulae and frequencies as high as 2.9×10^{27} Hz have been detected from astrophysical sources.

Rationale

Electromagnetic radiation interacts with matter in different ways in different parts of the spectrum. The types of interaction can be so different that it seems to be justified to refer to different types of radiation. At the same time, there is a continuum containing all these "different kinds" of electromagnetic radiation. Thus we refer to a spectrum, but divide it up based on the different interactions with matter.

Table 2.1

Region of the Spectrum	Main Interactions with Matter
Radio	Collective oscillation of charge carriers in bulk material (plasma oscillation). An example would be the oscillation of the electrons in an antenna.
Microwave through far infrared	Plasma oscillation, molecular rotation
Near infrared	Molecular vibration, plasma oscillation (in metals only)
Visible	Molecular electron excitation (including pigment molecules found in the human retina), plasma oscillations (in metals only)
Ultraviolet	Excitation of molecular and atomic valence electrons, including ejection of the electrons (photoelectric effect)
X-rays	Excitation and ejection of core atomic electrons, Compton scattering (for low atomic numbers)
Gamma rays	Energetic ejection of core electrons in heavy elements, Compton scattering (for all atomic numbers), excitation of atomic nuclei, including dissociation of nuclei
High-energy gamma rays	Creation of particle-antiparticle pairs. At very high energies a single photon can create a shower of high-energy particles and antiparticles upon interaction with matter.

TYPES OF RADIATION

Boundaries

The regions (or bands or types) of the electromagnetic spectrum. Note that there are no precisely defined boundaries between the bands of the electromagnetic spectrum; rather they fade into each other like the bands in a rainbow (which is the sub-spectrum of visible light). Radiation of each frequency and wavelength (or in each band) will have a mixture of properties of two regions of the spectrum that bound it. For example, red light resembles infrared radiation in that it can resonate some chemical bonds.

Regions of the Spectrum

The types of electromagnetic radiation are broadly classified into the following classes:

- Gamma radiation
- X-ray radiation
- Ultraviolet radiation
- Visible radiation
- Infrared radiation
- Microwave radiation
- Radio waves.

This classification goes in the increasing order of wavelength, which is characteristic of the type of radiation. While, in general, the classification scheme is accurate, in reality there is often some overlap between neighbouring types of electromagnetic energy. For example, SLF radio waves at 60 Hz may be received and studied by astronomers, or may be ducted along wires as electric power, although the latter is, in the strict sense, not electromagnetic radiation at all.

The distinction between X-rays and gamma rays is partly based on sources: the photons generated from nuclear decay or other nuclear and subnuclear/particle process, are always termed gamma rays, whereas X-rays are generated by electronic transitions involving highly energetic inner atomic electrons.In general, nuclear transitions are much more energetic than electronic transitions, so gamma-rays are more energetic than X-rays, but exceptions exist. By analogy to electronic transitions, muonic atom transitions are also said to produce X-rays, even though their energy may exceed 6 megaelectronvolts (0.96 pJ), whereas there are many [77 known to be less than 10 keV (1.6 fJ)] low-energy nuclear transitions (*e.g.*, the 7.6 eV (1.22 aJ) nuclear transition of thorium-229), and, despite being one million-fold less energetic than some muonic X-rays, the emitted photons are still called gamma rays due to their nuclear origin.

The convention that EM radiation that is known to come from the nucleus, is always called "gamma ray" radiation is the only convention that is universally respected, however. Many astronomical gamma ray sources (such as gamma ray bursts are known to be too energetic (in both intensity and wavelength) to be of nuclear origin. Quite often, in high energy physics and in medical radiotherapy, very high energy EMR (in the >10 MeV region) which is of higher energy than any nuclear gamma ray, is not referred to as either X-ray or gamma-ray, but instead by the generic term of "high energy photons."

The region of the spectrum in which a particular observed electromagnetic radiation falls, is reference frame-dependent (due to the Doppler shift for light), so EM radiation that one observer would say is in one region of the spectrum could appear to an observer moving at a substantial fraction of the speed of light with respect to the first to be in another part of the spectrum. For example, consider the cosmic microwave background. It was produced, when matter and radiation decoupled, by the de-excitation of hydrogen atoms to the ground state.

These photons were from Lyman series transitions, putting them in the ultraviolet (UV) part of the electromagnetic spectrum. Now this radiation has undergone enough cosmological red shift to put it into the microwave region of the spectrum for observers moving slowly (compared to the speed of light) with respect to the cosmos. However, for particles moving near the speed of light, this radiation will be blue-shifted in their rest frame. The highest-energy cosmic ray protons are moving such that, in their rest frame, this radiation is blueshifted to high-energy gamma rays, which interact with the proton to produce bound quark-antiquark pairs (pions). This is the source of the GZK limit.

Radio Frequency

Radio waves generally are utilised by antennas of appropriate size (according to the principle of resonance), with wavelengths ranging from hundreds of meters to about one millimeter. They are used for transmission of data, via modulation. Television, mobile phones, wireless networking, and amateur radio all use radio waves. The use of the radio spectrum is regulated by many governments through frequency allocation.

Radio waves can be made to carry information by varying a combination of the amplitude, frequency, and phase of the wave within a frequency band. When EM radiation impinges upon a conductor, it couples to the conductor, travels along it, and induces an electric current on the surface of that conductor by exciting the electrons of the conducting material. This effect (the skin effect) is used in antennas.

Microwaves

The super-high frequency (SHF) and extremely high frequency (EHF) of microwaves come after radio waves. Microwaves are waves that are typically short enough to employ tubular metal waveguides of reasonable diameter. Microwave energy is produced with klystron and magnetron tubes, and with solid state diodes such as Gunn and IMPATT devices.

Microwaves are absorbed by molecules that have a dipole moment in liquids. In a microwave oven, this effect is used to heat food. Low-intensity microwave radiation is used in Wi-Fi, although this is at intensity levels unable to cause thermal heating.

Volumetric heating, as used by microwave ovens, transfers energy through the material electromagnetically, not as a thermal heat flux. The benefit of this is a more uniform heating and reduced heating time; microwaves can heat material in less than 1 per cent of the time of conventional heating methods.

When active, the average microwave oven is powerful enough to cause interference at close range with poorly shielded electromagnetic fields such as those found in mobile medical devices and cheap consumer electronics.

Terahertz Radiation

Terahertz radiation is a region of the spectrum between far infrared and microwaves. Until recently, the range was rarely studied and few sources existed for microwave energy at the high end of the band (sub-millimeter waves or so-called terahertz waves), but applications such as imaging and communications are now appearing. Scientists are also looking to apply terahertz technology in the armed forces, where high-frequency waves might be directed at enemy troops to incapacitate their electronic equipment.

Infrared Radiation

The infrared part of the electromagnetic spectrum covers the range from roughly 300 GHz (1 mm) to 400 THz (750 nm). It can be divided into three parts:

- **Far-infrared**, from 300 GHz (1 mm) to 30 THz (10 μm). The lower part of this range may also be called microwaves. This radiation is typically absorbed by so-called rotational modes in gas-phase molecules, by molecular motions in liquids, and by phonons in solids. The water in Earth's atmosphere absorbs so strongly in this range that it renders the atmosphere in effect opaque. However, there are certain wavelength ranges ("windows") within the opaque range that allow partial transmission, and can be used for astronomy. The wavelength range from approximately 200 μm up to a few mm is often referred to as "sub-millimeter" in astronomy, reserving far infrared for wavelengths below 200 μm.
- **Mid-infrared**, from 30 to 120 THz (10 to 2.5 μm). Hot objects (black-body radiators) can radiate strongly in this range. It is absorbed by molecular vibrations, where the different atoms in a molecule vibrate around their equilibrium positions. This range is sometimes called the *fingerprint region*, since the mid-infrared absorption spectrum of a compound is very specific for that compound.
- **Near-infrared**, from 120 to 400 THz (2,500 to 750 nm). Physical processes that are relevant for this range are similar to those for visible light.

Visible Radiation (Light)

Above infrared in frequency comes visible light. This is the range in which the sun and other stars emit most of their radiation and the spectrum that the human eye is the most sensitive to.

Visible light (and near-infrared light) is typically absorbed and emitted by electrons in molecules and atoms that move from one energy level to another. The light we see with our eyes is really a very small portion of the electromagnetic spectrum. A rainbow shows the optical (visible) part of the electromagnetic spectrum; infrared would be located just beyond the red side of the rainbow with ultraviolet appearing just beyond the violet end. Electromagnetic radiation with a wavelength between 380 nm and 760 nm (790–400 terahertz) is detected by the human eye and perceived as visible light. Other wavelengths, especially near infrared (longer than 760 nm) and ultraviolet (shorter than 380 nm) are also sometimes referred to as light, especially when the visibility to humans is not relevant.

White light is a combination of lights of different wavelengths in the visible spectrum. Passing white light through a prism splits it up in to the several colours of light observed in the visible spectrum between 400 nm and 780 nm.

If radiation having a frequency in the visible region of the EM spectrum reflects off an object, say, a bowl of fruit, and then strikes our eyes, this results in our visual perception of the scene. Our brain's visual system processes the multitude of reflected frequencies into different shades and hues, and through this insufficiently-understood psychophysical phenomenon, most people perceive a bowl of fruit.

At most wavelengths, however, the information carried by electromagnetic radiation is not directly detected by human senses. Natural sources produce EM radiation across the spectrum, and our technology can also manipulate a broad range of wavelengths. Optical fibre transmits light that, although not necessarily in the visible part of the spectrum, can carry information. The modulation is similar to that used with radio waves.

Ultraviolet Light

Next in frequency comes ultraviolet (UV). The wavelength of UV rays is shorter than the violet end of the visible spectrum but longer than the X-ray.

UV in the very shortest range (next to X-rays) is capable even of ionising atoms, greatly changing their physical behavior.

At the middle range of UV, UV rays cannot ionise but can break chemical bonds, making molecules to be unusually reactive. Sunburn, for example, is caused by the disruptive effects of middle range UV radiation on skin cells, which is the main cause of skin cancer. UV rays in the middle range can irreparably damage the complex DNA molecules in the cells producing thymine dimers making it a very potent mutagen.

The sun emits a large amount of UV radiation, which could potentially turn Earth's land surface into a barren desert (although ocean water would provide some protection for life there). However, most of the Sun's most-damaging UV wavelengths are absorbed by the atmosphere's nitrogen, oxygen, and ozone layer before they reach the surface. The higher ranges of UV (vacuum UV) are absorbed by nitrogen and, at longer wavelengths, by simple diatomic oxygen in the air.

Most of the UV in this mid-range is blocked by the ozone layer, which absorbs strongly in the important 200–315 nm range, the lower part of which is too long to be absorbed by ordinary oxygen in air.

The range between 315 nm and visible light (called UV-A) is not blocked well by the atmosphere, but does not cause sunburn and does less biological damage. However, it is not harmless and does cause oxygen radicals, mutation and skin damage.

X-rays

After UV come X-rays, which, like the upper ranges of UV are also ionising. However, due to their higher energies, X-rays can also interact with matter by means of the Compton effect. Hard X-rays have shorter wavelengths than soft X-rays.

As they can pass through most substances, X-rays can be used to 'see through' objects, the most notable use being diagnostic X-ray images in medicine (a process known as radiography), as well as for high-energy physics and astronomy. Neutron stars and accretion disks around black holes emit X-rays, which enable us to study them. X-rays are given off by stars and are strongly emitted by some types of nebulae.

Gamma Rays

After hard X-rays come gamma rays, which were discovered by Paul Villard in 1900. These are the most energetic photons, having no defined lower limit to their wavelength. They are useful to astronomers in the study of high-energy objects or regions, and find a use with physicists thanks to their penetrative ability and their production from radioisotopes. Gamma rays are also used for the irradiation of food and seed for sterilisation, and in medicine they are used in radiation cancer therapy and some kinds of diagnostic imaging such as PET scans. The wavelength of gamma rays can be measured with high accuracy by means of Compton scattering.

LIGHT ABSORPTION, REFLECTION, AND TRANSMISSION

Visible light waves consist of a continuous range of wavelengths or frequencies. When a light wave with a single frequency strikes an object, a number of things could happen.

The light wave could be absorbed by the object, in which case its energy is converted to heat. The light wave could be reflected by the object. And the light wave could be transmitted by the object. Rarely however does just a single frequency of light strike an object. While it does happen, it is more usual that visible light of many frequencies or even all frequencies is incident towards the surface of objects. When this occurs, objects have a tendency to selectively absorb, reflect or transmit light certain frequencies.

That is, one object might reflect green light while absorbing all other frequencies of visible light. Another object might selectively transmit blue light while absorbing all other frequencies of visible light. The manner in which visible light interacts with an object is dependent upon the frequency of the light and the nature of the atoms of the object. The light of certain frequencies can be selectively absorbed, reflected or transmitted.

Atoms and molecules contain electrons. It is often useful to think of these electrons as being attached to the atoms by springs. The electrons and their attached springs have a tendency to vibrate at specific frequencies.

Similar to a tuning fork or even a musical instrument, the electrons of atoms have a natural frequency at which they tend to vibrate. When a light wave with that same natural frequency impinges upon an atom, then the electrons of that atom will be set into vibrational motion. If a light wave of a given frequency strikes a material with electrons having the same vibrational frequencies, then those electrons will absorb the energy of the light wave and transform it into vibrational motion.

During its vibration, the electrons interact with neighbouring atoms in such a manner as to convert its vibrational energy into thermal energy. Subsequently, the light wave with that given frequency is absorbed by the object, never again to be released in the form of light. So the selective absorption of light by a particular material occurs because the selected frequency of the light wave matches the frequency at which electrons in the atoms of that material vibrate.

Since different atoms and molecules have different natural frequencies of vibration, they will selectively absorb different frequencies of visible light.

Reflection and transmission of light waves occur because the frequencies of the light waves do not match the natural frequencies of vibration of the objects. When light waves of these frequencies strike an object, the electrons in the atoms of the object begin vibrating. But instead of vibrating in resonance at a large amplitude, the electrons vibrate for brief periods of time with small amplitudes of vibration; then the energy is reemitted as a light wave.

If the object is transparent, then the vibrations of the electrons are passed on to neighbouring atoms through the bulk of the material and reemitted on the opposite side of the object. Such frequencies of light waves are said to be transmitted. If the object is opaque, then the vibrations of the electrons are not passed from atom to atom through the bulk of the material. Rather the electrons of atoms on the material's surface vibrate for short periods of time and then reemit the energy as a reflected light wave. Such frequencies of light are said to be reflected.

The colour of the objects that we see are largely due to the way those objects interact with light and ultimately reflect or transmit it to our eyes. The colour of an object is not actually within the object itself. Rather, the colour is in the light that shines upon it and is ultimately reflected or transmitted to our eyes. We know that the visible light spectrum consists of a range of frequencies, each of which corresponds to a specific colour.

When visible light strikes an object and a specific frequency becomes absorbed, that frequency of light will never make it to our eyes. Any visible light that strikes the object and becomes reflected or transmitted to our eyes will contribute to the colour appearance of that object. So the colour is not in the object itself, but in the light that strikes the object and ultimately reaches our eye.

The only role that the object plays is that it might contain atoms capable of selectively absorbing one or more frequencies of the visible light that shine upon it. So if an object absorbs all of the frequencies of visible light except for the frequency associated with green light, then the object will appear green in the presence of ROYGBIV. And if an object absorbs all of the frequencies of visible light except for the frequency associated with blue light, then the object will appear blue in the presence of ROYGBIV.

The diagrams depict a sheet of paper being illuminated with white light (ROYGBIV). The papers are impregnated with a chemical capable of absorbing one or more of the colours of white light. Such chemicals that are capable of selectively absorbing one or more frequency of white light are known as pigments.

Transparent materials are materials that allow one or more of the frequencies of visible light to be transmitted through them; whatever colour(s) is/are not transmitted by such objects, are typically absorbed by them. The appearance of a transparent object is dependent upon what colour(s) of light is/are incident upon the object and what colour(s) of light is/are transmitted through the object.

The colours perceived of objects are the results of interactions between the various frequencies of visible light waves and the atoms of the materials that objects are made of. Many objects contain atoms capable of either selectively absorbing, reflecting or transmitting one or more frequencies of light. The frequencies of light that become transmitted or reflected to our eyes will contribute to the colour that we perceive.

REFLECTION AND ABSORPTION OF LIGHT FIG

As well as emitting radiation, bodies also absorb it, some absorb everything, which falls on them, and are called black bodies, but others absorb only, certain wavelengths and reflect the rest of the radiation. Most colours do not originate directly from a light source. They are created by an interplay of light, the human eye and colourants. Trees, flowers and fruits, human beings and animals, stones and even earth allow us to see countless colours without themselves generating light. They exhibit colours through colourants. These substances have the property of absorbing a particular part of the spectrum and reflecting another.The behaviour of a body can be characterised by its absorption spectrum, which shows what proportion of the light of a particular wavelength is absorbed by the body.

Thus a body, which is not self-luminous, can appear coloured because it absorbs light of some wavelengths and reflects the rest of the light, which falls on it from an external source. Two theories of colour mixing depend upon these twin ideas of reflection and absorption, *viz.* The light theory and the pigment theory respectively. In mixing the differently coloured lights reflected by a body the colours are added, whereas in mixing pigments, as in dyeing, the absorptions are added and, so far as colour is concerned, the process is subtractive. If we know the composition of the illuminating light and the absorption spectrum of a body, we can tell exactly what light the body will reflect. But this really tells us very little about what colour it will appeal to be.

What About White, Black and Grey

In theory these are not colours. A white object contains a substance which does not absorb any colour in the spectrum. The whole spectrum is reflected. With black we see the opposite. No colour is reflected, all the colours in the spectrum are absorbed. Grey is somewhere between white and black. An equal quantity of each colour is reflected, the rest is absorbed. The reflected colours mix to become grey. The lighter the grey (the further in the direction of white), the more of each colour is reflected and *vice versa*.

However, these examples are purely theoretical. In reality there are no substances which totally absorb a certain part of the spectrum and reflect a hundred percent of another. We can illustrate this with the colour red. From the many shades of red we shall select vermilion to begin with. If we check what portion of the spectrum is reflected in this red, we find that the red portion is the main one. But we see too that all the other colours are also present, especially orange and yellow. Let us now look at the pink colour magenta. Here too the red portion of the spectrum again proves to be most evident. But equally all the other colours, notably purple and blue are also found.

EMISSION OF LIGHT

AN OVERVIEW OF LIGHT EMISSION

Light can be produced by matter which is in an excited state and as it will be shown excitation can come from a variety of sources. The atoms and molecules that make up matter typically emit light at characteristic energies. The light emission can be spontaneous or stimulated. In spontaneous emission matter at a sufficiently high energy level can relax by emitting photons of a characteristic energy, this is the process which occurs in flames, or discharge lamps. Stimulated emission occurs when matter in an excited state is perturbed by a photon of light and gives rise to a further photon of light, typically at the same energy and phase as the perturbing photon. This phenomenon is the process which gives rise to laser emission where you have many photons at the same wavelength and in phase with each other.

A body at a given temperature also emits a characteristic spectrum of light called black body radiation. Consider an electric filament as current is applied to it. As the electric current supplies energy to the filament and it heats up, it starts to glow red, and as it gets hotter it then turns orange and then white. The process underlying this is well understood for a theoretical body known as a 'black body'. Our filament will approximate a black body and as the filament gains energy from the electrical power it tries to equalise its energy with its surroundings by radiating its excess energy. It does this by emitting light starting first in the infrared and as the filament gets hotter or has more energy the radiation moves more into the visible spectrum. The spectral radiance emittance M in $Wm^{-2}\ nm^{-1}\ sr^{-1}$ of a black body of Temperature T in Kelvin is given by Planck's Law below:

$$M = \frac{2\pi c^2 h}{\lambda^5}\left(\exp\left(\frac{hc}{\lambda kT}\right) - 1\right)$$

Where c is the speed of light, h = Planck's constant and K = Boltzmann constant

The spectral irradiance for artificial sources in general deviate from a perfect black body radiation but the approximation is useful in many applications and by measuring the spectral output of a heated body its temperature can be remotely measured. For example Sunlight is due to the black body radiation characteristic of a body at approximately 5,800K: The source of the excitation to produce light emission can come from a variety of sources. Table 2.2 below provides some of the sources and examples where they can be used.

Table 2.2: The Source of the Excitation

Name	*Excitation source*	*Examples of use*
Chemiluminescence	Chemical reactions	Emergency lighting
Cathodeluminescence	Electron beam	Electron beam
Sonoluminescence	Sound energy	Possible chemical reactions
Triboluminescence	Friction energy	Gives rise to light emission seen when opening gum labels in the dark.
Bioluminescence	Biological processes	Light emission seen from Fireflies or some jellyfish
Thermoluminescence	Heat energy	Used for Archeological dating
Electroluminescence	Electric Voltage	Source of light seen in LED's
Photoluminescence	Photons of Light	Fluorescence markers

Light can also be produced by the acceleration of a free charged particle, such as an electron. The light emission is known as Bremsstrahlung or 'braking radiation'. The emission is characteristically seen in X-ray emission tubes which work by accelerating electrons with a high voltage and then by decelerating them very fast by directing them onto a metal target. A special variety of particle accelerators known as Synchrotrons can be used to generate a wide range of light frequencies of very high power for use in the study of matter. A related effect is Cherenkov radiation which occurs when charged particles move through a medium faster than the speed of light. This produces the characteristic blue light seen in water ponds containing nuclear fuel.

EMITTED LIGHT

The colour that we see around us are from objects that are either original sources (luminous objects) or secondary sources (illuminated objects). Luminous objects are things that emit light; candles, light bulbs, and stars are some examples. Illuminated objects, on the other hand, have colour because they reflect light. How does something emit light? In order to answer this, we must go to the atomic level. Over the years, many different models of the atom have been developed by scientists to explain different things.

To explain how light waves originate, Niel Bohr's model of the atom probably works the best. In this model, atoms are made up of protons and nutrons scrunched into the central nucleus, and electrons orbit this nucleus in set "orbits." Now, usually, an atom with low energy has all of its electrons in a low and stable energy level. These electrons are in their ground state, and stay in orbits that are close about the nucleus. When the atom receives energy from the surrounding (in the form of heat, electricity, etc...), its electrons are boosted into a higher energy level. They actually move to a new orbit that is farther away from the nucleus.

Now, this situation, like all good things, doesn't last forever. The electrons eventually move back down to their ground state. In order to do so, they must release energy in the form of photons, which, of course, our eyes perceive as coloured light. As stated before, the amount of energy in the released photon is the thing that determines its colour. All of the different elements in this world give off different colours when their respective atoms are given energy. This is because each element has its own electron orbitals, and therefor, different amounts of energy that it gives off. In fact, scientists can determine the composition of stars simply by the colours of the light they give off.

REFLECTED LIGHT

What about illuminated objects? The same basic mechanisms apply, but the energy that excites the atoms of an illuminated object is actually other light waves! A photon of light is absorbed by an atom, the electron is elevated to a higher energy level, then it drops to it original state, and a photon is released. This photon may or may not be of the same frequency that the atom first absorbed.

Looking at the bigger picture, reflected light can also be depicted in another manner. Light can be thought of as a series of rays. When it strikes an object, each ray is reflected off the object in many different directions. Those that reach our eyes allow us to "see" the object in question.

THE BASICS OF LIGHT

LIGHT AS ENERGY

Light is remarkable. It is something we take for granted every day, but it's not something we stop and think about very often or even try and define. Let's take a few minutes and try and understand some things about light. Simply stated, light is nature's way of transferring energy through space. We can complicate it by talking about interacting electric and magnetic fields, quantum mechanics, and all of that, but just remember—*light is energy.*

Light travels very rapidly, but it does have a finite velocity. In vacuum, the speed of light is 186,282 miles per *second* (or nearly 300,000 kilometers per second), which is really humming along! However, when we start talking about the incredible distances in astronomy, the finite nature of light's velocity becomes readily apparent. It takes about two and a half seconds, for instance, for a radio communication travelling at the speed of light to get to the moon and back.

You might find it interesting to remember, the next time you watch a beautiful sunrise or sunset, that the sun itself actually dipped below the horizon eight minutes earlier—it takes that long for the light to reach the Earth! And, of course, every newspaper article you ever read about astronomy will always include the required statement, "A light year is the distance light travels in one year at the speed of 186,282 miles per second, about 6 trillion miles." (Well, 5.8 trillion miles actually, but what's 200 billion miles among friends?) We should also highlight right up front that light is more generally referred to as *electromagnetic radiation*. Okay, we used a big word.

It had to happen sooner or later. But too often when we say "light" it is mistaken to mean "optical light," which is roughly the radiation visible to our eyes. Visible light is a tiny portion of a huge smorgasboard of light called the *electromagnetic spectrum*. For our convenience, we break this smorgasboard up into different courses (appetiser, salad, etc.) and refer to them by name, such as gamma-rays, X-rays, ultraviolet, optical, infrared, and radio. However, it is important to remember that they are all just *light*. There are no "breaks" and no hard boundaries in the electromagnetic spectrum—just a continuous range of energy.

PARTICLES AND WAVES

Physics experiments over the past hundred years or so have demonstrated that light has a dual nature. In many instances, it is convenient to represent light as a "particle" phenomenon, thinking of light as discrete "packets" of energy that we call *photons*. Now in this way of thinking, not all photons are created equal, at least in terms of how much energy they contain. Each photon of X-ray light contains a lot of energy in comparison with, say, an optical or radio photon. It is this "energy content per photon" that is one of the distinguishing characteristics of the different ranges of light. Even though it is not strictly correct, it is hard not to think of a beam of light as a collection of little "light bullets" all strung together in a row.

The other way of representing light is as a *wave* phenomenon. This is somewhat more difficult for most people to understand, but perhaps an analogy with sound waves will be useful. When you play a high note and a low note on the piano, they both produce sound, but the main thing that is different between the two notes is the *frequency* of the vibrating string producing the sound waves—the faster the vibration the higher the pitch of the note. If we now shift our focus to the sound waves themselves instead of the vibrating string, we would find that the higher pitched notes have shorter *wavelengths*, or distances between each successive wave. Likewise (and restricting ourselves to optical light for the moment), blue light and red light are both just light, but the blue light has a higher frequency of vibration (or a shorter wavelength) than the red light.

It's the same way as we move throughout the electromagnetic spectrum. Each range of light we have defined above corresponds to a range of frequencies (or wavelengths) of light vibrations. These wavelengths are one of the primary indicators we use to describe light and spectra on a graph. Displaying a spectrum as a graph instead of just a colour bar allows us to measure the light.

For instance, the "rainbow" of colour shown in the figure above is what you see when you pass white light through a prism. What may not be obvious, however, is that the "intensity" or brightness of the light is also changing along with the colours. If we converted the "rainbow" into a graph of light intensity versus wavelength, it would look like this:

Notice that the spectrum is brightest in the middle (yellow-green region) and drops off in both directions (towards red and blue). This was not obvious from the rainbow version of the spectrum! Also notice that the "intensity" of the light in the graph does not stop at the "ends" of the rainbow spectrum that is visible to our eyes! The light continues beyond what we can see in both directions, which we can see in the graph but not by looking at the rainbow.

Astronomers use graphical spectra most of the time because they can get more information out of the light this way, and because they can still plot and analyse light that is not directly visible to our eyes! Now we mentioned that the energy of each photon of light was also a basic property. It turns out that there is a simple relationship between the energy of a photon and the corresponding wavelength of that photon:

$$E(\text{photon}) = (\text{constant})/\,(\text{wavelength}).$$

This simple equation basically ties together the particle and wave nature of light by permitting us to convert back and forth from wavelengths to photons and photons to their corresponding wavelengths. This equation is also in accord with what we said earlier an X-ray photon has a large energy (and a small wavelength) compared with a photon of optical light.

INTERACTION OF LIGHT WITH MATTER: ABSORPTION AND EMISSION OF LIGHT

It should come as no surprise to you that atoms and *molecules* (which are simply bound collections of two or more atoms) can absorb light (= energy!). If they didn't, you could simply flick a light on and off, and then sit back while the photons continued to bounce around the room! Likewise, infrared light (= heat = energy!) wouldn't do any good in heating up your home in the winter if it didn't get absorbed by matter. Higher energy light photons, like X-rays, tend to want to plow through more matter before they get absorbed. (Hence, their use in medical imaging: they can pass through your "soft" tissue, but are more readily absorbed in your bones, which are denser.) How and why do photons get absorbed by matter?

Well, it's time to develop another conceptual device to help us understand this process. In physics, we often find it helpful to pretend we are looking at a single atom. Atoms are made up of protons, neutrons, and electrons, and each chemical element has a specific number of them—that's what makes them different! Protons (and neutrons) are more massive than electrons, and so we sometimes visualise an atom as a miniature solar system, with the heavy particles at the center (the nucleus) and the electrons whizsing around in specific "orbits" like planets. (In reality, this picture is not very accurate. Electrons are *not* thought to be little balls "in orbit" around a nuclear "sun." However, if you get the idea that the electrons are only found at specific, discrete "distances" from the nucleus, and that each allowed distance corresponds to a different "energy level" for the electron, that would be closer to reality.)

Without delving into atomic physics and quantum mechanics too far, let us just take the following statement for granted for now: *the electrons bound to any particular atom can only be found in certain, specific energy levels with respect to the atom's nucleus*. The hydrogen atom only contains one proton and one electron, and is the simplest (and most common) element in the Universe, so let's use it as an example. A schematic hydrogen atom where instead of drawing the allowed "orbits" for the electron we draw vertically-displaced lines to represent the allowed energy levels for the electron.

If left undisturbed, our hydrogen atom likes to bind its electron as tightly as it can, and so we would find the electron in the lowest energy level, which is called the "ground state." However, if our atom is immersed in a beam of light from, say, a nearby star, sooner or later the atom will encounter a photon with an energy that is just the right amount to jump the electron up to the next higher energy level. *Voila!* The photon gets absorbed, and is "gone" from the beam of light coming from the star! Since the absorbed photon had a specific energy, this absorption occurs at a specific wavelength in the spectrum.

Now our hydrogen atom is in what is called an "excited" state, sort of like a kid right before Halloween. However, as all parents know, this is not the natural state of a child, and it's not the natural state of an atom either. If no other photons are absorbed by the atom, the electron will eventually drop back down to the lower energy ground state. However, the atom has to lose energy to do this, and so it releases a photon of the same energy as the one it absorbed (albeit most likely into some other direction from which it was absorbed). This process is called *emission* because a photon of light is emitted by the atom, again at a very specific wavelength.

Of course, the atom could have absorbed another photon with just the right energy to jump up another energy level, or even two or three or more. Likewise, after each of these possible excitations of the atom, the electron could jump back down one or more steps, emitting photons as it went.

If a photon with a sufficiently large energy gets absorbed, it can even cause an electron to become unbound from its nucleus, a process that is called *ionisation*. Our crippled hydrogen atom could then no longer absorb or emit light until it manages to capture a free electron back into a bound energy level.

We have been discussing one specific transition or "energy jump" in one atom, but of course in any physical system there are many atoms. In a hydrogen gas, all of the separate atoms could be absorbing and emitting photons corresponding to the whole group of "allowed" transitions between the various energy levels, each of which would absorb or emit at the specific wavelengths corresponding to the energy differences between the energy levels.

This pattern of absorptions (or emissions) is unique to hydrogen—no other element can have the same pattern—and causes a recognisable pattern of absorption (or emission) *lines* in a spectrum.

This graphic demonstrates the optical spectrum one would see from glowing neon gas, both in colourbar and graphical formats. As with hydrogen, neon shows a specific set of spectral lines. Note how each bright coloured line in the colour bar corresponds to an upward "spike" in the graphical format. Since most of the lines are in the yellow and red regions of the optical spectrum, a neon lamp appears "orange" to your eye. The presence of this pattern of lines in the spectrum of a glowing cloud in space would tell astronomers that the cloud contains neon in the gas.

This diagram shows how the spectrum of neon would appear in the spectrum of a star. Here, the background "rainbow" comes from the atmosphere of the star, and the neon atoms in the star's atmosphere (or outer layers) absorb the stars light, leaving dark lines. Note how the graph shows dips at each line position, producing the characteristic pattern of lines expected from neon.

Extending this a bit, it should become clear that since every chemical element has its own unique set of allowed energy levels, each element also has its own distinctive pattern of spectral absorption (and emission) lines! It is this spectral "fingerprint" that astronomers use to identify the presence of the various chemical elements in astronomical objects. Spectral lines are what allows us, from a "spectrum," to derive so much information about the object being observed!

3

Atomic Spectroscopy

ATOMIC ABSORPTION, EMISSION AND FLUORESCENCE TECHNIQUES

Atomic spectroscopy is the determination of elemental composition by its electromagnetic or mass spectrum. The study of the electromagnetic spectrum of elements is called Optical Atomic Spectroscopy. Electrons exist in energy levels within an atom. These levels have well defined energies and electrons moving between them must absorb or emit energy equal to the difference between them.

In optical spectroscopy, the energy absorbed to move an electron to a more energetic level and/or the energy emitted as the electron moves to a less energetic energy level is in the form of a photon. The wavelength of the emitted radiant energy is directly related to the electronic transition which has occurred. Since every element has a unique electronic structure, the wavelength of light emitted is a unique property of each individual element. As the orbital configuration of a large atom may be complex, there are many electronic transitions which can occur, each transition resulting in the emission of a characteristic wavelength of light.

The science of atomic spectroscopy has yielded three techniques for analytical use: Atomic Absorption. Atomic Emission. Atomic Fluorescence. The process of excitation and decay to the ground state is involved in all three fields of atomic spectroscopy. Either the energy absorbed in the excitation process, or the energy emitted in the decay process is measured and used for analytical purposes.

If light of just the right wavelength impinges on a free, ground state atom, the atom may absorb the light as it enters an excited state in a process known as atomic absorption. This process is illustrated on the right.Atomic absorption measures the amount of light at the resonant wavelength which is absorbed as it passes through a cloud of atoms. As the number of atoms in the light path increases, the amount of light absorbed increases in a predictable way. By measuring the amount of light absorbed, a quantitative determination of the amount of analyte element present can be made. The use of special light sources and careful selection of wavelength allow the specific quantitative determination of individual elements in the presence of others.The atom cloud required for atomic absorption measurements is produced by supplying enough thermal energy to the sample to dissociate the chemical compounds into free atoms.

Aspirating a solution of the sample into a flame aligned in the light beam serves this purpose. Under the proper flame conditions, most of the atoms will remain in the ground state form and are capable of absorbing light at the analytical wavelength from a source lamp. The ease and speed at which precise and accurate determinations can be made with this technique have made atomic absorption one of the most popular methods for the determination of metals.

In atomic emission, a sample is subjected to a high energy, thermal environment in order to produce excited state atoms, capable of emitting light. The energy source can be an electrical arc, a flame, or more recently, a plasma. The emission spectrum of an element exposed to such an energy source consists of a collection of the allowable emission wavelengths, commonly called emission lines, because of the discrete nature of the emitted wavelengths. This emission spectrum can be used as a unique characteristic for qualitative identification of the element.

Atomic emission using electrical arcs has been widely used in qualitative analysis.Emission techniques can also be used to determine how much of an element is present in a sample. For a "quantitative" analysis, the intensity of light emitted at the wavelength of the element to be determined is measured. The emission intensity at this wavelength will be greater as the number of atoms of the analyte element increases. The technique of flame photometry is an application of atomic emission for quantitative analysis.

The third field of atomic spectroscopy is atomic fluorescence. This technique incorporates aspects of both atomic absorption and atomic emission. Like atomic absorption, ground state atoms created in a flame are excited by focusing a beam of light into the atomic vapor. Instead of looking at the amount of light absorbed in the process, however, the emission resulting from the decay of the atoms excited by the source light is measured.

The intensity of this "fluorescence" increases with increasing atom concentration, providing the basis for quantitative determination. The source lamp for atomic fluorescence is mounted at an angle to the rest of the optical system, so that the light detector sees only the fluorescence in the flame and not the light from the lamp itself.

It is advantageous to maximize lamp intensity since sensitivity is directly related to the number of excited atoms which in turn is a function of the intensity of the exciting radiation.

While atomic absorption is the most widely applied of the three techniques and usually offers several advantages over the other two, particular benefits may be gained with either emission or fluorescence in special analytical situations.

ATOMIC SPECTROSCOPY: INSTRUMENTATION, TECHNIQUES, AND THEORY

Atomic spectroscopy exploits different energetic transitions experienced by atoms that are associated with either the absorption or emission of photons. When these transitions involve the excitation and relaxation of the valence (outer or bonding) shell electrons of metal atoms and ions, the corresonding photons have energies within the ultraviolet and visible regions of the spectrum.

A good example of this is the dark absorption lines in the solar spectrum, which are caused by heavier elements present in the outer layers of the sun.

The figure on the right shows a high energy photon with $E_{photon} = h\nu$ being absorbed, resulting in a 2s→3s electron excitation; similarly, a 3d→3p electron relaxation results in the emission of a lower energy photon. By convention, the change in electron energy $\Delta E = E_f - E_i$, where f and i refer to the final and initial states, respectively; so $\Delta E = E_{photon}$, and the sign of E_{photon} tells you whether the photon is being absorbed or emitted. Since E_f and E_i depend on the number electrons and protons within an atom (or monatomic ion), the wavelengths associated with atomic absorption and emission are considered characteristic for a particular element.

ABSORPTION AND EMISSION:

In atomic absorption (AA) spectroscopy, absorption of a photon results in excitation of an electron from a lower to higher energy atomic orbital (AO). An instrument measures the absorbance, A, which is defined as the logarithm of the ratio of incident to transmitted radiant power of the photon beam, $A = \log(P_0 \div P)$, at a wavelength specific to the element of interest. Samples are typically analysed using a flame atomic absorption spectrophotometer.

In atomic emission (AE) spectroscopy, thermal or electrical energy from an arc, flame, spark, or plasma is used to excite and electron from a lower to higher energy AO; when the excited electron returns to its original AO (*i.e.*, the ground state), it may do so by emitting a photon. The instrument measures the intensity, I, of these emitted photons as a function of wavelength.

Because AO energies are well-defined, atomic absorption and emission spectra consist of discrete, narrow lines. This allows the concentration of metallic elements in different samples to be determined selectively, with lower limits at or below 1 mg/L (1 ppm). Techniques such as graphite furnace atomic absorption spectrophotometry (GFAAS) allow concentration to be measured down to μg/L (ppb) levels. Actual limits-of-detection vary with both element, technique, and sample matrix.

OPTICAL SPECTROSCOPY

Electrons exist in energy levels within an atom. These levels have well defined energies and electrons moving between them must absorb or emit an energy equal to the difference between them. In optical spectroscopy, the energy absorbed to move an electron to a more energetic level and/or the energy emitted as the electron moves to a lower energy level is in the form of a photon (a particle of light). Because this energy is well-defined, an atom's identity can be found by the energy of this transition. The wavelength of light can be related to its energy. It is usually easier to measure the wavelength of light than to directly measure its energy.

Optical spectroscopy can be further divided into absorption, emission, and fluorescence.

In atomic absorption spectroscopy, light is passed through a collection of atoms. If the wavelength of the light has energy corresponding to the energy difference between two energy levels in the atoms, a portion of the light will be absorbed. The relationship between the concentration of atoms, the distance the light travels through the collection of atoms, and the portion of the light absorbed is given by the Beer-Lambert law.

The energy stored in the atoms can be released in a variety of ways. When it is released as light, this is known as fluorescence. Atomic fluorescence spectroscopy measures this emitted light. Fluorescence is generally measured at a 90° angle from the excitation source to minimize collection of scattered light from the excitation source, often such a rotation is provided by a Pellin-Broca prism on a turntable which will also separate the light into its spectrum for closer analysis. The wavelength once again tells you the identity of the atoms.

For low absorbances (and therefore low concentrations) the intensity of the fluoresced light is directly proportional to the concentration of atoms. Atomic fluorescence is generally more sensitive (*i.e.,* it can detect lower concentrations) than atomic absorption. Strictly speaking, any measurement of the emitted light is emission spectroscopy, but atomic emission spectroscopy usually does not include fluorescence and rather refers to emission after excitation by thermal means. The intensity of the emitted light is directly proportional to the concentration of atoms.

MASS SPECTROMETRY

Atomic mass spectrometry is similar to other types of mass spectrometry in that it consists of an ion source, a mass analyser, and a detector. Atoms' identities are determined by their mass-to-charge ratio (via the mass analyser) and their concentrations are determined by the number of ions detected. Although considerable research has gone into customising mass spectrometers for atomic ion sources, it is the ion source that differs most from other forms of mass spectrometry. These ion sources must also atomise samples, or an atomisation step must take place before ionisation. Atomic ion sources are generally modifications of atomic optical spectroscopy atom sources.

Ion and Atom Sources

Sources can be adapted in many ways, but the lists below give the general uses of a number of sources. Of these, flames are the most common due to their low cost and their simplicity. Although significantly less common, inductively-coupled plasmas, especially when used with mass spectrometers, are recognised for their outstanding analytical performance and their versatility.

For all atomic spectroscopy, a sample must be vaporised and atomised. For atomic mass spectrometry, a sample must also be ionised. Vaporisation, atomisation, and ionisation are often, but not always, accomplished with a single source. Alternatively, one source may be used to vaporise a sample while another is used to atomise (and possibly ionise). An example of this would be laser ablation inductively-coupled plasma atomic emission spectrometry, where a laser is used to vaporise a solid sample and an inductively-coupled plasma is used to atomise the vapor.

With the exception of flames and graphite furnaces, which are most commonly used for atomic absorption spectroscopy, most sources are used primarily for atomic emission spectroscopy.

Liquid-sampling sources include:

- Flames and sparks (atom source)
- Inductively-coupled plasma (atom and ion source)
- Graphite furnace (atom source)
- Microwave plasma (atom and ion source)
- Direct-current plasma (atom and ion source)

Solid-sampling sources include:

- Lasers (atom and vapor source)
- Glow discharge (atom and ion source)
- Arc (atom and ion source)
- Spark (atom and ion source)
- Graphite furnace (atom and vapor source)

Gas-sampling sources include:

- Flame (atom source)
- Inductively-coupled plasma (atom and ion source)
- Microwave plasma (atom and ion source)
- Direct-current plasma (atom and ion source)
- Glow discharge (atom and ion source)

ATOMIC EMISSION SPECTRA - ORIGIN OF SPECTRAL LINES

By the early 1900s, scientists had made the following observations:

- When a sample of gaseous atoms of an element at low pressure is subjected to an input of energy, such as from an electric discharge, the atoms are themselves found to emit electromagnetic radiation.
- On passing through a very thin slit and then through a prism the light (electromagnetic radiation) emitted by the excited atoms is separated into its component frequencies.

The familiar dispersion of white light is illustrated below:

- Solids, liquids and dense gases glow at high temperatures. The emitted light, examined using a spectroscope, consists of a *continuous band of colours* as in a rainbow. A continuous spectrum is observed.

This is typical of matter in which the atoms are packed closely together. Gases at *low* pressure behave quite differently.

- The excited atoms emit only certain frequencies, and when these are placed as discreet lines along a frequency scale an atomic emission spectrum is formed.
- Spectral lines exist in series in the different regions (infra-red, visible and ultra-violet) of the spectrum of electromagnetic radiation.
- The spectral lines in a series get closer together with increasing frequency.
- Each element has its own unique atomic emission spectrum.

It was necessary to explain how electrons are situated in atoms and why atoms are stable. Much of the following discussion refers to hydrogen atoms as these contain only one proton and one electron making them convenient to study.

In 1913, it was Neils Bohr who solved many of the problems at the time by proposing that the electron revolves around the nucleus of the atom with a definite fixed energy in a fixed path, without emitting or absorbing energy. The electron in the hydrogen atom exists only in certain definite energy levels. These energy levels are called Principal Quantum Levels, denoted by the Principal Quantum Number, n. Principal Quantum Level n = 1 is closest to the nucleus of the atom and of lowest energy. When the electron occupies the energy level of lowest energy the atom is said to be in its ground state. An atom can have only one ground state. If the electron occupies one of the higher energy levels then the atom is in an excited state. An atom has many excited states.

When a gaseous hydrogen atom in its ground state is excited by an input of energy, its electron is 'promoted' from the lowest energy level to one of higher energy. The atom does not remain excited but re-emits energy as electromagnetic radiation. This is as a result of an electron 'falling' from a higher energy level to one of lower energy. This electron transition results in the release of a photon from the atom of an amount of energy ($E = h\nu$) equal to the difference in energy of the electronic energy levels involved in the transition. In a sample of gaseous hydrogen where there are many trillions of atoms all of the possible electron transitions from higher to lower energy levels will take place many times. A prism can now be used to separate the emitted electromagnetic radiation into its component frequencies (wavelengths or energies). These are then represented as spectral lines along an increasing frequency scale to form an atomic emission spectrum.

The Bohr Theory

The Bohr theory was a marvellous success in explaining the spectrum of the hydrogen atom. His calculated wavelengths agreed perfectly with the experimentally measured wavelengths of the spectral lines. Bohr knew that he was on to something; matching theory with experimental data is successful science. More recent theories about the electronic structure of atoms have refined these ideas, but Bohr's 'model' is still very helpful to us. For clarity, it is normal to consider electron transitions from higher energy levels to the same Principal Quantum Level. The formation of a series of spectral lines in the visible region of the spectrum of electromagnetic radiation for hydrogen, called the Balmer Series.

The Spectral Lines are in Series

The hydrogen atoms, electron transitions form higher energy levels all to the n = 2 level produce a series of lines in the visible region of the electromagnetic spectrum, called the Balmer Series. The series of lines in the ultra-violet region, called the Lyman Series, are due to electron transitions from higher energy levels all to the n = 1 level, and these were discovered after Bohr predicted their existence.

Within each series, the spectral lines get closer together with increasing frequency. This suggests that the electronic energy levels get closer the more distant they become from the nucleus of the atom.

No two elements have the same atomic emission spectrum; the atomic emission spectrum of an element is like a fingerprint.

SPECTROSCOPY: ELEMENT IDENTIFICATION AND EMISSION SPECTRA

The energy levels in atoms and ions are the key to the production and detection of light. Energy levels or "shells"exist for electrons in atoms and molecules. The colours of dyes and other compounds results from electron jumps between these shells or levels. The colours of fireworks result from jumps of electrons from one shell to another. Observations of light emitted by the elements is also evidence for the existence of shells, subshsells and energy levels. The kinds of light that interact with atoms indicate the energy differences between shells and energy levels in the quantum theory model of the atom. Typically the valence electrons are the ones involved in these jumps.

The "quantum" theory was proposed more than 90 years ago, and has been confirmed by thousands of experiments. Science and education has failed to clearly describe the energy level concept to almost four generations of citizens. This experiment is an exercise aimed at throwing a little more light on the subject. Atoms have two kinds of states; a ground state and an excited state. The ground state is the state in which the electrons in the atom are in their lowest energy levels possible (atoms naturally are in the ground state). This means the electrons have the lowest possible values for "n" the principal quantum number.

Specific quantised amounts of energy are needed to excite an electron in an atom and produce an excited state. The animation shows the opposite of excitation. It shows how the excited hydrogen atom with an electron in the n = 3 shell can release energy. If the electron in hydrogen only drops to then = 2 shell the energy matches a pulse of red light.

Note the size of the electron cloud in the excited atom changes when the electron moves from shell to shell. The size of the atom decreases in volume when the electron goes from the n = 3 shell to the n = 2 shell. On average the electrons are closer to the nucleus for lower values of "n". The electron cloud is related to the most probable distance between the nucleus and the electron.

The most probable distance increases with increasing "n" value. The excited electron is still "in" the atom even in an excited state. The valence electron will only escape the atom if the electron is given an amount of energy equal to the ionisation energy for that atom.

Energy can be added to atoms many different ways. It can be in the form of light, an electric discharge or heat. This added or extra energy is emitted when the excited electrons in the atoms give off light and fall back to lower shells. The light emitted has wavelengths and colours that depend on the amount of energy originally absorbed by the atoms. Usually each individual excited atom will emit one type of light. Since we have billions and billions of atoms we get billions of excitations and emissions. return to top of page

Not all atoms in a sample will absorb or be excited exactly the same. For example in hydrogen the ground state has the electron in the n = 1 shell. The electron in some hydrogen atoms may be excited into the n = 2 level. Other hydrogen atoms can have the electron excited into the n = 4 shell.

Different elements emit different emission spectra when they are excited because each type of element has a unique energy shell or energy level system. Each element has a different set of emission colours because they have different energy level spacings. We will see the emission spectra or pattern of wavelengths (atomic spectra) emitted by six different elements in this lab. We will then identify an unknown element by comparing the colour of the unknown with the flame colour of our knowns.

You need to know that white light is the combination of all colours of the spectrum.

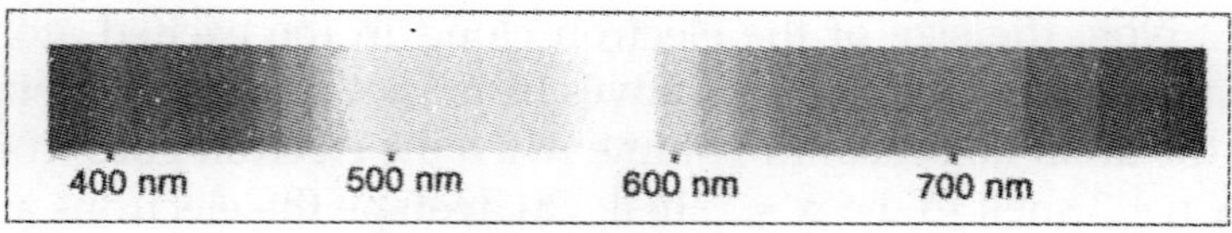

Fig. 3.1

Each colour has a characteristic wavelength. The wavelength is the distance between the beginning and end of a complete cycle of the light wave. All colours of light travel at the same speed, 3.0×10^8 meters/ second. The animation shows how a prism separates photons of red light from photons of blue light.

The photons of different colours fall in different positions on the colour spectrum. The position is determined by the wavelength.

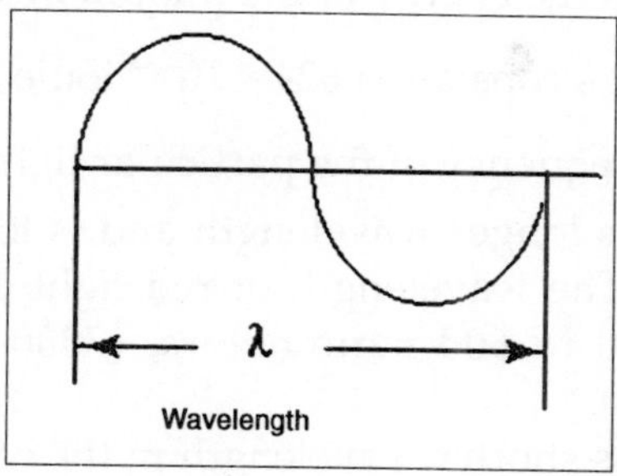

Fig. 3.2 **Return to top of Page**

The wavelength for a particular color of visible light is read off the calibration on the scale for the spectrum.

The position on the scale indicates λ, the wavelength.

Fig. 3.3

The speed of light frequency and wavelength are related by the formula,

$$c = \lambda \nu$$

where c is the speed of light 3.00×10^8 meters/ second.

ν is the frequency of the light wave in cycles per second

Lambda, λ, is the wavelength in meters/cycle.

The frequency,ν, equals the number of cycles that pass an observer in a second. These individual cycles each carry a specific small amount of energy. The particles of light are called photons. The energy of a light photon or particle is different for each colour. If you have ever seen a Star Trek movie you may have heard of "photon torpedoes". The science fiction writers suggest that bundles of light energy could be harnessed and used as projectiles.return to top of page

We can calculate the energy of a photon or wave packet using the Planck energy relation shown here. Planck won a Nobel Prize for this work. This relation allows us to tell how much energy a single photon can carry.

$$E = h\nu$$

here E is the energy of the photon in joules

h is Planck's constant 6.624×10^{-34} joule seconds

ν is the frequency of the particular light wave

Red light has longer wavelength and is lower in energy than blue light. The wavelength of red light corresponds to the range of 700 to 600 nanometers, (7000 Ångstrom or 0.0000007 meters).

Blue light has shorter wavelength in the range of 400 nm (4000 Ångstrom or 0.00000004 meter,

$1\ \text{Å} = 1 \times 10^{-10}$ m = 0.0000000001 meter = 1×10^{-1} nanometer).

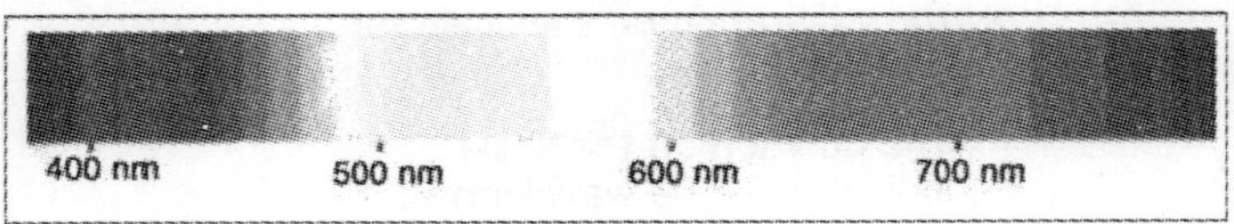

Fig. 3.4

Spectroscopy is the analysis of light spectra and the way in which light interacts with matter. When light is analysed it is commonly separated into its component colours. The light source is directed on a slit and the "beam" of light is separated using a prism or grating.

The reason that the images are lines is that the light from the lamp is focused on a narrow slit. The illustration shows the separation of a light beam into its component colours.

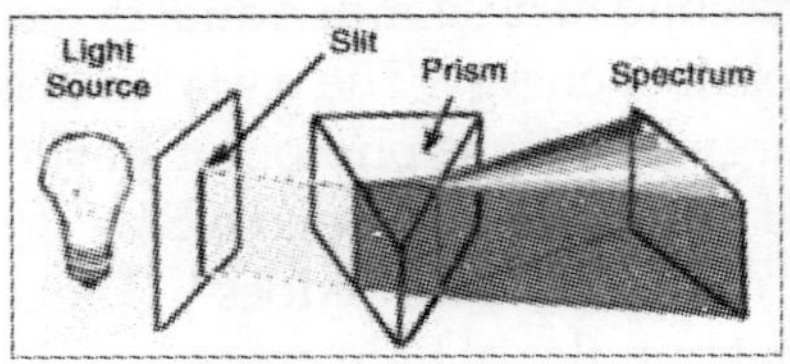

Fig. 3.5

This produces an image of the slit which has the shape of a line. The resulting beam of light can be broken into the colour spectrum. or into its components of the spectrum emitted by the atom. You can see the specific colours emitted by the light source. The emission spectrum for sodium shows only two colours in the visible colour range. The two colours are yellow and have wavelengths of about 590 nm. The continuous spectrum and calibration scale is shown to give approximate wavelength values.

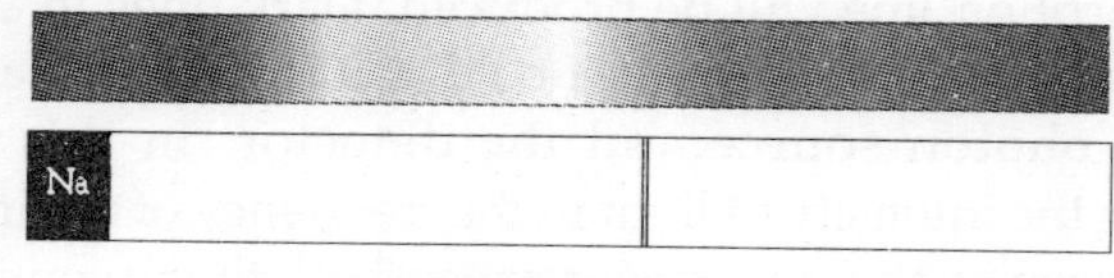

Fig. 3.6

A CD-ROM mirrored surface behaves like a grating or prism. If you look at the surface of the CD-ROM under a light, you can see the colour spectrum.

Street lights are sodium vapor lamps in many communities. These lamps have an orange yellow tint. You can see from the emission spectrum why the sodium vapor lamps would appear yellow and not white. These lamps consume less energy than the older blue coloured mercury vapor lamps. Mercury vapor lamps have been sold in hardware stores for yard lighting.

SPECTRAL LINE

A spectral line is a dark or bright line in an otherwise uniform and continuous spectrum, resulting from a deficiency or excess of photons in a narrow frequency range, compared with the nearby frequencies.

TYPES OF LINE SPECTRA

Spectral lines are the result of interaction between a quantum system (usually atoms, but sometimes molecules or atomic nuclei) and a single photon. When a photon has about the right amount of energy to allow a change in the energy state of the system (in the case of an atom this is usually an electron changing orbitals), the photon is absorbed. Then it will be spontaneously re-emitted, either in the same frequency as the original or in a cascade, where the sum of the energies of the photons emitted will be equal to the energy of the one absorbed (assuming the system returns to its original state). The direction and polarisation of the new photons will, in general, correlate with those of the original photon.

Depending on the type of gas, the photon source and what reaches the detector of the instrument, either an emission line or an absorption line will be produced. Dark lines in a broad spectrum are produced when a cold gas is between a broad spectrum photon source and the detector. In this case a decrease in the intensity of light in the frequency of the incident photon is seen as the photons are absorbed, then reemitted in random directions, which are mostly in directions different from the original one. This results in an *absorption line,* since the narrow frequency band of light initially traveling towards the detector, has been effectively scattered in other directions. Absorption lines are produced even during reflection from an illuminated cold gas, as after reflection there is still the opportunity for a selective absorption (and re-scatter) between the point of reflection and the detector. In this case the cold gas need not be directly interposed between light source and the detector, but it is required to not act as a significant independent source of light. By contrast, if the detector sees photons emitted directly from a (hot) glowing gas, then the detector often sees photons emitted in a narrow frequency range by quantum emission processes in atoms in the gas, and this results in an *emission line.*

Spectral lines are highly atom-specific, and can be used to identify the chemical composition of any medium capable of letting light pass through it (typically gas is used). Several elements were discovered by spectroscopic means, such as helium, thallium, and cerium. Spectral lines also depend on the physical conditions of the gas, so they are widely used to determine the chemical composition of stars and other celestial bodies that cannot be analysed by other means, as well as their physical conditions.

Mechanisms other than atom-photon interaction can produce spectral lines. Depending on the exact physical interaction (with molecules, single particles, etc.) the frequency of the involved photons will vary widely, and lines can be observed across the electromagnetic spectrum, from radio waves to gamma rays.

Nomenclature

Strong spectral lines in the visible part of the spectrum often have a unique Fraunhofer line designation, such as K for a line at 393.366 nm emerging from singly ionised Ca^+, though some of the Fraunhofer "lines" are blends of multiple lines from several different species.

In other cases the lines are designated according to the level of ionisation adding a Roman numeral to the designation of the chemical element, so that Ca^+ also has the designation Ca II. Neutral atoms are denoted with the roman number I, singly ionised atoms with II, and so on, so that for example Fe IX (IX, roman 9) represents eight times ionised iron. The line wavelength and may include a multiplet number (for atomic lines) or band designation (for molecular lines). Many spectral lines of atomic hydrogen also have designations within their respective series, such as the Lyman series or Balmer series.

Spectral line Broadening and Shift

A spectral line extends over a range of frequencies, not a single frequency (*i.e.,* it has a non-zero linewidth). In addition, its center may be shifted from its nominal central wavelength. There are several reasons for this broadening and shift. These reasons may be divided into two broad categories- broadening due to local conditions and broadening due to extended conditions.

Broadening due to local conditions is due to effects which hold in a small region around the emitting element, usually small enough to assure local thermodynamic equilibrium. Broadening due to extended conditions may result from changes to the spectral distribution of the radiation as it traverses its path to the observer. It also may result from the combining of radiation from a number of regions which are far from each other.

Broadening Due to Local Effects

- *Natural broadening:* The uncertainty principle relates the lifetime of an excited state (due to the spontaneous radiative decay or the Auger process) with the uncertainty of its energy. This broadening effect results in an unshifted Lorentzian profile. The natural broadening can be experimentally altered only to the extent that decay rates can be artificially suppressed or enhanced.
- Thermal Doppler broadening: The atoms in a gas which are emitting radiation will have a distribution of velocities. Each photon emitted will be "red"- or "blue"-shifted by the Doppler effect depending on the velocity of the atom relative to the observer. The higher the temperature of the gas, the wider the distribution of velocities in the gas. Since the spectral line is a combination of all of the emitted radiation, the higher the temperature of the gas, the broader will be the spectral line emitted from that gas. This broadening effect is described by a Gaussian profile and there is no associated shift.
- Pressure broadening: the presence of nearby particles will affect the radiation emitted by an individual particle. There are two limiting cases by which this occurs:
  - *Impact pressure broadening*: The collision of other particles with the emitting particle interrupts the emission process, and by shortening the characteristic time for the process, increases the uncertainty in the energy emitted (as occurs in natural broadening). The duration of the collision is much shorter than the lifetime of the emission process. This effect depends on both the density and the temperature of the gas. The broadening effect is described by a Lorentzian profile and there may be an associated shift.

- *Quasistatic pressure broadening*: The presence of other particles shifts the energy levels in the emitting particle, thereby altering the frequency of the emitted radiation. The duration of the influence is much longer than the lifetime of the emission process. This effect depends on the density of the gas, but is rather insensitive to temperature. The form of the line profile is determined by the functional form of the perturbing force with respect to distance from the perturbing particle. There may also be a shift in the line center. A stable distribution is a general expression for the lineshape resulting from quasistatic pressure broadening

Pressure broadening may also be classified by the nature of the perturbing force as follows:

- Linear Stark broadening occurs via the linear Stark effect which results from the interaction of an emitter with an electric field, which causes a shift in energy which is linear in the field strength. $(\Delta E \sim 1/r^2)$
- Resonance broadening occurs when the perturbing particle is of the same type as the emitting particle, which introduces the possibility of an energy exchange process. $(\Delta E \sim 1/r^3)$
- Quadratic Stark broadening occurs via the quadratic Stark effect which results from the interaction of an emitter with an electric field, which causes a shift in energy which is quadratic in the field strength. $(\Delta E \sim 1/r^4)$
- Van der Waals broadening occurs when the emitting particle is being perturbed by van der Waals forces. For the quasistatic case, a van der Waals profile is often useful in describing the profile. The energy shift as a function of distance is given in the wings by, *e.g.*, the Lennard-Jones potential $(\Delta E \sim 1/r^6)$.
- Inhomogeneous broadening is a general term for broadening because some emitting particles are in

a different local environment than others, and therefore emit at a different frequency. This term is used especially for solids, where surfaces, grain boundaries, and stoichiometry variations can create a variety of local environments for a given atom to occupy. In liquids, the effects of inhomogeneous broadening is sometimes reduced by a process called motional narrowing.

Broadening Due to Non-local Effects

Certain types of broadening are the result of conditions over a large region of space rather than simply upon conditions that are local to the emitting particle.

- *Opacity broadening*: Electromagnetic radiation emitted at a particular point in space can be absorbed as it travels through space. This absorption depends on wavelength. The line is broadened because photons at the line wings have a smaller reabsorption probability than photons at the line center. Indeed, the absorption near line center may be so great as to cause a self reversal in which the intensity at the center of the line is less than in the wings. This process is also sometimes called self-absorption.
- *Macroscopic Doppler broadening*: Radiation emitted by a moving source is subject to Doppler shift due to a finite line-of-sight velocity projection. If different parts of the emitting body have different velocities (along the line of sight), the resulting line will be broadened, with the line width proportional to the width of the velocity distribution. For example, radiation emitted from a distant rotating body, such as a star, will be broadened due to the line-of-sight variations in velocity on opposite sides of the star. The greater the rate of rotation, the broader the line. Another example is an imploding plasma shell in a Z-pinch.

Combined Effects

Each of these mechanisms can act in isolation or in combination with others. Assuming each effect is independent, the observed line profile is a convolution of the line profiles of each mechanism. For example, a combination of the thermal Doppler broadening and the impact pressure broadening yields a Voigt profile.

However, the different line broadening mechanisms are not always independent. For example, the collisional effects and the motional Doppler shifts can act in a coherent manner, resulting under some conditions even in a collisional *narrowing*, known as the Dicke effect.

THE VECTOR MODEL OF NMR

The vector model of nmr spectroscopy is a simple, very visual way of comprehending the results of pulses and delay times in many modern nmr experiments. We start by considering the state of the spins in solution when the sample is inserted into the magnet.

Just after the sample is put into the magnet the spins begin precessing about the external magnetic field, which is usually taken as the z-axis. In a sample of normal concentration there are something on the order of 10^{16} spins in the sample, all precessing out of phase with their magnetic moments pointing in random directions:

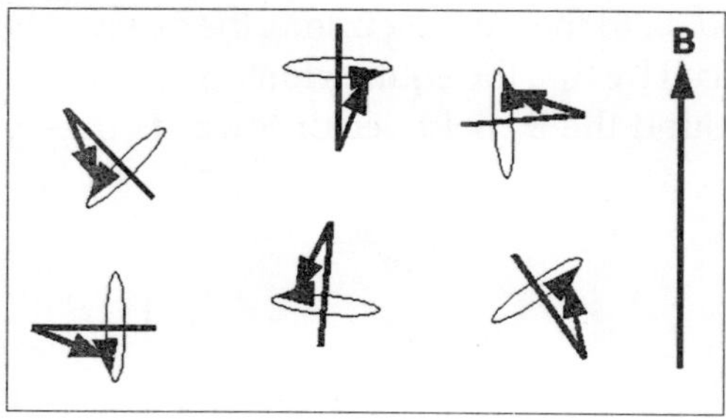

Fig. 3.7

At this point, addition of these magnetic moment vectors will result in a net magnetic moment (or magnetisation, as it is frequently called) of zero since there are so many of them pointed in random directions... we say that the spin distribution is *isotropic*. Over time, however, the axis about which the magnetic moments are precessing will change so that there are slightly more spins with a component of their magnetic moment aligned with the external field than against the field. Even though the spins are still precessing with random phases, these component vectors along the field axis add up to give a net magnetisation. At this point we say that the spin distribution is *anisotropic*. In order to simplify the road to understanding the vector model we need an understanding of the rotating coordinate frame. Once having done this we can proceed:

In the rotating frame, if we choose the correct rotational frequency, the magnetic moment vector will appear to be motionless. Application of an rf pulse in the transverse (xy) plane will result in an oscillating magnetic field, B_1, which can viewed (in the laboratory frame) as a rotating vector. If we view this in the rotating frame this magnetic field will appear to be motionless, however, if the rotating frame frequency is chosen to be identical to that of B_1... also the effective external magnetic field will be zero. It is as if the external field vanishes and is replaced by B_1 which is at 90 degrees to the external field. What will happen? Well, what always happens with spin magnetic moments... they will precess about the field that they find themselves in. If we are starting at equilibrium, there will be a net magnetisation aligned along the z-axis parallel to the external field, B. In the rotating frame, the external field vanishes and is replaced by B_1... the equilibrium magnetisation will begin to rotate around the B_1 field vector towards the $-$y axis:

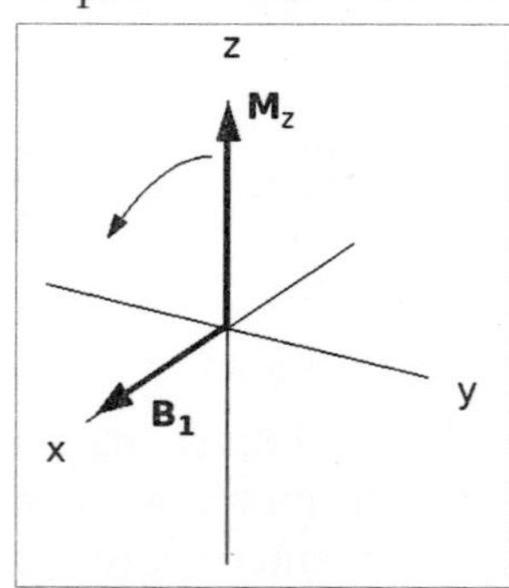

Fig. 3.8 To Determine the Direction of Rotation we Use the Right-hand Rule: Line up the Thumb along the B_1 Axis and the Direction of Rotation is Indicated by the Fingers

If we leave the B_1 field on long enough the magnetisation vector will reach the transverse or xy plane. In this case we say that we have issued a 90 degree pulse. How do we know how long to leave the transmitter on to do this? Well, the signal that we see from the magnetisation is only the portion that is projected onto the transverse plane because of the orientation of the receiver coils.

Thus, if the equilibrium magnetisation is tipped by a small amount, only a small portion of this will be detectable in the form of a small signal. The further we tip the equilibrium magnetisation towards the transverse plane the larger the projection on the transverse plane and the larger the signal we will observe. Obviously it will be at a maximum when the tip angle is 90 degrees. Any more than that, and the signal strength will begin to decrease:

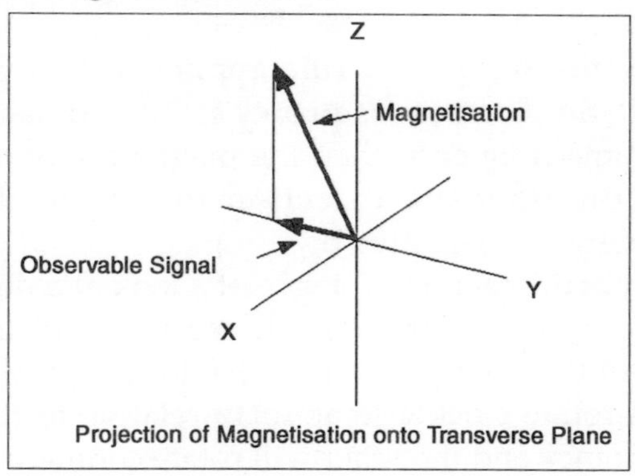

Fig. 3.9

What now? With the magnetisation tipped towards the transverse plane what happens? Well, let's take the simplest case in which the magnetisation is tipped 90 degrees into the plane. If the larmor frequency of the nucleus is identical to that of the B_1 field the transverse magnetisation vector will be motionless and will simply decay back to the equilibrium condition.

That is, the transverse magnetisation will decrease in size and the z-axis magnetisation will increase. If, on the other hand, the Larmor frequency of the nucleus is not the same as that of the B_1 field, but is say, 100 Hz more, then the effective magnetic field will be non-zero but small. This means that the transverse magnetisation will precess about B_{eff} with frequency gB_{eff}. This is known as chemical shift evolution:

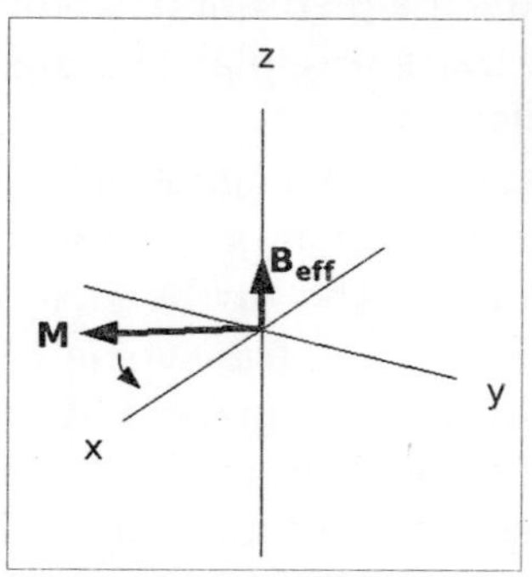

Fig. 3.10

Again, the right-hand rule applies to the direction of rotation. If the Larmor frequency is 100 Hz less than the rotating frame frequency then the magnetisation vector will rotate in the opposite direction to that in the figure, corresponding to a negative B_{eff}.

What about scalar coupling? Let's look at a doublet with a coupling constant of 20Hz. If we issue a pulse at the frequency of the chemical shift of the doublet then one of the peaks will rotate clockwise at 10Hz relative to the rotating frame frequency and the other will rotate counterclockwise at -10Hz, again relative to the rotating frame frequency:

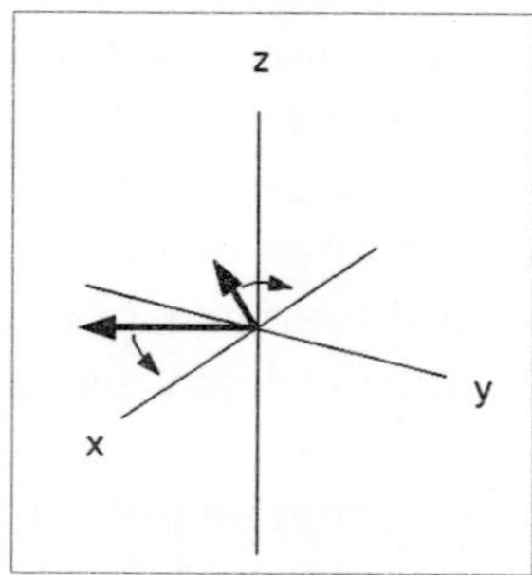

Fig. 3.11

We now have the tools needed to analyse the effects of pulses and evolution times on pulse sequences. Let's give it a try.

The spin-echo pulse sequence is simple but most useful in a multitude of nmr experiments. The sequence is:

$$(p/2)_{-x} – \text{delay} – p_x – \text{delay} – \text{acquire}$$

where p/2 and p refer to 90 degree and 180 degree pulses respectively. The x and y subscripts refer to the phases of the pulses. This can be viewed as the axis along which the B_1 field is applied. Now, consider what will happen to our doublet. During the delay after the initial $(p/2)_{-x}$ pulse the counter rotating vectors travel through an angle at their precession frequencies.

The angle is determined by the length of the delay but, as we shall see, this time is unimportant to the result. The p_x pulse rotates each vector through 180 degrees about the x-axis. Then, during the next delay which is equal to the first delay, the vectors continue their precession through the same angle as they travelled during the first delay. They end up colinear or on top of on another on the -y axis. What is interesting here is that this result is not dependent on the value of J or the delay times. This will *always* be the case for any doublet, as long as the delay times are equal. (The first vector diagram here represents the state of the system after the initial $(p/2)_{-x}$ pulse)

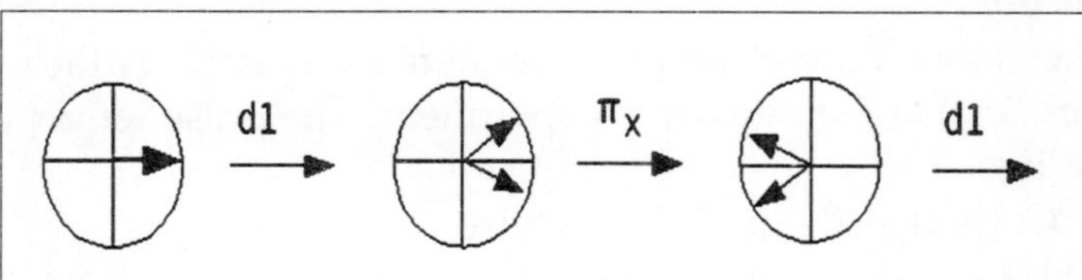

Fig. 3.12

What will happen if the B_1 field is not at the same frequency as the chemical shift of the doublet? The two vectors will rotate, each with their own frequency as before. This time however, their frequencies relative to the rotating frame will be different... they may not even be counter-rotating from the rotating frame point of view. This being the case one, labelled a in the diagram, will rotate faster than the other, labelled b. As before, they will each rotate through some angle during the first delay and then the p_x pulse will rotate them 180 degrees. Finally, the during the second delay, the vectors will rotate towards the -y axis and end up colinear, just as in the first case:

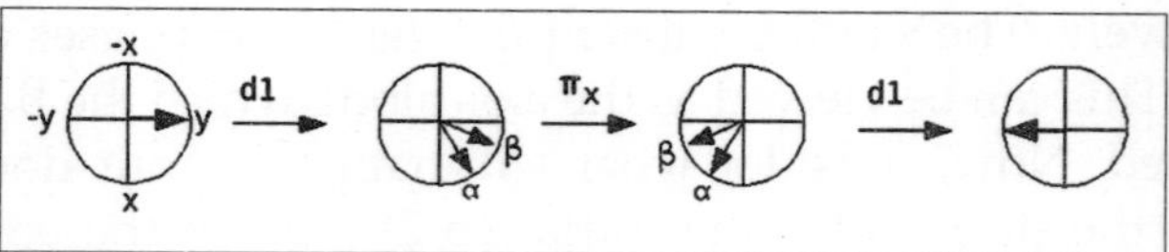

Fig. 3.13

This is very interesting. It means that no matter where in the spectrum the double appears the two vectors that represent the doublet peaks will *always* realign at the end of the pulse sequence. In other words, the result of the experiment is *chemical shift independent*. This is of such importance that this particular pulse sequence is built in to many larger pulse sequences as a 'building block' that will get rid of chemical shift effects. Why would we want to do this? Well, in a long sequence of pulses and delays lasting perhaps milliseconds chemical shift evolution will contribute to frequency dependent phase errors in the resulting spectrum. The simple expedient of including a spin-echo building block will get rid of this effect.

Let's look at another pulse sequence, the APT (Attached Proton Test) or J-modulation experiment. The pulse sequence looks like:

^{13}C: $(p/2)_x$ – d – p_x – d – acquire

^{1}H: - - - - - - - - - decoupler on

Of particular interest is the situation when the delay, d, is equal to 1/J. Without using the ^{1}H decoupler, the pulse sequence would be identical to those above... a simple spin-echo. With it, interesting things happen. Let's again consider the fate of a doublet and for simplicity, we assume that the rotating frame frequency is set at the chemical shift of the doublet. For the first part of the sequence, prior to the application of the decoupler things will be as they were above. Each doublet vector will rotate in a direction opposite to the other a J/2 Hz. The equation for calculating the rotation angle of such a vector is:

$$f = 2pt_dJ$$

where J is rotational frequency of the vector and t_d is the time of rotation.

If the delay time is 1/J then the angle that the doublet vectors will rotate through is 2p(1/J)(J/2) or p radians. The application of ^1H decoupling will cause the ^1H-^{13}C coupling to collapse into a singlet (which doesn't evolve in the rotating frame since we are using a pulse which is on the chemical shift of the doublet):

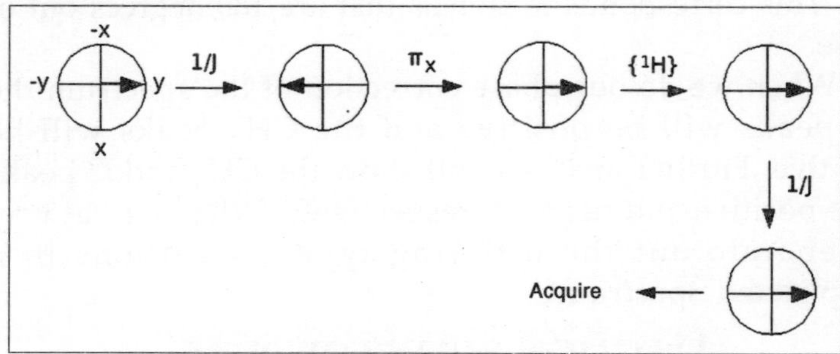

Fig. 3.14

where {^1H} represents the ^1H decoupler.

So, the coupling evolution takes place during the first delay but not the second. Let's now look at the situation for a triplet. Again, for simplicity, we assume that the transmitter frequency (and therefore the rotating frame frequency) is set exactly on the chemical shift.

Of the three vectors representing the triplet, on will rotate clockwise at J Hz, one will remain motionless and one will rotate counterclockwise at J Hz. If we use a t_d value of 1/J again, the angle of rotation will be 2p(1/J)J or 2p radians. Also, during the second delay time, with the $_1H$ decoupler on the vectors will collapse to one vector that is motionless in the rotating frame:

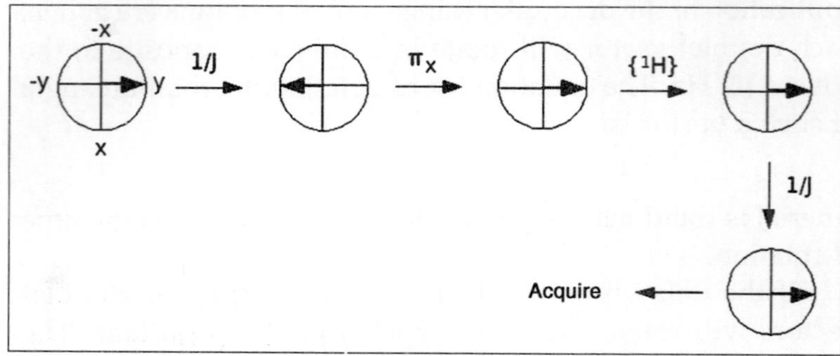

Fig. 3.15

This is interesting. For the doublet, the vector ends up lying along the +y axis and for the triplet it lies along the -y axis. This corresponds to signals that are 180 degrees out of phase.

When we do our phase correction of the spectrum the CH peaks will be positive and the CH_2 peaks will be negative. Further analysis will show the CH_3 and C peaks to be positive and negative respectively. What a great way to separate out the differing types of carbons in a complicated spectrum!

ELECTION RULES FOR PURE ROTATIONAL SPECTRA

A molecule must have a transitional dipole moment that is in resonance with an electromagnetic field for rotational spectroscopy to be used. *Polar* molecules have a dipole moment. A transitional dipole moment not equal to zero is possible.

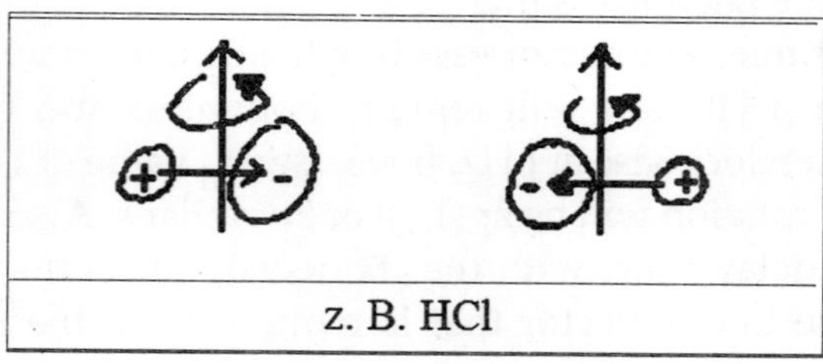

Fig. 3.16

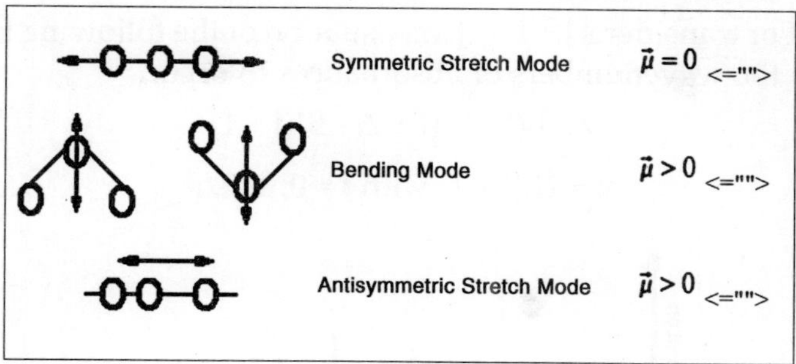

Fig. 3.17

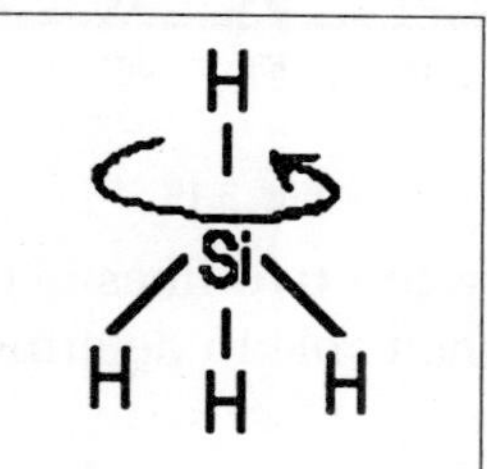

Fig. 3.18 With high Rotational Speed, an Originally Spherical Symmetry of a Molecule is Distorted

In contrast, no rotational spectra are displayed by homonuclear diatomics; the same is true for spherical tops. Nevertheless, certain states of a such molecules allow unexpected interactions with the electromagnetic field; *i.e.*

- Some vibrations, that introduce a time-dependent dipole moment
- High rotational speeds that cause some distortion of an originally spherical symmetry. A (weak) dipole moment emerges.

The conservation of the angular momentum is fundamental for the selection rules that allow or prohibit transitions of a linear molecule:

$$\Delta J = \pm 1 \qquad \Delta M_J = 0, \pm 1$$

For a symmetric top, an existing dipole moment is always parallel to the molecule's axis. Thus, with respect to this axis, no changes of the rotational state occur.

$$\Delta K = 0$$

For transitions J + 1 ← J, an equation of the following kind rules the wavenumbers of absorbances to occur.

$$\nu = B(J + 1)(J + 2) - BJ(J + 1)$$

$$\nu = 2B(J + 1) \text{ with } J = 0, 1, 2...$$

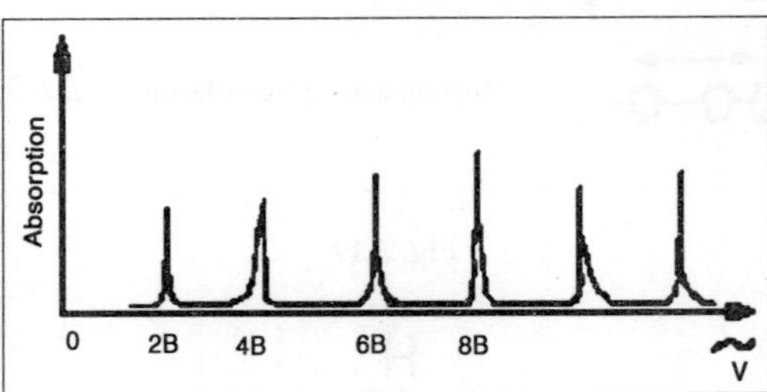

Fig. 3.19

The distance between two lines is constant. $\Delta\nu = \nu(J) - \nu(J-1) = 2B$. We are then able to determine the bond's length r as $I = \mu r^2$.

For high rotational speeds and centrifugal forces that stretch a molecule, a more accurate equation for ν is,

$$\nu = B(J+1)(J+2) - D(J+1)^2(J+2)^2 - BJ(J+1) + DJ^2(J+1)^2$$

$$\nu = 2B(J + 1) - 4D(J + 1)^3$$

i.e., the distance between the lines,

$$\Delta\nu = \nu(J) - \nu(J - 1)$$

$$\Delta\nu = 2B - 4D(3J^2 + 9J + 7)$$

decreases with J. Thus, the centrifugal constant D for diatomic molecules is in connection with the wavenumber ν_S that corresponds with the molecule's vibration.

$$D = \frac{4B^3}{V_s^2}$$

Conversely, D provides information on ν_s. Of course, the intensity of an absorption is dependent on the transitional dipole moment and on the occupancy of the initial and the final state.

SELECTION RULE

In physics and chemistry a selection rule, or transition rule, formally constrains the possible transitions of a system from one state to another. Selection rules have been derived for electronic, vibrational, and rotational transitions. The selection rules may differ according to the technique used to observe the transition.

OVERVIEW

In quantum mechanics the basis for a spectroscopic selection rule is the value of the transition moment integral.

$$\int_{-\infty}^{\infty} \psi^*_1 \mu \psi_2 dr$$

where ψ and ψ_2 are the wave functions of the two states involved in the transition and μ is the transition moment operator. If the value of this integral is zero the transition is forbidden. In practice, the integral itself does not need to be calculated to determine a selection rule. It is sufficient to determine the symmetry of transition moment function, $\Psi^*_1 \mu \psi_2$. If the symmetry of this function spans the totally symmetric representation of the point group to which the atom or molecule belongs then its value is not zero and the transition is allowed. Otherwise, the transition is forbidden. The idea of symmetry is important when considering the integral of odd functions (which equal zero when integrated over the whole of space). The transition moment integral is non-zero if and only if the transition moment function, $\Psi^*_1 \mu \psi_2$., is not anti-symmetric, as when $y(x) = -y(-x)$. The symmetry of the transition moment function is the direct product of the symmetries of its three components. The symmetry characteristics of each component can be obtained from standard character tables. Rules for obtaining the symmetries of a direct product can be found in texts on character tables.

Table 3.1

Symmetry characteristics of transition moment operator

Transition type	μ Transforms as	Note
Electric dipole	x, y, z	Optical spectra
Electric quadrupole	x^2, y^2, z^2, xy, xz, yz	Constraint $x^2 + y^2 + z^2 = 0$
Electric polarizability	x^2, y^2, z^2, xy, xz, yz	Raman spectra
Magnetic dipole	R_x, R_y, R_z	Optical spectra (weak)

Electronic Spectra

The Laporte rule is a selection rule formally-stated as follows: In a centrosymmetric environment transitions between like atomic orbitals such as *s-s*,*p-p*, *d-d*, or *f-f* transitions are forbidden. The Laporte rule applies to electric dipole transitions, so the operator has *u* symmetry. *p* orbitals also have *u* symmetry, so the symmetry of the transition moment function is given by the triple product $u \times u \times u$, which has *u* symmetry. The transitions are therefore forbidden. Likewise, *d* orbitals have *g* symmetry, so the triple product $g \times u \times g$ also has *u* symmetry and the transition is forbidden.

The wave function of a single electron is the product of a space-dependent wave function and a spin wave function. Spin is directional and can be said to have odd parity. It follows that transitions in which the spin "direction" changes are forbidden. In formal terms, only states with the same total spin quantum number are "spin-allowed". In crystal field theory, *d-d* transitions that are spin-forbidden are very much weaker than spin-allowed transitions. Both can be observed, in spite of the Laporte rule, because the actual transitions are coupled to vibrations that are anti-symmetric and have the same symmetry as the dipole moment operator.

Vibrational Spectra

In vibrational spectroscopy, transitions are observed between different vibrational states. In a fundamental vibration, the molecule is excited from its ground state ($v = 0$) to the first excited state ($v = 1$). The symmetry of the ground-state wave function is the same as that of the molecule. It is, therefore, a basis for the totally symmetric representation in the point group of the molecule. It follows that, for a vibrational transition to be allowed, the symmetry of the excited state wave function must be the same as the symmetry of the transition moment operator.

In infrared spectroscopy, the transition moment operator transforms as either *x* and/or *y* and/or *z*. The excited state wave function must also transform as at least one of these vectors. In

Raman spectroscopy, the operator transforms as one of the second-order terms in the right-most column of the character table, below.

Table 3.2

Character Table for the T_d Point Group							
	E	8 C_3	3 C_2	6 S_4	6 σ_d		
A_1	1	1	1	1	1		$x^2 + y^2 + z^2$
A_2	1	1	1	-1	-1		
E	2	-1	2	0	0		$(2z^2 - x^2 - y^2, x^2 - y^2)$
T_1	3	0	-1	1	-1	(R_x, R_y, R_z)	
T_2	3	0	-1	-1	1	(x, y, z)	(xy, xz, yz)

The molecule methane, CH_4, may be used as an example to illustrate the application of these principles. The molecule is tetrahedral and has T_d symmetry. The vibrations of methane span the representations A_1 + E + $2T_2$. Examination of the character table shows that all four vibrations are Raman-active, but only the T_2 vibrations can be seen in the infrared spectrum.

In the harmonic approximation, it can be shown that overtones are forbidden in both infrared and Raman spectra. However, when anharmonicity is taken into account, the transitions are weakly allowed.

Rotational Spectra

The selection rule for rotational transitions, derived from the symmetries of the rotational wave functions in a rigid rotor, is $\Delta J = \pm 1$, where J is a rotational quantum number.

Coupled Transitions

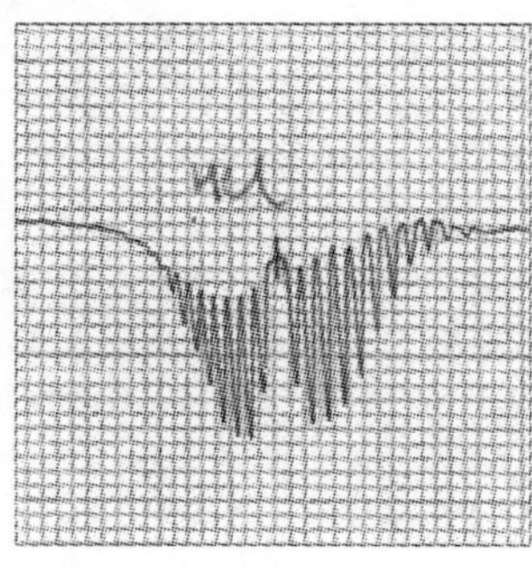

Fig. 3.20 The Infrared Spectrum of HCl Gas

There are many types of coupled transition such as are observed in vibration-rotation spectra. The excited-state wave function is the product of two wave functions such as vibrational and rotational. The general principle is that the symmetry of the excited state is obtained as the direct product of the symmetries of the component wave functions. In rovibronic transitions, the excited states involve three wave functions.

The infrared spectrum of hydrogen chloride gas shows rotational fine structure superimposed on the vibrational spectrum. This is typical of the infrared spectra of heteronuclear diatomic molecules. It shows the so-called *P* and *R* branches.

The *Q* branch, located at the vibration frequency, is absent. Symmetric top molecules display the *Q* branch. This follows from the application of selection rules.

Resonance Raman spectroscopy involves a kind of vibronic coupling. It results in much-increased intensity of fundamental and overtone transitions as the vibrations "steal" intensity from an allowed electronic transition. In spite of appearances, the selection rules are the same as in Raman spectroscopy.

Angular Momentum

In general, electric (charge) radiation or magnetic (current, magnetic moment radiation) can be classified into multipoles Eλ (electric) or Mλ (magnetic) of order 2^λ, *e.g.*, E1 for electric dipole, E2 for quadrupole, or E3 for octupole. In transitions where the change in angular momentum between the initial and final states makes several multipole radiations possible, usually the lowest-order multipoles are overwhelmingly more likely, and dominate the transition.

The emitted particle carries away an angular momentum λ, which for the photon must be at least 1, since it is a vector particle (*i.e.*, it has $J^P = 1^-$). Thus, there is no E0 (electric monopoles) or M0 (magnetic monopoles, which do not seem to exist) radiation.

Since the total angular momentum has to be conserved during the transition, we have that,

$$J_i = J_f + \lambda$$

where $\|\lambda\| = \sqrt{\lambda(\lambda+1)}\hbar$, and its z-projection is given by $\lambda_z = \mu\hbar$; J_i and J_f are, respectively, the initial and final angular momenta of the atom. The corresponding quantum numbers λ and μ (z-axis angular momentum) must satisfy,

$$|J_i - J_f| \le \lambda \le J_i + J_f$$

and,

$$\mu = M_i - M_f.$$

Parity is also preserved. For electric multipole transitions,

$$\pi(E\lambda) = \pi_i \pi_f = (-1)^{\lambda}$$

while for magnetic multipoles,

$$\pi(M\lambda) = \pi_i \pi_f = (-1)^{\lambda+1}$$

Thus, parity does not change for E-even or M-odd multipoles, while it changes for E-odd or M-even multipoles.

These considerations generate different sets of transitions rules depending on the multipole order and type. The expression *forbidden transitions* is often used; this does not mean that these transitions cannot occur, only that they are *electric-dipole-forbidden.*

These transitions are perfectly possible; they merely occur at a lower rate. If the rate for an E1 transition is non-zero, the transition is said to be permitted; if it is zero, then M1, E2, etc., transitions can still produce radiation, albeit with much lower transitions rates. These are the so-called forbidden transitions. The transition rate decreases by a factor of about 1000 from one multipole to the next one, so the lowest multipole transitions are most likely to occur.

Semi-forbidden transitions (resulting in so-called intercombination lines) are electric dipole (E1) transitions for which the selection rule that the spin does not change is violated. This is a result of the failure of LS coupling.

ZEEMAN EFFECT

Zeeman effect, in physics and astronomy, the splitting of a spectral line into two or more components of slightly different frequency when the light source is placed in a magnetic field. It was first observed in 1896 by the Dutch physicist Pieter Zeeman as a broadening of the yellow D-lines of sodium in a flame held between strong magnetic poles. Later the broadening was found to be a distinct splitting of spectral lines into as many as 15 components.

Zeeman's discovery earned him the 1902 Nobel Prize for Physics, which he shared with a former teacher, Hendrik Antoon Lorentz, another Dutch physicist. Lorentz, who had earlier developed a theory concerning the effect of magnetism on light, hypothesised that the oscillations of electrons inside an atom produce light and that a magnetic field would affect the oscillations and thereby the frequency of the light emitted. This theory was confirmed by Zeeman's research and later modified by quantum mechanics, according to which spectral lines of light are emitted when electrons change from one discrete energy level to another. Each of the levels, characterised by an angular momentum (quantity related to mass and spin), is split in a magnetic field into substates of equal energy. These substates of energy are revealed by the resulting patterns of spectral line components.

The Zeeman effect has helped physicists determine the energy levels in atoms and identify them in terms of angular momenta. It also provides an effective means of studying atomic nuclei and such phenomena as electron paramagnetic resonance. In astronomy, the Zeeman effect is used in measuring the magnetic field of the Sun and of other stars.

STARK EFFECT

Computed regular (non-chaotic) Rydberg atom energy level spectra of hydrogen in an electric field near n = 15 for magnetic quantum number m = 0. Each n-level consists of n-1 degenerate sublevels; application of an electric field breaks the degeneracy. Note that energy levels can cross due to underlying symmetries of dynamical motion.

"Stark shift" is not to be confused with Stokes shift.

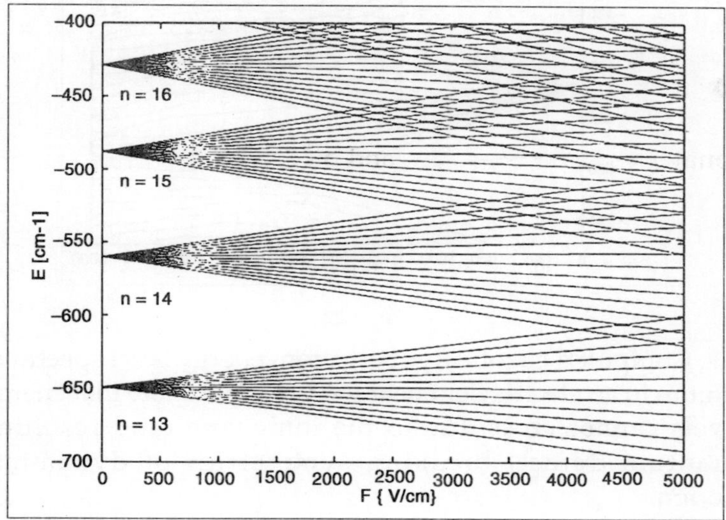

Fig. 3.21

The Stark effect is the shifting and splitting of spectral lines of atoms and molecules due to presence of an external static electric field. The amount of splitting and or shifting is called the Stark splitting or Stark shift. In general one distinguishes first- and second-order Stark effects. The first-order effect is linear in the applied electric field, while the second-order effect is quadratic in the field.

The Stark effect is responsible for the pressure broadening (Stark broadening) of spectral lines by charged particles. When the split/shifted lines appear in absorption, the effect is called the inverse Stark effect.

The Stark effect is the electric analogue of the Zeeman effect where a spectral line is split into several components due to the presence of a magnetic field.

The Stark effect can be explained with fully quantum mechanical approaches, but it has also been a fertile testing ground for semiclassical methods.

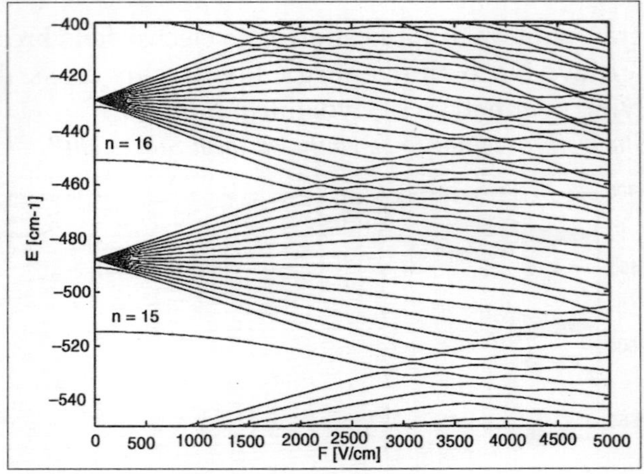

Fig. 3.22

Computed chaotic Rydberg atom energy level spectra of lithium in an electric field near n=15 for m=0. Note that energy levels cannot cross due to the ionic core (and resulting quantum defect) breaking symmetries of dynamical motion.

HISTORY

The effect is named after Johannes Stark, who discovered it in 1913. It was independently discovered in the same year by the Italian physicist Antonino Lo Surdo, and in Italy it is thus sometimes called the Stark-Lo Surdo effect. The discovery of this effect contributed importantly to the development of quantum theory. Ironically, soon after their discoveries, both Stark and Lo Surdo rejected developments in modern physics and allied themselves with the political and racial programmes of Hitler and Mussolini.

Inspired by the magnetic Zeeman effect, and especially by Lorentz's explanation of it, Woldemar Voigt performed classical mechanical calculations of quasi-elastically bound electrons in an electric field. By using experimental indices of refraction he gave an estimate of the Stark splittings. This estimate was a few orders of magnitude too low. Not deterred by this prediction, Stark undertook measurements on excited states of the hydrogen atom and succeeded in observing splittings. By the use of the Bohr-Sommerfeld ("old") quantum theory Paul Epstein and Karl Schwarzschild were independently able to derive equations for the linear and quadratic Stark effect in hydrogen.

Four years later, Hendrik Kramers derived formulas for intensities of spectral transitions. Kramers also included the effect of fine structure, which includes corrections for relativistic kinetic energy and coupling between electron spin and orbit.

The first quantum mechanical treatment (in the framework of Heisenberg's matrix mechanics) was by Wolfgang Pauli. Erwin Schrödinger discussed at length the Stark effect in his third paper on quantum theory (in which he introduced his perturbation theory), once in the manner of the 1916 work of Epstein (but generalised from the old to the new quantum theory) and once by his (first-order) perturbation approach. Finally, Epstein reconsidered the linear and quadratic Stark effect from the point of view of the new quantum theory. He derived equations for the line intensities which were a decided improvement over Kramers' results obtained by the old quantum theory.

While first-order perturbation effects for the Stark effect in hydrogen are in agreement for the Bohr-Sommerfeld model and the quantum-mechanical theory of the atom, higher order effects are not. Measurements of the Stark effect under high field strengths confirmed the correctness of the quantum theory over the Bohr model.

FINE AND HYPERFINE STRUCTURE OF SPECTRA

Although the gross energies of the electron in hydrogen are fixed by the mutual electrostatic attraction of the electron and the nucleus, there are significant magnetic effects on the energies.

An electron has an intrinsic magnetic dipole moment and behaves like a tiny bar magnet aligned along its spin axis.

Also, because of its orbital motion within the atom, the electron creates a magnetic field in its vicinity. The interaction of the electron's magnetic moment with the magnetic field created by its motion (the spin-orbit interaction) modifies its energy and is proportional to the combination of the orbital angular momentum and the spin angular momentum.

Small differences in energies of levels arising from the spin-orbit interaction sometimes cause complexities in spectral lines that are known as the fine structure. Typically, the fine structure is on the order of one-millionth of the energy difference between the energy levels given by the principal quantum numbers.

The hyperfine structure is the result of two effects:

1. The magnetic interactions between the total (orbital plus spin) magnetic moment of the electron and the magnetic moment of the nucleus and
2. The electrostatic interaction between the electric quadrupole moment of the nucleus and the electron.

FINE STRUCTURE

Fine structure, in spectroscopy, the splitting of the main spectral lines of an atom into two or more components, each representing a slightly different wavelength. Fine structure is produced when an atom emits light in making the transition from one energy state to another.

The split lines, which are called the fine structure of the main lines, arise from the interaction of the orbital motion of an electron with the quantum mechanical "spin" of that electron. An electron can be thought of as an electrically charged spinning top, and hence it behaves as a tiny bar magnet. The spinning electron interacts with the magnetic field produced by the electron's rotation about the atomic nucleus to generate the fine structure.

The amount of splitting is characterised by a dimensionless constant called the fine-structure constant. This constant is given by the equation $\alpha = ke^2/hc$, where k is

Coulomb's constant, *e* is the charge of the electron, *h* is Planck's constant, and *c* is the speed of light. The value of the constant α is $7.29735254 \times 10^{-3}$, which is nearly equal to 1/137. In the atoms of alkali metals such as sodium and potassium, there are two components of fine structure (called doublets), while in atoms of alkaline earths there are three components (triplets).

This arises because the atoms of alkali metals have only one electron outside a closed core, or shell, of electrons, while the atoms of alkaline earths have two such electrons. Doublet separation for corresponding lines increases with atomic number; thus, with lithium (atomic number 3), a doublet may not be resolved by an ordinary spectroscope, whereas with rubidium (atomic number 37), a doublet may be widely separated.

HYPERFINE STRUCTURE

The term hyperfine structure refers to a collection of different effects leading to small shifts and splittings in the energy levels of atoms, molecules and ions. The name is a reference to the *fine structure* which results from the interaction between the magnetic moments associated with electron spin and the electrons' orbital angular momentum. Hyperfine structure, with energy shifts typically orders of magnitude smaller than the fine structure, results from the interactions of the nucleus (or nuclei, in molecules) with internally generated electric and magnetic fields.

In atoms, hyperfine structure occurs due to the energy of the nuclear magnetic dipole moment in the magnetic field generated by the electrons, and the energy of the nuclear electric quadrupole moment in the electric field gradient due to the distribution of charge within the atom.

Molecular hyperfine structure is generally dominated by these two effects, but also includes the energy associated with the interaction between the magnetic moments associated with different magnetic nuclei in a molecule, as well as between the nuclear magnetic moments and the magnetic field generated by the rotation of the molecule.

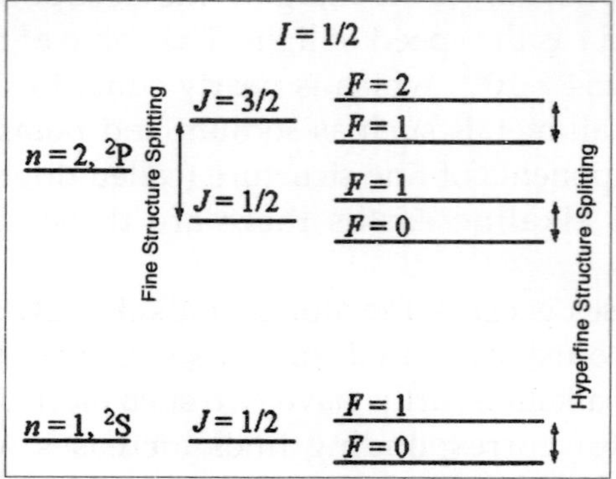

Fig. 3.23 Schematic Illustration of fine and Hyperfine Structure in Hydrogen

HISTORY

The optical hyperfine structure was already observed in 1881 by Albert Abraham Michelson. It could, however, only be explained in terms of quantum mechanics when Wolfgang Pauli proposed the existence of a small nuclear magnetic moment in 1924.

In 1935, M. Schüler and Theodour Schmidt proposed the existence of a nuclear quadrupole moment in order to explain anomalies in the hyperfine structure.

THEORY

The theory of hyperfine structure comes directly from electromagnetism, consisting of the interaction of the nuclear multipole moments (excluding the electric monopole) with internally generated fields. The theory is derived first for the atomic case, but can be applied to *each nucleus* in a molecule.

ATOMIC HYPERFINE STRUCTURE

Magnetic Dipole

The dominant term in the hyperfine Hamiltonian is typically the magnetic dipole term. Atomic nuclei with a non-zero nuclear spin have a magnetic dipole moment, given by:

$$\mu_1 = g_1 \mu_N I.$$

There is an energy associated with a magnetic dipole moment in the presence of a magnetic field. For a nuclear magnetic dipole moment, μ_I, placed in a magnetic field, B, the relevant term in the Hamiltonian is given by:

$$\hat{H}_D = -\mu_I . B$$

In the absence of an externally applied field, the magnetic field experienced by the nucleus is that associated with the orbital (l) and spin (s) angular momentum of the electrons:

$$B \equiv BB_{el} = B'_{el} + B^s_{el.}$$

Electron orbital angular momentum results from the motion of the electron about some fixed external point that we shall take to be the location of the nucleus. The magnetic field at the nucleus due to the motion of a single electron, with charge *-e* at a position r relative to the nucleus, is given by:

$$B^l_{el} = \frac{\mu_0}{4\pi} \frac{(-e)V \times (-r)}{r^3},$$

where -r gives the position of the nucleus relative to the electron. Written in terms of the Bohr magneton, this gives:

$$B^l_{el} = -2\mu_B \frac{\mu_0}{4\pi} \frac{1}{r^3} \frac{r \times m_e V}{\hbar}.$$

Recognising that m_ev is the electron momentum, p, and that r×p/$\hbar$ is the orbital angular momentum in units of $\hbar$ l, we can write:

$$B^l_{el} = -2\mu_B \frac{\mu_0}{4\pi} \frac{1}{r^3} 1.$$

For a many electron atom this expression is generally written in terms of the total orbital angular momentum, L, by summing over the electrons and using the projection operator, ϕ^l_i where $\Sigma_i I_i + = \Sigma i \phi^l_i L$. For states with a well defined projection of the orbital angular momentum, L_z, we can write $\phi^l_i = \hat{I}z_i / Lz$, giving:

$$B^l_{el} = -2\mu_B \frac{\mu_0}{4\pi} \frac{1}{L\approx} \sum_i \frac{\hat{I}\approx i}{r_i^3} L$$

The electron spin angular momentum is a fundamentally different property that is intrinsic to the particle and therefore does not depend on the motion of the electron. Nonetheless it is angular momentum and any angular momentum associated with a charged particle results in a magnetic dipole moment, which is the source of a magnetic field. An electron with spin angular momentum, s, has a magnetic moment, μ_s, given by:

$$\mu_s = -g_s \mu_B S,$$

where g_s is the electron spin *g*-factor and the negative sign is because the electron is negatively charged (consider that negatively and positively charged particles with identical mass, travelling on equivalent paths, would have the same angular momentum, but would result in currents in the opposite direction).

The magnetic field of a dipole moment,μ_s, is given by:

$$B_{el}^{s} = \frac{\mu_o}{4\pi r^3}\left(3(\mu_s.\hat{r})\hat{r} - \mu_s\right) + \frac{2\mu_o}{3}\mu_s \delta^3(r).$$

The complete magnetic dipole contribution to the hyperfine Hamiltonian is thus given by:

$$\hat{H}_D = 2g_I \mu_N \mu_B \frac{\mu_o}{4\pi}\frac{1}{L\approx}\sum_i \frac{\hat{I}\approx i}{r_i^3} I.L$$

$$+g_I\mu NgsmB\frac{\mu_o}{4\pi}\frac{1}{S\approx}\sum_i \frac{\hat{S}\approx i}{r_i^3}\{3(I.\hat{r})(S.\hat{r}) - I.S\}$$

$$+\frac{2}{3}g I \mu_N g_s \mu_B \mu_o \frac{1}{S\approx}\sum_i \hat{s}\approx i\delta^3(r_i)I.S.$$

The first term gives the energy of the nuclear dipole in the field due to the electrnnic orbital angular momentum. The second term gives the energy of the "finite distance" interaction of the nuclear dipole with the field due to the electron spin magnetic moments.

The final term, often known as the "Fermi contact" term relates to the direct interaction of the nuclear dipole with the spin dipoles and is only non-zero for states with a finite electron spin density at the position of the nucleus (those with unpaired electrons in *s*-subshells). It has been argued that one may get a different expression when taking into account the detailed nuclear dipole moment distribution.

For states with $l \neq 0$ this can be expressed in the form,

$$\hat{H}_D = 2gI\mu_B\mu N \frac{\mu_0}{4\pi}\frac{I.N}{r^3},$$

where $N = 1-(g_s/2)s + 3(s.\hat{r})\hat{r}$.

If hyperfine structure is small compared with the fine structure (sometimes called *IJ*-coupling by analogy with *LS*-coupling), *I* and *J* are good quantum numbers and matrix elements of $\hat{H}_D$ can be approximated as diagonal in *I* and *J*. In this case (generally true for light elements), we can project N onto J (where J = L + S is the total electronic angular momentum) and we have:

$$\hat{H}_D = 2g_I\mu_B\mu_N \frac{\mu_0}{4\pi}\frac{N.J}{J.J}\frac{I.J}{r^3}$$

This is commonly written as,

$$\hat{H}_D = \hat{A}I.J,$$

with $\langle\hat{A}\rangle$ determined by experiment. Since I.J = ½{F.F - I.I - J.J} (where F = I + J is the total angular momentum), this gives an energy of,

$$\Delta E_D = \frac{1}{2}\langle\hat{A}\rangle\left[F(F+1)-(I+1)-(J+1)\right].$$

In this case the hyperfine interaction satisfies the Landé interval rule.

Electric Quadrupole

Atomic nuclei with spin $I \geq 1$ have an electric quadrupole moment. In the general case this is represented by a rank-2 tensor, $\underline{\underline{Q}}$, with components given by:

$$Q_{ij} = \frac{1}{e}\int\left(3x'_i x'_j\right)-\left(r'\right)^2\delta_{ij})\rho\left(r'\right)d^3r',$$

where *i* and *j* are the tensor indices running from 1 to 3, x_i and x_j are the spatial variables *x*, *y* and *z* depending on the values of i and j respectively, δ_{ij} is the Kronecker delta and $\rho(r)$ is the charge density. Being a 3-dimensional rank-2 tensor, the quadrupole moment has $3^2 = 9$ components. From the definition of the components it is clear that the quadrupole tensor is a symmetric matrix ($Q_{ij} = Q_{ji}$) that is also traceless $\left(\sum_i Q_{ii} = 0\right)$, giving only five components in the irreducible representation. Expressed using the notation of irreducible spherical tensors we have:

$$T_m^2(Q) = \sqrt{\frac{4\pi}{5}} \int \rho(r')(r')^2 Y_m^2(\phi', \Phi') d^3r'$$

The energy associated with an electric quadrupole moment in an electric field depends not on the field strength, but on the electric field gradient, confusingly labelled $\underline{\underline{q}}$, another rank-2 tensor given by the outer product of the del operator with the electric field vector:

$$\underline{\underline{q}} = \nabla \otimes E,$$

with components given by:

$$q_{ij} = \frac{\partial^2 V}{\partial x_i \partial x_j}.$$

Again it is clear this is a symmetric matrix and, because the source of the electric field at the nucleus is a charge distribution entirely outside the nucleus, this can be expressed as a 5-component spherical tensor, $T^2(q)$, with:

$$T_0^2(q) = \frac{\sqrt{6}}{2} q_{zz}$$

$$T_{+1}^2(q) = -q_{xz} - iq_{yz}$$

$$T_{+2}^2(q) = \frac{1}{2}\left(q_{xx} - q_{yy}\right) + iq_{xy},$$

where:

$$T_{-m}^2(q) = (-1)^m T_{+m}^2(q)^*.$$

The quadrupolar term in the Hamiltonian is thus given by:

$$\hat{H}_Q = -eT^2(Q).T^2(q) = -e\sum_m (-1)^m T^2_m(Q)T^2_{-m}(q)$$

A typical atomic nucleus closely approximates cylindrical symmetry and therefore all off-diagonal elements are close to zero. For this reason the nuclear electric quadrupole moment is often represented by Q_{zz}.

Molecular Hyperfine Structure

The molecular hyperfine Hamiltonian includes those terms already derived for the atomic case with a magnetic dipole term for each nucleus with I > 0 and an electric quadrupole term for each nucleus with I ≥ 1. The magnetic dipole terms were first derived for diatomic molecules by Frosch and Foley and the resulting hyperfine parameters are often called the Frosch and Foley parameters.

Direct Nuclear Spin-spin

Each nucleus with I > 0 has a non-zero magnetic moment that is both the source of a magnetic field and has an associated energy due to the presence of the combined field of all of the other nuclear magnetic moments. A summation over each magnetic moment dotted with the field due to each *other* magnetic moment gives the direct nuclear spin-spin term in the hyperfine Hamiltonian, $\hat{H}_{II}$.

$$\hat{H}_{II} = -\sum_{\alpha \neq \alpha'} \mu_\alpha . \mathbf{B}\alpha'$$

where α and α' are indices representing the nucleus contributing to the energy and the nucleus that is the source of the field respectively. Substituting in the expressions for the dipole moment in terms of the nuclear angular momentum and the magnetic field of a dipole, both given above, we have:

$$\hat{H}_{II} = \frac{\mu_o \mu_N^2}{4\pi} \sum_{\alpha \neq \alpha'} \frac{g_\alpha g_{\alpha'}}{R^3_{\alpha\alpha'}} \{I_\alpha . I_{\alpha'} - 3(I_\alpha . \hat{R}_{\alpha\alpha'})(I_{\alpha'} . \hat{R}_{\alpha\alpha'})\}$$

Nuclear Spin-rotation

The nuclear magnetic moments in a molecule exist in a magnetic field due to the angular momentum, T (R is the internuclear displacement vector), associated with the bulk rotation of the molecule.

$$\hat{H}_{IR} = \frac{e\mu_o\mu_N\hbar}{4\pi}\sum_{\alpha\neq\alpha}\frac{1}{R^3_{\alpha\alpha'}}\left\{\frac{Z_\alpha g_{\alpha'}}{M_\alpha}I_{\alpha'} + \frac{Z_{\alpha'}g_\alpha}{M_{\alpha'}}I_\alpha\right\}.T$$

MEASUREMENTS

Hyperfine interactions can be measured, among other ways, in atomic and molecular spectra and in electron paramagnetic resonance spectra of free radicals and transition-metal ions.

APPLICATIONS

Astrophysics

As the hyperfine splitting is very small, the transition frequencies usually are not optical, but in the range of radio- or microwave frequencies. Hyperfine structure gives the 21 cm line observed in H I regions in interstellar medium.

Carl Sagan and Frank Drake considered the hyperfine transition of hydrogen to be a sufficiently universal phenomenon so as to be used as a base unit of time and length on the Pioneer plaque and later Voyager Golden Record.

In radio astronomy, heterodyne receivers are widely used in detection of the electromagnetic signals from celestial objects. The separations among various components of a hyperfine structure are usually small enough to fit into the receiver's IF band. Because optical depth varies with frequency, strength ratios among the hyperfine components differ from that of their intrinsic intensities. From this we can derive the object's physical parameters.

Nuclear Technology

The AVLIS process uses the hyperfine splitting between optical transitions in uranium-235 and uranium-238 to selectively photo-ionise only the uranium-235 atoms and then separate the ionised particles from the non-ionised ones. Precisely tuned dye lasers are used as the sources of the necessary exact wavelength radiation.

Use in Defining the SI Second and Meter

The hyperfine structure transition can be used to make a microwave notch filter with very high stability, repeatability and Q factor, which can thus be used as a basis for very precise atomic clocks. Typically, the hyperfine structure transition frequency of a particular isotope of caesium or rubidium atoms is used as a basis for these clocks.

Due to the accuracy of hyperfine structure transition-based atomic clocks, they are now used as the basis for the definition of the second. One second is now *defined* to be *exactly* 9,192,631,770 cycles of the hyperfine structure transition frequency of caesium-133 atoms.

Since 1983, the meter is defined by declaring the speed of light in a vacuum to be exactly 299,792,458 metres per second. Thus:

The metre is the length of the path travelled by light in vacuum during a time interval of 1/299,792,458 of a second.

Precision Tests of Quantum Electrodynamics

The hyperfine splitting in hydrogen and in muonium have been used to measure the value of the fine structure constant α. Comparison with measurements of α in other physical systems provides a stringent test of QED.

Qubit in ion-trap Quantum Computing

The hyperfine states of a trapped ion are commonly used for storing qubits in ion-trap quantum computing. They have the advantage of having very long lifetimes, experimentally exceeding ~10 min (compared to ~1 s for metastable electronic levels).

The frequency associated with the states' energy separation is in the microwave region, making it possible to drive hyperfine transitions using microwave radiation.

However, at present no emitter is available that can be focused to address a particular ion from a sequence. Instead, a pair of laser pulses can be used to drive the transition, by having their frequency difference (*detuning*) equal to the required transition's frequency. This is essentially a stimulated Raman transition.

4

Molecular Spectroscopy

INTRODUCTION

Spectroscopy is the use of the absorption, emission, or scattering of electromagnetic radiation by atoms or molecules (or atomic or molecular ions) to qualitatively or quantitatively study the atoms or molecules, or to study physical processes. The interaction of radiation with matter can cause redirection of the radiation and/or transitions between the energy levels of the atoms or molecules.

A transition from a lower level to a higher level with transfer of energy from the radiation field to the atom or molecule is called absorption. A transition from a higher level to a lower level is called emission if energy is transfered to the radiation field, or non-radiative decay if no radiation is emitted. Redirection of light due to its interaction with matter is called scattering, and may or may not occur with transfer of energy, *i.e.*, the scattered radiation has a slightly different or the same wavelength.

The combination of atoms into molecules leads to the creation of unique types of energetic states and therefore unique spectra of the transitions between these states. Molecular spectra can be obtained due to electron spin states (electron paramagnetic resonance), molecular rotations, molecular vibration and electronic states.

Rotations are collective motions of the atomic nuclei and typically lead to spectra in the microwave and millimeter-wave spectral regions; rotational spectroscopy and microwave spectroscopy are synonymous. Vibrations are relative motions of the atomic nuclei and are studied by both infrared and Raman spectroscopy. Electronic excitations are studied using visible and ultraviolet spectroscopy as well as fluorescence spectroscopy.

ABSORPTION

When atoms or molecules absorb light, the incoming energy excites a quantised structure to a higher energy level. The type of excitation depends on the wavelength of the light. Electrons are promoted to higher orbitals by ultraviolet or visible light, vibrations are excited by infrared light, and rotations are excited by microwaves.

An absorption spectrum is the absorption of light as a function of wavelength. The spectrum of an atom or molecule depends on its energy level structure, and absorption spectra are useful for identifying of compounds.

Measuring the concentration of an absorbing species in a sample is accomplished by applying the Beer-Lambert Law.

Emission

Atoms or molecules that are excited to high energy levels can decay to lower levels by emitting radiation (emission or luminescence). For atoms excited by a high-temperature energy source this light emission is commonly called atomic or optical emission, and for atoms excited with light it is called atomic fluorescence. For molecules it is called fluorescence if the transition is between states of the same spin and phosphorescence if the transition occurs between states of different spin.

The emission intensity of an emitting substance is linearly proportional to analyte concentration at low concentrations, and is useful for quantitating emitting species.

Scattering

When electromagnetic radiation passes through matter, most of the radiation continues in its original direction but a small fraction is scattered in other directions. Light that is scattered at the same wavelength as the incoming light is called Rayleigh scattering.

Light that is scattered in transparent solids due to vibrations (phonons) is called Brillouin scattering. Brillouin scattering is typically shifted by 0.1 to 1 cm^{-1} from the incident light.

Light that is scattered due to vibrations in molecules or optical phonons in solids is called Raman scattering. Raman scattered light is shifted by as much as 4000 cm^{-1} from the incident light.

BORN OPPENHEIMER APPROXIMATION

The Born-Oppenheimer approximation is a way to simplify the complicated Schrödinger equation for a molecule. The nucleus and electrons are attracted to each other with the same magnitude of electric charge, thus they exert the same force and momentum.

While exerting the same kind of momentum, the nucleus, with a much larger mass in comparison to electron's mass, will have a very small velocity that is almost negligible. Born-Oppenheimer takes advantage of this phenomenon and makes the assumption that since the nucleus is way heavier in mass compared to the electron, its motion can be ignored while solving the electronic Schrödinger equation; that is, the nucleus is assumed to be stationary while electrons move around it. The motion of the nuclei and the electrons can be separated and the electronic and nuclear problems can be solved with independent wavefunctions.

The wavefunction for the molecule thus becomes:

$$\psi_{molecule} = \psi_{electron} \times \psi_{nuclei}$$

The principle of Born-Oppenheimer can be applied to calculate the bond length energy between molecules. By focusing on the specific separation between nucleus and electron, their wavefunction can be calculated. Thus, a molecule's energy in relationship with its bond length can be examined.

THE BORN-OPPENHEIMER APPROXIMATION

Exact solutions in quantum mechanics are hard to come by. In almost all cases, approxi-mation is needed. The Born-

Oppenheimer approximation in particular is a key part of real-life quantum analysis of atoms and molecules and the like. The basic idea is that the uncertainty in the nuclear positions is too small to worry about when you are trying to find the wave function for the electrons. That was already assumed in the earlier approximate solutions for the hydrogen molecule and molecular ion.

The Hamiltonian

The strictly non-relativistic case. Corrections for relativistic effects on energy, including those involving spin, can in principle be added later, though that is well beyond the scope of this book. The physical problem to be addressed is that there are a finite number *I* of electrons around a finite number *J* of nuclei in otherwise empty space. That describes basic systems of atoms and molecules, but modifi-cations would have to be made for ambient electric and magnetic fields and electro-magnetic waves, or for the infinite systems of electrons and nuclei used to describe solids.

The electrons will be numbered using an index *i*, and whenever there is a second electron involved, its index will be called $\underline{i}$. Similarly, the nuclei will be numbered with an index j, or $\underline{j}$ where needed. The nuclear charge of nucleus number j, *i.e.*, the number of protons in that nucleus, will be indicated by Z_j, and the mass of the nucleus by m_j^n. Roughly speaking, the mass m_j^n will be the sum of the masses of the protons and neutrons in the nucleus; however, inter-nal nuclear energies are big enough that there are noticeable relativistic deviations in total nuclear rest mass from what you would think. All the electrons have the same mass me since relativistic mass changes due to motion are ignored.

Under the stated assumptions, the Hamiltonian of the system consists of a number of contributions that will be looked at one by one. First there is the kinetic energy of the electrons, the sum of the kinetic energy operators of the individual electrons:

$$\hat{T}^{E} = -\sum_{i=1}^{I} \frac{\hbar^2}{2m_e} \nabla_i^2 = -\sum_{i=1}^{I} \frac{\hbar^2}{2m_e} \left(\frac{\partial^2}{\partial r_{1i}^{\ 2}} + \frac{\partial^2}{\partial r_{2i}^{\ 2}} + \frac{\partial^2}{\partial r_{3i}^{\ 2}} \right)$$

where $\vec{r_i} = (r_{1i}, r_{2i}, r_{3i})$ is the position of electron number *i*. Note the use of (r_1, r_2, r_3) as the notation for the components of position, rather than x, y, z. For more elaborate mathematics, the index notation $r_{1,} r_{2,} r_3$ is often more convenient, since you can indicate any generic component by the single expression $r_{\alpha'}$ (with the under-standing that α =1, 2, or 3,) instead of writing them out all three separately.

Similarly, there is the kinetic energy of the nuclei,

$$\hat{T}^{N} = -\sum_{j=1}^{j} \frac{\hbar 2}{2m_j^n} \nabla_j^{n^2} = -\sum_{j=1}^{j} \frac{\hbar^2}{2m_j^n} \left(\frac{\partial^2}{\partial r_{i\ j}^{n2}} + \frac{\partial^2}{\partial r_{2\ j}^{n2}} + \frac{\partial^2}{\partial r_{2\ j}^{n2}} \right)$$

where $\vec{r}_j^{\,n} = (r_1^n j, r_2^n j, r_{3j}^n)$ is the position of nucleus number j.

Next there is the potential energy due to the attraction of the *I* electrons by the *J* nuclei. That potential energy is, summing over all electrons and over all nuclei:

$$V^{NE} = -\sum_{i=1}^{I} \sum_{j=1}^{J} \frac{Z_j e^2}{4\pi \in_0} \frac{1}{r_{ij}}$$

where $r_{ij} \equiv \left| \vec{r}_i - \vec{r}_j^{\,n} \right|$ is the distance between electron number i and nucleus number j, and $\in 0 = 8.8510^{-12}\ C^2/J$ m is the permittivity of space. Next there is the potential energy due to the electron-electron repulsions:

$$V^{EE} = \frac{1}{2} \sum_{i=1}^{I} \sum_{\substack{\underline{i}=1 \\ \underline{i} \neq i}}^{I} \frac{e2}{4\pi \in_0} \frac{1}{r_{i\underline{i}}}$$

where $r_{i\underline{i}} \equiv \left| \vec{r}_i - \vec{r}_{\underline{i}} \right|$ is the distance between electron number *i* and electron number $\underline{i}$ Half of this repulsion energy will be attributed to electron *i* and half to electron $\underline{i}$, accounting for the factor ½.

Finally, there is the potential energy due to the nucleus-nucleus repulsions,

$$V^{NN} = \frac{1}{2}\sum_{j=1}^{J}\sum_{\substack{\underline{j}=1 \\ \underline{j}\neq 1}}^{J} \frac{ZjZ\underline{j}e^2}{4\pi\epsilon_0}\frac{1}{r_{j\underline{j}}},$$

where $r_{J\underline{J}} \equiv \left|\vec{r}_j^{\,n} - \vec{r}_{\underline{j}}^{\,n}\right|$ is the distance between nucleus number j and nucleus number $\underline{j}$.

Solving the full quantum problem for this system of electrons and nuclei exactly would involve finding the eigenfunctions ψ to the Hamiltonian eigenvalue problem,

$$\left[\hat{T}+\hat{T}^{N}+V^{NE}+V^{EE}+V^{EE}+V^{NN}\right]\psi = E\psi$$

Here ψ is a function of the position and spin coordinates of all the electrons and all the nuclei, in other words:

$$\psi = \psi\left(\vec{r}_1, Sz_1, \vec{r}_2, Sz_2, \ldots, \vec{r}_1, S_{zI}, \vec{r}_1^{\,n}, S_{z1}^{n}, \vec{r}_2^{\,n}, S_{z2,\ldots,}^{n} \vec{r}_j^{\,n}, S_z^{1}\right)$$

You might guess solving this problem is a tall order, and you would be perfectly right. It can only be done analytically for the very simplest case of one electron and one nucleus. That is the hydrogen atom solution, using an effective electron mass to include the nuclear motion. For any decent size system, an accurate numerical solution is a formidable task too.

The Basic Born-Oppenheimer Approximation

The general idea of the Born-Oppenheimer approximation is simple. First note that the nuclei are thousands of times heavier than the electrons. A proton is almost two thousand times heavier than an electron, and that does not even count any neutrons in the nuclei.

So, if you take a look at the kinetic energy operators of the two,

$$\hat{T}^{E} = -\sum_{i=1}^{I}\frac{\hbar^2}{2m_e}\left(\frac{\partial^2}{\partial r_{Ii}{}^2}+\frac{\partial^2}{\partial r_{2i}{}^2}+\frac{\partial^2}{\partial r_{3i}{}^2}\right)$$

$$\hat{T}^{N} = -\sum_{j=1}^{j}\frac{\hbar^2}{2m_j^n}\left(\frac{\partial^2}{\partial r_{j\,j}^{n2}}+\frac{\partial^2}{\partial r_{2\,j}^{n2}}+\frac{\partial^2}{\partial r_{3\,j}^{n2}}\right)$$

Then what would seem more reasonable than to ignore the kinetic energy $\hat{T}^N$ of the nuclei? It has those heavy masses in the bottom.

An alternative, and better, way of phrasing the assumption that $\hat{T}^N$ can be ignored is to say that you ignore the uncertainty in the positions of the nuclei. For example, visualise the hydrogen molecule. The two protons, the nuclei, have pretty well defined positions in the molecule, while the electron wave function extends over the entire region like a big blob of possible measurable positions. So how important could the uncertainty in position of the nuclei really be?

Assuming that the nuclei do not suffer from quantum uncertainty in position is really equivalent to putting $\hbar$ to zero in their kinetic energy operator above, making the operator disappear, because $\hbar$ is nature's measure of uncertainty. And without a kinetic energy term for the nuclei, there is nothing left in the mathematics to force them to have uncertain positions. Indeed, you can now just guess numerical *values* for the positions of the nuclei, and solve the approximated eigenvalue problem $H\psi = E\psi$ for those assumed values.

That thought is the Born-Oppenheimer approximation in a nutshell. Just do the electrons, assuming suitable positions for the nuclei a priori. The solutions that you get doing so will be called ψ^E to distinguish them from the true solutions ψ that do not use the Born-Oppenheimer approximation. Mathematically ψ^E will still be a function of the electron and nuclear positions:

$$\psi^E = \psi^E\left(\vec{r}_1, S_{z1}, \vec{r}_2, S_{z2}, \ldots \vec{r}_I, S_{zI}; \vec{r}_1^{\,n}, S_z^n 1, \vec{r}_2^{\,n}, S_z^n 2, \ldots, \vec{r}_I, S_{zI}; \vec{r}_2^{\,n}, S_{z2}^n, \ldots, \vec{r}_J^{\,n}\right)$$

But physically it will be a quite different thing: it describes the probability of finding the electrons, *given* the positions of the nuclei. That is why there is a semi-colon between the electron positions and the nuclear positions. The nuclear positions are here assumed positions, while the electron positions are potential positions, for which the square magnitude of the wave function ψ^E gives the probability. This is an electron wave function only.

In application, it is usually most convenient to write the Hamiltonian eigenvalue problem for the electron wave function as,

$$\left[\hat{T}^{E}+V^{NE}+V^{EE}+V^{NN}\right]\psi^{E}=\left(E^{E}+V^{NN}\right)\psi^{E},$$

which just means that the eigen-value is called $E^{E}+V^{NN}$ instead of simply E^{E}. The reason is that you can then get rid of V^{NN}, and obtain the electron wave function eigen-value problem in the more concise form,

$$\left[\hat{T}^{E}+V^{NE}+V^{EE}\right]\psi^{E}=E^{E}\psi^{E} \tag{a}$$

After all, for given nuclear coordinates, V^{NN} is just a bothersome constant in the solution of the electron wave function that you may just as well get rid of.

Of course, after you compute your electron eigen-functions, you want to get something out of the results. Maybe you are looking for the ground state of a molecule, like was done earlier for the hydrogen molecule and molecular ion. In that case, the simplest approach is to try out various nuclear positions and for each likely set of nuclear positions compute the electronic ground state energy E_{gs}^{E}, the lowest eigenvalue of the electronic problem (a).

For different assumed nuclear positions, you will get different values for the electronic ground state energy, and the nuclear positions corresponding to the actual ground state of the molecule will be the ones for which the total energy is least:

$$\text{Nominal Ground State Condition}: E_{gs}^{E}+V^{NN} \text{ is Minimal}$$

This is what was used to solve the hydrogen molecule; a computer programme was written to print out the energy $E_{gs}^{E}+V^{NN}$ for a lot of different spacings between the nuclei, allowing the spacing that had the lowest total energy to be found by skimming down the print-out. That identified the ground state. The biggest error in those cases was not in using the Born-Oppenheimer approximation or the nominal ground state condition above, but in the crude way in which the electron wave function for given nuclear positions was approximated.

Going One Better

Solving the wave function for electrons only, given positions of the nuclei is definitely a big simplification. But identifying the ground state as the position of the nuclei for which the electron energy plus nuclear repulsion energy is minimal is much less than ideal.

Such a procedure ignores the motion of the nuclei, so it is no use for figuring out any molecular dynamics beyond the ground state. And even for the ground state, it is really wrong to say that the nuclei are at the position of minimum energy, because the uncertainty principle does not allow precise positions for the nuclei.

Instead, the nuclei behave much like the particle in a harmonic oscillator. They are stuck in an electron blob that wants to push them to their nominal positions. But uncertainty does not allow that, and the wave function of the nuclei spreads out a bit around the nominal positions, adding both kinetic and potential energy to the molecule. One example effect of this "zero point energy" is to lower the required dissociation energy a bit from what you would expect otherwise. It is not a big effect, maybe on the order of tenths of electron volts, compared to typical electron energies · described in terms of multiple electron volts (and much more for the inner electrons in all but the lightest atoms.) But it is not as small as might be guessed based on the fact that the nuclei are at least thousands of times heavier than the electrons.

Moreover, though relatively small in energy, the motion of the nuclei may actually be the one that is physically the important one. One reason is that the electrons tend to get stuck in single energy states. That may be because the differences between electron energy levels tend to be so large compared to a typical unit ½ of thermal energy, about one hundredth of an electron volt, or otherwise because they tend to get stuck in states for which the next higher energy levels are already filled with other electrons. The interesting physical effects then become due to the seemingly minor nuclear motion.

For example, the heat capacity of typical diatomic gases, like the hydrogen molecule or air under normal conditions, is not in any direct sense due to the electrons; it is kinetic energy of translation of the molecules plus a comparable energy due to angular momentum of the molecule; read, angular motion of the nuclei around their mutual center of gravity. The heat capacity of solids too is largely due to nuclear motion, as is the heat conduction of non-metals.

For all those reasons, you would really, really, like to actually compute the motion of the nuclei, rather than just claim they are at fixed points. Does that mean that you need to go back and solve the combined wave function for the complete system of electrons plus nuclei anyway? Throw away the Born-Oppenheimer approximation results?

Fortunately, the answer is mostly no. It turns out that nature is quite cooperative here, for a change. After you have done the electronic structure computations for all relevant positions of the nuclei, you can proceed with computing the motion of nuclei as a separate problem. For example, if you are interested in the ground state nuclear motion, it is governed by the Hamiltonian eigenvalue problem,

$$\left[\hat{T}^{N} + V^{NN} + E_1^{E}\right]\psi_1^{N} = E\psi_1^{N}$$

where ψ_1^N is a wave function involving the nuclear coordinates only, *not* any electronic ones. The trick is in the potential energy to use in such a computation; it is not just the potential energy of nucleus to nucleus repulsions, but you must include an additional energy E_1^E.

So, what is this E_1^E? Easy, it is the electro-nic ground state energy E_{gs}^E that you computed for assumed positions of the nuclei. So it will depend on where the nuclei are, but it does *not* depend on where the electrons are. You can just computed E_1^E for a sufficient number of relevant nuclear positions, tabulate the results somehow, and inter-polate them as needed. E_1^E is then a known function function of the nuclear positions and so is V^{NN}. Proceed to solve for the wave function for the nuclei ψ_1^N as a problem not directly involving any electrons.

And it does not necessarily have to be just to compute the ground state. You might want to study thermal motion or whatever. As long as the electrons are not kicked strongly enough to raise them to the next energy level, you can assume that they are in their ground state, even if the nuclei are not. The usual way to explain this is to say something like that the electrons "move so fast compared to the slow nuclei that they have all the time in the world to adjust themselves to whatever the electronic ground state is for the current nuclear positions."

You might even decide to use classical molecular dynamics based on the potential $V^{NN} + E_1^E$ instead of quantum mechanics. It would be much faster and easier, and the results are often good enough.

So what if you are interested in what your molecule is doing when the electrons are at an elevated energy level, instead of in their ground state? Can you still do it? Sure. If the electrons are in an elevated energy level E_n^E, (for simplicity, it will be assumed that the electron energy levels are numbered with a single index n,) just solve,

$$\left[\hat{T}^N + V^{NN} + E_n^E\right]\psi_n^N = E\psi_n^N$$

or equivalent.

Note that for a different value of η, this is truly a different motion problem for the nuclei, since the potential energy will be different. If you are a visual sort of person, you might vaguely visualise the potential energy for a given value of η plotted as a surface in some high-dimensional space, and the state of the nuclei moving like a roller-coaster along that potential energy surface, speeding up when the surface goes down, slowing down if it goes up. There is one such surface for each value of η. Anyway. The bottom line is that people refer to these different potential energies as "potential energy surfaces." They are also called "adiabatic surfaces" because "adiabatic" normally means processes sufficiently fast that heat transfer can be ignored. So, some quantum physicists figured that it would be a good idea to use the same term for quantum processes that are so slow that quasi-equilibrium conditions persist throughout, and that have nothing to do with heat transfer.

Of course, any approxi-mation can fail. It is possible to get into trouble solving your problem for the nuclei as explained above. The difficulties arise if two electron energy levels, call them E^E_η and $E^E_{\underline{\eta}}$, become almost equal, and in particular when they cross. In simple terms, the difficulty is that if energy levels are equal, the energy eigen-functions are not unique, and the slightest thing can throw you from one eigen-function to the completely different one.

You might now get alarmed, because for example the hydrogen molecular ion *does* have two different ground state solutions with the same energy. Its single electron can be in either the spin-up state or the spin down state, and it does not make any difference for the energy because the assumed Hamiltonian does not involve spin. In fact, all systems with an odd number of electrons will have a second solution with all spins reversed and the same energy. There is no need to worry, though; these reversed-spin solutions go their own way and do not affect the validity. It is spatial, rather than spin non-uniqueness that is a concern.

There is a derivation of the nuclear eigenvalue problem in derivation, showing what the ignored terms are and why they can usually be ignored.

MOLECULAR STRUCTURE AND SPECTRA

Until the advent of quantum theory, ideas about the structure of molecules evolved gradually from analysis and interpretation of the facts of chemistry. Chemists developed the concept of molecules as built from atoms in definite proportions, and identified and constructed (synthesised) a great variety of molecules. Later, when the structure of atoms as built from nuclei and electrons began to be understood with the help of quantum theory, a beginning was made in seeing why atoms can combine in definite ways to form molecules; also, infrared spectra began to be used to obtain information about the dimensions and the nuclear motions (vibrations) in molecules. However, a fundamental understanding of chemical bonding and molecular structure became possible only by application of the present form of quantum theory, called quantum mechanics. This theory makes it possible to obtain from the spectra of molecules a great deal of information about the nature of molecules in their normal as well as excited states, and about dissociation energies and other characteristics of molecules.

MOLECULAR SIZES

The size of a molecule varies approximately in proportion to the numbers and sizes of the atoms in the molecule. Simplest are diatomic molecules. These may be thought of as built of two spherical atoms of radii r and r^2, flattened where they are joined. The equilibrium value R_e of the distance R between their nuclei is then smaller than the sum of the atomic radii. However, the nuclei of atoms in two different molecules cannot normally approach more closely than a distance $r + r^2$; r and r^2 are called the van der Waals radii of the atoms.

To describe a polyatomic molecule, one must specify not merely its size but also its shape or configuration. For example, carbon dioxide (CO_2) is a linear symmetrical molecule, the O—C—O angle being 180°. The H—O—H angle in the non-linear water (H_2O) molecule is 105°. Many molecules which are essential for life contain thousands or even millions of atoms. Proteins are often coiled or twisted and cross-linked in ways which are important for their biological functioning.

Dipole Moments

Most molecules have an electric dipole moment. In atoms, the electron cloud surrounds the nucleus so symmetrically that its electrical center coincides with the nucleus, giving zero dipole moment; in a molecule, however, these coincidences are disturbed, and a dipole moment usually results.

Thus, when the atoms of HCl come together, there is some shifting of the H-atom electron towards the Cl. A complete shift would give H^+Cl^-, which would constitute an electric dipole of magnitude eR_e, where e is the electronic charge. But in fact the dipole moment is only 0. 17 eR_e. This is because the actual electronic shift is only fractional.

Molecular Polarizability

In the preceding consideration of dipole moments, the discussion has been in terms of atoms and molecules free from external forces. An electric field pulls the electrons of an atom or molecule towards it and pushes the nuclei away, or vice versa. This action creates a small induced dipole moment, whose magnitude per unit strength of the field is called the polarizability.

Molecular Energy Levels

The states of motion of nuclei and electrons in a molecule, or of electrons in an atom, are restricted by quantum mechanics to special forms with definite energies. The state of lowest energy is called the ground state; all others are excited states. In analogy to water levels, one speaks of energy levels. Excited states exist only momentarily, following an electrical or other stimulus.

Excitation of an atom consists of a change in the state of motion of its electrons. Electronic excitation of molecules can also occur, but alternatively or additionally, molecules can be excited to discrete states of vibration and rotation.

The total energy of any molecule can be written as Equation,

$$\mathrm{E = Ee/+Ev+\left(Er+E\int s+Eh\int s+Eest\right)}$$

Both the electronic energy E_{el} and vibration energy E_v can be discrete or continuous. The quantities E_r,break E_{fs}, and E_{hfs} denote rotational, fine-structure, and hyperfine-structure energies. The last two appear as small or minute splittings of the rotation levels. The spacings ΔE of adjacent discrete levels of each type are usually in the order given in notation

$$\Delta \mathrm{E_{el}} >> \Delta \mathrm{E_v} >> \Delta \mathrm{Er} >> \Delta \mathrm{E}\int \mathrm{s} >> \Delta \mathrm{Eh}\int \mathrm{s}$$

The E_{ext} term to additional fine structure which appears on subjecting molecules to external magnetic fields (Zeeman effect) or electric fields (Stark effect).

Polyatomic molecules have much more complicated patterns of vibrational and (usually) rotational energy levels than diatomic molecules.

Molecular Spectra

The frequencies cv (c = speed of light) of electromagnetic spectra obey the Einstein-Bohr equation,

$$hc\nu = E' - E''$$

where h is Planck's constant. Molecular emission spectra accompany jumps in energy from higher to lower levels; absorption spectra accompany jumps from lower to higher levels.

Molecular spectra can be classified as fine-structure or low-frequency spectra, rotation spectra, vibration-rotation spectra, and electronic spectra. Transitions between energy levels differing only in rotational state give rise to pure rotation spectra. These typically consist of a sequence of lines spaced almost equidistantly, and lying in the far infrared or the microwave region.

Spectra involving only vibrational and rotational state changes consist of bands which lie mainly in the infrared. Each band consists of two sets of closely spaced rotational lines, one on each side of a central frequency. Vibration-rotation absorption bands of liquids and solutions are widely used in chemical analysis. Here the rotational structure is blurred out, and only an "envelope" is seen.

Electronic band spectra are the most general type of molecular spectra. For any one electronic transition, the spectrum consists typically of many bands.

RAMAN SPECTROSCOPY

Energy level diagram showing the states involved in Raman signal. The line thickness is roughly proportional to the signal strength from the different transitions.

Raman spectroscopy is a spectroscopic technique used to study vibrational, rotational, and other low-frequency modes in a system. It relies on inelastic scattering, or Raman scattering, of monochromatic light, usually from a laser in the visible, near infrared, or near ultraviolet range. The laser light interacts with molecular vibrations, phonons or other excitations in the system, resulting in the energy of the laser photons being shifted up or down. The shift in energy gives information about the vibrational modes in the system. Infrared spectroscopy yields similar, but complementary, information.

Typically, a sample is illuminated with a laser beam. Light from the illuminated spot is collected with a lens and sent through a monochromator. Wavelengths close to the laser line due to elastic Rayleigh scattering are filtered out while the rest of the collected light is dispersed onto a detector.

Spontaneous Raman scattering is typically very weak, and as a result the main difficulty of Raman spectroscopy is separating the weak inelastically scattered light from the intense Rayleigh scattered laser light. Historically, Raman spectrometers used holographic gratings and multiple dispersion stages to achieve a high degree of laser rejection. In the past, photomultipliers were the detectors of choice for dispersive Raman setups, which resulted in long acquisition times. However, modern instrumentation almost universally employs notch or edge filters for laser rejection and spectrographs (either axial transmissive (AT), Czerny-Turner (CT) monochromator, or FT (Fourier transform spectroscopy based), and CCD detectors.

There are a number of advanced types of Raman spectroscopy, including surface-enhanced Raman, resonance Raman, tip-enhanced Raman, polarised Raman, stimulated Raman (analogous to stimulated emission), transmission Raman, spatially offset Raman, and hyper Raman.

The Raman effect occurs when light impinges upon a molecule and interacts with the electron cloud and the bonds of that molecule. For the spontaneous Raman effect, which is a form of light scattering, a photon excites the molecule from the ground state to a virtual energy state.

When the molecule relaxes it emits a photon and it returns to a different rotational or vibrational state. The difference in energy between the original state and this new state leads to a shift in the emitted photon's frequency away from the excitation wavelength. The Raman effect, which is a light scattering phenomenon, should not be confused with absorption (as with fluorescence) where the molecule is excited to a discrete (not virtual) energy level.

If the final vibrational state of the molecule is more energetic than the initial state, then the emitted photon will be shifted to a lower frequency in order for the total energy of the system to remain balanced. This shift in frequency is designated as a Stokes shift. If the final vibrational state is less energetic than the initial state, then the emitted photon will be shifted to a higher frequency, and this is designated as an Anti-Stokes shift. Raman scattering is an example of inelastic scattering because of the energy transfer between the photons and the molecules during their interaction.

A change in the molecular polarisation potential - or amount of deformation of the electron cloud - with respect to the vibrational coordinate is required for a molecule to exhibit a Raman effect. The amount of the polarizability change will determine the Raman scattering intensity. The pattern of shifted frequencies is determined by the rotational and vibrational states of the sample. This dependence on the polarizability differs from Infrared spectroscopy where the interaction between the molecule and light is determined by the dipole moment; this contrasting feature allows to analyse transitions that might not be IR active via Raman spectroscopy, as exemplified by the rule of mutual exclusion in centrosymmetric molecules.

HISTORY

Although the inelastic scattering of light was predicted by Adolf Smekal in 1923, it is not until 1928 that it was observed in practice. The Raman effect was named after one of its discoverers, the Indian scientist Sir C.V. Raman who observed the effect by means of sunlight (1928, together with K. S. Krishnan and independently by Grigory Landsberg and Leonid Mandelstam). Raman won the Nobel Prize in Physics in 1930 for this discovery accomplished using sunlight, a narrow band photographic filter to create monochromatic light, and a "crossed filter" to block this monochromatic light. He found that a small amount of light had changed frequency and passed through the "crossed" filter.

Systematic pioneering theory of the Raman effect was developed by Czechoslovak physicist George Placzek between 1930 and 1934. The mercury arc became the principal light source, first with photographic detection and then with spectrophotometric detection. At the present time, lasers are used as light sources.

RAMAN SHIFT

In colloquial usage, Raman shifts are typically in wavenumbers, which have units of inverse length. In order to convert between spectral wavelength and wavenumbers of shift in the Raman spectrum, the following formula can be used:

$$\Delta w = \left(\frac{1}{\lambda_0} - \frac{1}{\lambda_1}\right),$$

where Δw is the Raman shift expressed in wavenumber, λ_0 is the excitation wavelength, and λ_1 is the Raman spectrum wavelength. Most commonly, the units chosen for expressing wavenumber in Raman spectra is inverse centimeters (cm^{-1}). Since wavelength is often expressed in units of nanometers (nm), the formula above can scale for this units conversion explicitly, giving,

$$\Delta w = \left(cm^{-1}\right) = \left(\frac{1}{\lambda_0(nm)} - \frac{1}{\lambda_1(nm)}\right) \times 10^7, \text{effectively multiplying by} \frac{(nm)}{(cm)}.$$

APPLICATIONS

Raman spectroscopy is commonly used in chemistry, since vibrational information is specific to the chemical bonds and symmetry of molecules. Therefore, it provides a fingerprint by which the molecule can be identified. For instance, the vibrational frequencies of SiO, Si_2O_2, and Si_3O_3 were identified and assigned on the basis of normal coordinate analyses using infrared and Raman spectra. The fingerprint region of organic molecules is in the (wavenumber) range 500–2000 cm^{-1}. Another way that the technique is used is to study changes in chemical bonding, as when a substrate is added to an enzyme.

Raman gas analysers have many practical applications. For instance, they are used in medicine for real-time monitoring of anaesthetic and respiratory gas mixtures during surgery.

In solid-state physics, spontaneous Raman spectroscopy is used to, among other things, characterise materials, measure temperature, and find the crystallographic orientation of a sample. As with single molecules, a given solid material has characteristic phonon modes that can help an experimenter identify it. In addition, Raman spectroscopy can be used to observe other low frequency excitations of the solid, such as plasmons, magnons, and superconducting gap excitations. The spontaneous Raman signal gives information on the population of a given phonon mode in the ratio between the Stokes (downshifted) intensity and anti-Stokes (upshifted) intensity.

Raman scattering by an anisotropic crystal gives information on the crystal orientation. The polarisation of the Raman scattered light with respect to the crystal and the polarisation of the laser light can be used to find the orientation of the crystal, if the crystal structure (to be specific, its point group) is known.

Raman active fibres, such as aramid and carbon, have vibrational modes that show a shift in Raman frequency with applied stress. Polypropylene fibres also exhibit similar shifts. The radial breathing mode is a commonly used technique to evaluate the diameter of carbon nanotubes. In nanotechnology, a Raman microscope can be used to analyse nanowires to better understand the composition of the structures.

Spatially offset Raman spectroscopy (SORS), which is less sensitive to surface layers than conventional Raman, can be used to discover counterfeit drugs without opening their packaging, and for non-invasive monitoring of biological tissue. Raman spectroscopy can be used to investigate the chemical composition of historical documents such as the Book of Kells and contribute to knowledge of the social and economic conditions at the time the documents were produced. This is especially helpful because Raman spectroscopy offers a non-invasive way to determine the best course of preservation or conservation treatment for such materials.

Raman spectroscopy is being investigated as a means to detect explosives for airport security.

Raman spectroscopy has also been used to confirm the prediction of existence of low-frequency phonons in proteins and DNA, greatly stimulating the studies of low-frequency collective motion in proteins and DNA and their biological functions.

Raman reporter molecules with olefin or alkyne moieties are being developed to allow for tissue imaging with SERS-labeled antibodies.

MICROSPECTROSCOPY

Raman spectroscopy offers several advantages for microscopic analysis. Since it is a scattering technique, specimens do not need to be fixed or sectioned. Raman spectra can be collected from a very small volume (< 1 μm in diameter); these spectra allow the identification of species present in that volume. Water does not generally interfere with Raman spectral analysis.

Thus, Raman spectroscopy is suitable for the microscopic examination of minerals, materials such as polymers and ceramics, cells, proteins and forensic trace evidence. A Raman microscope begins with a standard optical microscope, and adds an excitation laser, a monochromator, and a sensitive detector (such as a charge-coupled device (CCD), or photomultiplier tube (PMT)). FT-Raman has also been used with microscopes. Ultraviolet microscopes and UV enhanced optics must be used when a UV laser source is used for Raman microspectroscopy.

In direct imaging, the whole field of view is examined for scattering over a small range of wavenumbers (Raman shifts).

For instance, a wavenumber characteristic for cholesterol could be used to record the distribution of cholesterol within a cell culture.

The other approach is hyperspectral imaging or chemical imaging, in which thousands of Raman spectra are acquired from all over the field of view. The data can then be used to generate images showing the location and amount of different components. Taking the cell culture example, a hyperspectral image could show the distribution of cholesterol, as well as proteins, nucleic acids, and fatty acids. Sophisticated signal- and image-processing techniques can be used to ignore the presence of water, culture media, buffers, and other interferents.

Raman microscopy, and in particular confocal microscopy, has very high spatial resolution. For example, the lateral and depth resolutions were 250 nm and 1.7 μm, respectively, using a confocal Raman microspectrometer with the 632.8 nm line from a Helium-Neon laser with a pinhole of 100 μm diameter. Since the objective lenses of microscopes focus the laser beam to several micrometres in diameter, the resulting photon flux is much higher than achieved in conventional Raman setups. This has the added benefit of enhanced fluorescence quenching. However, the high photon flux can also cause sample degradation, and for this reason some setups require a thermally conducting substrate (which acts as a heat sink) in order to mitigate this process.

By using Raman microspectroscopy, *in vivo* time- and space-resolved Raman spectra of microscopic regions of samples can be measured. As a result, the fluorescence of water, media, and buffers can be removed. Consequently *in vivo* time- and space-resolved Raman spectroscopy is suitable to examine proteins, cells and organs.

Raman microscopy for biological and medical specimens generally uses near-infrared (NIR) lasers (785 nm diodes and 1064 nm Nd:YAG are especially common). This reduces the risk of damaging the specimen by applying higher energy wavelengths. However, the intensity of NIR Raman is low (owing to the ω^4 dependence of Raman scattering intensity), and most detectors required very long collection times.

Recently, more sensitive detectors have become available, making the technique better suited to general use. Raman microscopy of inorganic specimens, such as rocks and ceramics and polymers, can use a broader range of excitation wavelengths.

Polarised Analysis

The polarisation of the Raman scattered light also contains useful information. This property can be measured using (plane) polarised laser excitation and a polarisation analyser. Spectra acquired with the analyser set at both perpendicular and parallel to the excitation plane can be used to calculate the depolarisation ratio. Study of the technique is useful in teaching the connections between group theory, symmetry, Raman activity, and peaks in the corresponding Raman spectra.

The spectral information arising from this analysis gives insight into molecular orientation and vibrational symmetry. In essence, it allows the user to obtain valuable information relating to the molecular shape, for example in synthetic chemistry or polymorph analysis. It is often used to understand macromolecular orientation in crystal lattices, liquid crystals or polymer samples.

Variations

Several variations of Raman spectroscopy have been developed. The usual purpose is to enhance the sensitivity (*e.g.*, surface-enhanced Raman), to improve the spatial resolution (Raman microscopy), or to acquire very specific information (resonance Raman).

- *Surface Enhanced Raman Spectroscopy (SERS)*: Normally done in a silver or gold colloid or a substrate containing silver or gold. Surface plasmons of silver and gold are excited by the laser, resulting in an increase in the electric fields surrounding the metal. Given that Raman intensities are proportional to the electric field, there is large increase in the measured signal (by up to 10^{11}). This effect was originally observed by Martin Fleischmann but the prevailing explanation was proposed by Van Duyne in 1977. A comprehensive theory of the effect was given by Lombardi and Birke.

- *Resonance Raman spectroscopy:* The excitation wavelength is matched to an electronic transition of the molecule or crystal, so that vibrational modes associated with the excited electronic state are greatly enhanced. This is useful for studying large molecules such as polypeptides, which might show hundreds of bands in "conventional" Raman spectra. It is also useful for associating normal modes with their observed frequency shifts.
- *Surface-Enhanced Resonance Raman Spectroscopy (SERRS):* A combination of SERS and resonance Raman spectroscopy that uses proximity to a surface to increase Raman intensity, and excitation wavelength matched to the maximum absorbance of the molecule being analysed.
- *Angle Resolved Raman Spectroscopy:* Not only are standard Raman results recorded but also the angle with respect to the incident laser. If the orientation of the sample is known then detailed information about the phonon dispersion relation can also be gleamed from a single test.
- *Hyper Raman*: A non-linear effect in which the vibrational modes interact with the second harmonic of the excitation beam. This requires very high power, but allows the observation of vibrational modes that are normally "silent". It frequently relies on SERS-type enhancement to boost the sensitivity.
- *Spontaneous Raman Spectroscopy (SRS):* Used to study the temperature dependence of the Raman spectra of molecules.
- *Optical Tweezers Raman Spectroscopy (OTRS):* Used to study individual particles, and even biochemical processes in single cells trapped by optical tweezers.

- *Stimulated Raman Spectroscopy*: A spatially coincident, two colour pulse (with polarisation either parallel or perpendicular) transfers the population from ground to a rovibrationally excited state, if the difference in energy corresponds to an allowed Raman transition, and if neither frequency corresponds to an electronic resonance. Two photon UV ionisation, applied after the population transfer but before relaxation, allows the intra-molecular or inter-molecular Raman spectrum of a gas or molecular cluster (indeed, a given conformation of molecular cluster) to be collected. This is a useful molecular dynamics technique.
- *Spatially Offset Raman Spectroscopy (SORS):* The Raman scattering beneath an obscuring surface is retrieved from a scaled subtraction of two spectra taken at two spatially offset points
- *Coherent anti-Stokes Raman spectroscopy (CARS):* Two laser beams are used to generate a coherent anti-Stokes frequency beam, which can be enhanced by resonance.
- *Raman optical activity (ROA):* Measures vibrational optical activity by means of a small difference in the intensity of Raman scattering from chiral molecules in right- and left-circularly polarised incident light or, equivalently, a small circularly polarised component in the scattered light.
- *Transmission Raman:* Allows probing of a significant bulk of a turbid material, such as powders, capsules, living tissue, etc. It was largely ignored following investigations in the late 1960s but was rediscovered in 2006 as a means of rapid assay of pharmaceutical dosage forms. There are also medical diagnostic applications.
- Inverse Raman spectroscopy.
- *Tip-Enhanced Raman Spectroscopy (TERS):* Uses a metallic (usually silver-/gold-coated AFM or STM) tip to enhance the Raman signals of molecules

situated in its vicinity. The spatial resolution is approximately the size of the tip apex (20-30 nm). TERS has been shown to have sensitivity down to the single molecule level and holds some promise for bioanalysis applications.

MOLECULAR VIBRATIONS

In order to predict equilibrium stable-isotope fractionations, it is necessary to know the characteristic frequencies of molecular vibrations. It is also necessary to know how much each vibrational frequency in a molecule changes when a heavy isotope is substituted for a light one. Vibrational frequencies for isotopically substituted molecules are not always known, so it is often necessary to use some type of force-field model to predict them.

Molecular vibrations are also important in understanding infrared absorption and the mechanisms and kinetics of chemical reactions. Frequencies are most commonly measured with infrared or Raman spectroscopy. Rotational-vibrational spectroscopy, isotope substitution, and many forms of force-field modeling are used to determine characteristic atomic motions. This page shows some results from quantum-mechanical force-field modeling.

Transition elements like iron are most commonly found in octahedral and tetrahedral coordination environments. Linear, trigonal-bipyramidal, square-planar, and cubic coordination also occur. The links below show typical vibrational motions for molecules with some of these geometries.

Most of the animations show electronically neutral, gas phase molecules with the highest possible symmetry. The animations should reasonably approximate vibrational motions of complexes that are less symmetric or otherwise complicated because they are charged, in solution or part of a weak crystal lattice. Vibrational motions were calculated by normal-coordinate analysis with the *ab initio* electronic structure packages GAMESS and Gaussian03. Joseph Ochterski has written a good tutorial explaining in detail how an *ab initio* software package (in this case, Gaussian 03) calculates vibrational frequencies and motions.

VIBRATIONAL COORDINATES

The coordinate of a normal vibration is a combination of *changes* in the positions of atoms in the molecule. When the vibration is excited the coordinate changes sinusoidally with a frequency ν, the frequency of the vibration.

INTERNAL COORDINATES

Internal coordinates are of the following types, illustrated with reference to the planar molecule ethylene,

```
H     H
 \   /
  C=C
 /   \
H     H
```

- *Stretching*: a change in the length of a bond, such as C-H or C-C
- *Bending*: a change in the angle between two bonds, such as the HCH angle in a methylene group
- *Rocking*: a change in angle between a group of atoms, such as a methylene group and the rest of the molecule.
- *Wagging*: a change in angle between the plane of a group of atoms, such as a methylene group and a plane through the rest of the molecule,
- *Twisting*: a change in the angle between the planes of two groups of atoms, such as a change in the angle between the two methylene groups.
- *Out-of-plane*: a change in the angle between any one of the C-H bonds and the plane defined by the remaining atoms of the ethylene molecule. Another example is in BF_3 when the boron atom moves in and out of the plane of the three fluorine atoms.

In a rocking, wagging or twisting coordinate the bond lengths within the groups involved do not change. The angles do. Rocking is distinguished from wagging by the fact that the atoms in the group stay in the same plane.

In ethene there are 12 internal coordinates: 4 C-H stretching, 1 C-C stretching, 2 H-C-H bending, 2 CH_2 rocking, 2 CH_2 wagging, 1 twisting. Note that the H-C-C angles cannot be used as internal coordinates as the angles at each carbon atom cannot all increase at the same time.

Symmetry-adapted Coordinates

Symmetry-adapted coordinates may be created by applying a projection operator to a set of internal coordinates. The projection operator is constructed with the aid of the character table of the molecular point group. For example, the four(un-normalised) C-H stretching coordinates of the molecule ethene are given by,

$$Q_{s1} = q_1 + q_2 + q_3 + q_4$$

$$Q_{s2} = q_1 + q_2 - q_3 - q_4$$

$$Q_{s3} = q_1 - q_2 + q_3 - q_4$$

$$Q_{s4} = q_1 - q_2 - q_3 + q_4$$

where $q_1 - q_4$ are the internal coordinates for stretching of each of the four C–H bonds.

Illustrations of symmetry-adapted coordinates for most small molecules can be found in Nakamoto.

Normal Coordinates

The normal coordinates, denoted as *Q*, refer to the positions of atoms away from their equilibrium positions, with respect to a normal mode of vibration. Each normal mode is assigned a single normal coordinate, and so the normal coordinate refers to the "progress" along that normal mode at any given time. Formally, normal modes are determined by solving a secular determinant, and then the normal coordinates (over the normal modes) can be expressed as a summation over the cartesian cordinates (over the atom positions). The advantage of working in normal modes is that they diagonalise the matrix governing the molecular vibrations, so each normal mode is an independent molecular vibration, associated with its own spectrum of quantum mechanical states.

If the molecule possesses symmetries, it will belong to a point group, and the normal modes will "transform as" an irreducible representation under that group. The normal modes can then be qualitatively determined by applying group theory and projecting the irreducible representation onto the cartesian coordinates. For example, when this treatment is applied to CO_2, it is found that the C=O stretches are not independent, but rather there is a O=C=O symmetric stretch and an O=C=O asymmetric stretch.

- *Symmetric stretching*: the sum of the two C-O stretching coordinates; the two C-O bond lengths change by the same amount and the carbon atom is stationary. $Q = q_1 + q_2$
- *Asymmetric stretching*: the difference of the two C-O stretching coordinates; one C-O bond length increases while the other decreases. $Q = q_1 - q_2$

When two or more normal coordinates belong to the same irreducible representation of the molecular point group (colloquially, have the same symmetry) there is "mixing" and the coefficients of the combination cannot be determined *a priori*.

For example, in the linear molecule hydrogen cyanide, HCN, The two stretching vibrations are

1. Principally C-H stretching with a little C-N stretching; $Q_1 = q_1 + a\, q_2$ $(a \ll 1)$
2. Principally C-N stretching with a little C-H stretching; $Q_2 = b\, q_1 + q_2$ $(b \ll 1)$

The coefficients a and b are found by performing a full normal coordinate analysis by means of the Wilson GF method.

NEWTONIAN MECHANICS

Perhaps surprisingly, molecular vibrations can be treated using Newtonian mechanics to calculate the correct vibration frequencies. The basic assumption is that each vibration can be treated as though it corresponds to a spring. In the harmonic approximation the spring obeys Hooke's law: the force required to extend the spring is proportional to the extension. The proportionality constant is known as a *force constant, k*. The anharmonic oscillator is considered elsewhere.

$$\text{Force} = -kQ$$

By Newton's second law of motion this force is also equal to a reduced mass, μ, times acceleration.

$$\text{Force} = \mu \frac{d^2Q}{dt^2}$$

Since this is one and the same force the ordinary differential equation follows.

$$\mu \frac{d^2Q}{dt^2} + kQ = 0$$

The solution to this equation of simple harmonic motion is,

$$Q(t) = A\cos(2\pi \nu t); \nu = \frac{1}{2\pi}\sqrt{\frac{k}{\mu}}.$$

A is the maximum amplitude of the vibration coordinate *Q*. It remains to define the reduced mass, μ. In general, the reduced mass of a diatomic molecule, AB, is expressed in terms of the atomic masses, m_A and m_B, as,

$$\frac{1}{\mu} = \frac{1}{m_A} + \frac{1}{m_B}.$$

The use of the reduced mass ensures that the centre of mass of the molecule is not affected by the vibration. In the harmonic approximation the potential energy of the molecule is a quadratic function of the normal coordinate. It follows that the force-constant is equal to the second derivative of the potential energy.

$$k = \frac{\partial^2 V}{\partial Q^2}$$

When two or more normal vibrations have the same symmetry a full normal coordinate analysis must be performed. The vibration frequencies, ν_i are obtained from the eigenvalues, λ_i, of the matrix product *GF*. *G* is a matrix of numbers derived from the masses of the atoms and the geometry of the molecule. *F* is a matrix derived from force-constant values.

QUANTUM MECHANICS

In the harmonic approximation the potential energy is a quadratic function of the normal coordinates. Solving the

Schrödinger wave equation, the energy states for each normal coordinate are given by,

$$E_n = h\left(n+\frac{1}{2}\right)v = h\left(\eta+\frac{1}{2}\right)\frac{1}{2}\sqrt{\frac{k}{m,}}$$

where *n* is a quantum number that can take values of 0, 1, 2... The difference in energy when *n* changes by 1 are therefore equal to the energy derived using classical mechanics. Knowing the wave functions, certain selection rules can be formulated. For example, for a harmonic oscillator transitions are allowed only when the quantum number *n* changes by one,

$$\Delta\eta = \pm 1$$

but this does not apply to an anharmonic oscillator; the observation of overtones is only possible because vibrations are anharmonic. Another consequence of anharmonicity is that transitions such as between states *n*=2 and *n*=1 have slightly less energy than transitions between the ground state and first excited state. Such a transition gives rise to a hot band.

Intensities

In an infrared spectrum the intensity of an absorption band is proportional to the derivative of the molecular dipole moment with respect to the normal coordinate. The intensity of Raman bands depends on polarizability.

ELECTRON TRAPPING BY MOLECULAR VIBRATION

In photoelectron spectroscopy experiments performed at the ALS, a group of researchers has found that electronic transitions normally thought to be forbidden can in fact be excited in conjunction with certain types of molecular vibrations. Specifically, they found that when the symmetry of a linear triatomic molecule is broken by asymmetric vibrational modes, photoelectrons can become temporarily trapped by the molecule before ultimately escaping, giving rise to a broad feature in the photoelectron spectrum known as a shape resonance.

This process represents a novel type of symmetry-breaking phenomenon that has not been observed previously but appears to be widespread. Such coupling between electronic motion and nuclear motion becomes increasingly important as scientists learn more about the geometry and dynamics of novel chemical structures such as those found in nanodevices and transient chemical species, and the results have implications for studies that use photoelectron spectroscopy as a diagnostic tool.

The researchers performed vibrationally resolved photoelectron spectroscopy studies of gas-phase carbon disulfide (CS_2), a simple molecule consisting of a central carbon atom with two sulfur atoms on each side, 180 degrees apart. This molecule has one "bending" vibrational mode and two "stretching" modes: one symmetric and one antisymmetric.

Using the High-Resolution Atomic and Molecular Electron Spectrometer (HiRAMES) endstation at ALS Beamline 10.0.1, the group investigated how the vibrational structure in the photoelectron spectrum changes as the incident photon energy is varied. They found that when the incident photon energy is tuned to the shape resonance (about 40 eV), the peaks corresponding to the bending and asymmetric stretch modes are dramatically enhanced.

This is a new resonance phenomenon: the observed shape resonance is the result of coupling between vibrational modes and electronic transitions that are "forbidden" by selection rules.

However, such rules are based on simplifying approximations, and nominally forbidden behavior can occur as the result of unanticipated processes. Thus, exceptions to the rules provide opportunities to gain deeper insight into how electronic motion and nuclear motion are intertwined. In the case of CS_2, the forbidden behavior is observed only when the photoelectrons are tuned to specific resonant energies and become trapped, or quasibound, when the molecule is distorted from its equilibrium geometry. This point is made dramatically clear in plots of the relative probabilities (branching ratios) of the various vibrational modes vs. incident photon energy. The resonance peak appears vividly for the two asymmetric vibrations but is absent in the plot for the symmetric vibrational mode.

In addition, the researchers note that the shape and width of the curves for the bending mode and the antisymmetric stretching mode are very similar; only their amplitudes are different. This indicates that the resonance trapping does not depend on the specific type of distortion in the molecular geometry, only on the fact that the motion breaks the molecule's symmetry. The researchers have found that this type of unprecedented behaviour is exhibited for other molecules and is likely to be a general phenomenon. In addition to these experimental results, they have performed accurate electron-molecule scattering calculations, and these theoretical results were largely responsible for the qualitative explanations provided here.

The results demonstrate that there are resonances with little sensitivity to distortions in bond length. Because it is common to correlate shape resonance position with changes in bond length, this has implications for studies that use vacuum ultraviolet or X-ray probes for analysing complex or exotic structures. More generally, the results provide a natural means of examining coupling between nuclear and electronic degrees of freedom and for developing tools based on the connections between them.

DIATOMIC MOLECULE

Diatomic molecules are molecules composed only of two atoms, of either the same or different chemical elements. The prefix di- is of Greek origin, meaning *two*. Common diatomic molecules are hydrogen (H_2), nitrogen (N_2), oxygen (O_2), and carbon monoxide (CO). Seven elements exist as homonuclear diatomic molecules at room temperature: H_2, N_2, O_2, F_2, Cl_2, Br_2, and I_2. Many elements and chemical compounds aside from these form diatomic molecules when evaporated. The noble gases do not form diatomic molecules: this can be explained using molecular orbital theory.

OCCURRENCE

Hundreds of diatomic molecules have been characterised in the terrestrial environment, laboratory, and interstellar medium. About 99 per cent of the Earth's atmosphere is composed of diatomic molecules, specifically oxygen and nitrogen at 21 per cent and 78 per cent, respectively. The natural abundance of hydrogen (H_2) in the Earth's atmosphere is only on the order of parts per million, but H_2 is, in fact, the most abundant diatomic molecule in nature. The interstellar medium is, indeed, dominated by hydrogen atoms.

If a diatomic molecule consists of two atoms of the same element, such as H_2 and O_2, then it is said to be homonuclear, but otherwise it is heteronuclear. The bond in a homonuclear diatomic molecule is non-polar. In most diatomic molecules, the elements are non-identical. Prominent examples include carbon monoxide, nitric oxide, and hydrogen chloride, but other important examples include gaseous MgO, SiO, and many other species not normally considered diatomic because they polymerise near room temperature.

Elements that consist of diatomic molecules, under typical laboratory conditions of 1 bar and 25 °C, include hydrogen (H_2), nitrogen (N_2), oxygen (O_2), and the halogens (although it is not yet known whether astatine forms diatomic astatine molecules). Other elements form homonuclear diatomics when evaporated, but these diatomic species repolymerise at lower temperatures. For example, heating ("cracking") elemental phosphorus gives diphosphorus, P_2.

MOLECULAR GEOMETRY

Diatomic molecules cannot have any geometry but linear, as any two points always lie in a line. This is the simplest spatial arrangement of atoms after the sphericity of single atoms.

Historical Significance

Diatomic elements played an important role in the elucidation of the concepts of element, atom, and molecule in the 19th century, because some of the most common elements, such as hydrogen, oxygen, and nitrogen, occur as diatomic molecules. John Dalton's original atomic hypothesis assumed that all elements were monatomic and that the atoms in compounds would normally have the simplest atomic ratios with respect to one another. For example, Dalton assumed that water's formula was HO, giving the atomic weight of oxygen as eight times that of hydrogen, instead of the modern value of about 16. As a consequence, confusion existed regarding atomic weights and molecular formulas for about half a century.

As early as 1805, Gay-Lussac and von Humboldt showed that water is formed of two volumes of hydrogen and one volume of oxygen, and by 1811 Amedeo Avogadro had arrived at the correct interpretation of water's composition, based on what is now called Avogadro's law and the assumption of diatomic elemental molecules. However, these results were mostly ignored until 1860. Part of this rejection was due to the belief that atoms of one element would have no chemical affinity towards atoms of the same element, and part was due to apparent exceptions to Avogadro's law that were not explained until later in terms of dissociating molecules.

At the 1860 Karlsruhe Congress on atomic weights, Cannizzaro resurrected Avogadro's ideas and used them to produce a consistent table of atomic weights, which mostly agree with modern values. These weights were an important pre-requisite for the discovery of the periodic law by Dmitri Mendeleev and Lothar Meyer.

Energy Levels

It is convenient, and common, to represent a diatomic molecule as two point masses (the two atoms) connected by a massless spring.

The energies involved in the various motions of the molecule can then be broken down into three categories.

- The translational energies.
- The rotational energies.
- The vibrational energies.

Translational Energies

The translational energy of the molecule is simply given by the kinetic energy expression:

$$E_{trans} = \frac{1}{2}mv^2$$

where m is the mass of the molecule and v is its velocity.

Rotational Energies

Classically, the kinetic energy of rotation is,

$$E_{rot} = \frac{L^2}{2I}$$

where

L is the angular momentum

I is the moment of inertia of the molecule

For microscopic, atomic-level systems like a molecule, angular momentum can only have specific discrete values given by,

$$L^2 = l(l+1)\hbar^2$$

where l is a non-negative integer and $\hbar$ is the reduced Planck constant.

Also, for a diatomic molecule the moment of inertia is,

$$I = \mu r_0^2$$

where

μ is the reduced mass of the molecule and

r_0 is the average distance between the two atoms in the molecule.

So, substituting the angular momentum and moment of inertia into E_{rot}, the rotational energy levels of a diatomic molecule are given by:

$$E_{rot} = \frac{\iota(\iota+1)\hbar^2}{2\mu r_0^2} \qquad \iota = 0,1,2,...$$

Vibrational Energies

Another way a diatomic molecule can move is to have each atom oscillate—or vibrate—along a line (the bond) connecting the two atoms. The vibrational energy is approximately that of a quantum harmonic oscillator:

$$E_{vib} = \left(\eta + \frac{1}{2}\right)\hbar w \qquad \eta = 0,1,2....$$

where

n is an integer

$\hbar$ is the reduced Planck constant and

w is the angular frequency of the vibration.

Comparison Between Rotational and Vibrational Energy Spacings

So the spacing, and the energy of a typical spectroscopic transition, between *vibrational* energy levels is about 100 times greater than that of a typical transition between *rotational energy* levels.

5

Visible and Ultraviolet Spectroscopy

BACKGROUND

An obvious difference between certain compounds is their colour. Thus, quinone is yellow; chlorophyll is green; the 2,4-dinitrophenylhydrazone derivatives of aldehydes and ketones range in colour from bright yellow to deep red, depending on double bond conjugation; and aspirin is colourless. In this respect the human eye is functioning as a spectrometer analysing the light reflected from the surface of a solid or passing through a liquid.

Although we see sunlight (or white light) as uniform or homogeneous in colour, it is actually composed of a broad range of radiation wavelengths in the ultraviolet (UV), visible and infrared (IR) portions of the spectrum. As shown on the right, the component colours of the visible portion can be separated by passing sunlight through a prism, which acts to bend the light in differing degrees according to wavelength. Electromagnetic radiation such as visible light is commonly treated as a wave phenomenon, characterised by a wavelength or frequency.

Wavelength is defined on the left below, as the distance between adjacent peaks (or troughs), and may be designated in meters, centimeters or nanometers (10^{-9} meters). Frequency is the number of wave cycles that travel past a fixed point per unit of time, and is usually given in cycles per second, or hertz

(Hz). Visible wavelengths cover a range from approximately 400 to 800 nm. The longest visible wavelength is red and the shortest is violet. Other common colours of the spectrum, in order of decreasing wavelength, may be remembered by the mnemonic: ROY G BIV. The wavelengths of what we perceive as particular colours in the visible portion of the spectrum are displayed and listed below:

- *Violet:* 400 - 420 nm
- *Indigo:* 420 - 440 nm
- *Blue:* 440 - 490 nm
- *Green:* 490 - 570 nm
- *Yellow:* 570 - 585 nm
- *Orange:* 585 - 620 nm
- *Red:* 620 - 780 nm

When white light passes through or is reflected by a coloured substance, a characteristic portion of the mixed wavelengths is absorbed. The remaining light will then assume the complementary colour to the wavelength(s) absorbed. This relationship is demonstrated by the colour wheel shown on the right.

Here, complementary colours are diametrically opposite each other. Thus, absorption of 420-430 nm light renders a substance yellow, and absorption of 500-520 nm light makes it red. Green is unique in that it can be created by absoption close to 400 nm as well as absorption near 800 nm. Early humans valued coloured pigments, and used them for decorative purposes. Many of these were inorganic minerals, but several important organic dyes were also known. These included the crimson pigment, kermesic acid, the blue dye, indigo, and the yellow saffron pigment, crocetin. A rare dibromo-indigo derivative, punicin, was used to colour the robes of the royal and wealthy. The deep orange hydrocarbon carotene is widely distributed in plants, but is not sufficiently stable to be used as permanent pigment, other than for food colouring.

THE ELECTROMAGNETIC SPECTRUM

The visible spectrum constitutes but a small part of the total radiation spectrum. Most of the radiation that surrounds us cannot be seen, but can be detected by dedicated sensing instruments. This electromagnetic spectrum ranges from very short wavelengths (including gamma and X-rays) to very long wavelengths (including microwaves and broadcast radio waves). The following chart displays many of the important regions of this spectrum, and demonstrates the inverse relationship between wavelength and frequency (shown in the top equation below the chart).

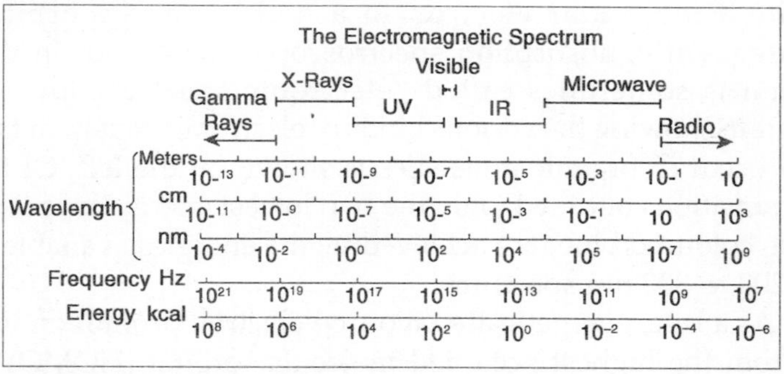

The Electromagnetic Spectrum

Gamma Rays, X-Rays, UV, Visible, IR, Microwave, Radio

Wavelength: Meters	10^{-13}	10^{-11}	10^{-9}	10^{-7}	10^{-5}	10^{-3}	10^{-1}	10
Wavelength: cm	10^{-11}	10^{-9}	10^{-7}	10^{-5}	10^{-3}	10^{-1}	10	10^{3}
Wavelength: nm	10^{-4}	10^{-2}	10^{0}	10^{2}	10^{4}	10^{5}	10^{7}	10^{9}
Frequency Hz	10^{21}	10^{19}	10^{17}	10^{15}	10^{13}	10^{11}	10^{9}	10^{7}
Energy kcal	10^{8}	10^{6}	10^{4}	10^{2}	10^{0}	10^{-2}	10^{-4}	10^{-6}

The energy associated with a given segment of the spectrum is proportional to its frequency. The bottom equation describes this relationship, which provides the energy carried by a photon of a given wavelength of radiation.

ν - c/ λ ν = frequency, λ = wavelength

c = velocity of light (c = 3. 1010 cm/sec)

$\Delta E = h\nu$ E=energy, ν = frequency,

h = planck's constant (h = 6,6.10 $^{-27}$ erg sec)

To obtain specific frequency, wavelength and energy values use this calculator.

UV-VISIBLE ABSORPTION SPECTRA

To understand why some compounds are coloured and others are not, and to determine the relationship of conjugation to colour, we must make accurate measurements of light absorption at different wavelengths in and near the visible part of the spectrum. Commercial optical spectrometers enable such experiments to be conducted with ease, and usually survey both the near ultraviolet and visible portions of the spectrum.

The visible region of the spectrum comprises photon energies of 36 to 72 kcal/mole, and the near ultraviolet region, out to 200 nm, extends this energy range to 143 kcal/mole. Ultraviolet radiation having wavelengths less than 200 nm is difficult to handle, and is seldom used as a routine tool for structural analysis.

The energies noted above are sufficient to promote or excite a molecular electron to a higher energy orbital. Consequently, absorption spectroscopy carried out in this region is sometimes called "electronic spectroscopy". A diagram showing the various kinds of electronic excitation that may occur in organic molecules is shown on the left. Of the six transitions outlined, only the two lowest energy ones (left-most, coloured blue) are achieved by the energies available in the 200 to 800 nm spectrum.

As a rule, energetically favoured electron promotion will be from the highest occupied molecular orbital (HOMO) to the lowest unoccupied molecular orbital (LUMO), and the resulting species is called an excited state. For a review of molecular orbitals click here. When sample molecules are exposed to light having an energy that matches a possible electronic transition within the molecule, some of the light energy will be absorbed as the electron is promoted to a higher energy orbital.

An optical spectrometer records the wavelengths at which absorption occurs, together with the degree of absorption at each wavelength. The resulting spectrum is presented as a graph of absorbance (A) versus wavelength, as in the isoprene spectrum.

Since isoprene is colourless, it does not absorb in the visible part of the spectrum and this region is not displayed on the graph. Absorbance usually ranges from 0 (no absorption) to 2 (99 per cent absorption), and is precisely defined in context with spectrometer operation.

Because the absorbance of a sample will be proportional to the number of absorbing molecules in the spectrometer light beam (*e.g.*, their molar concentration in the sample tube), it is necessary to correct the absorbance value for this and other operational factors if the spectra of different compounds are to be compared in a meaningful way.

The corrected absorption value is called "molar absorptivity", and is particularly useful when comparing the spectra of different compounds and determining the relative strength of light absorbing functions (chromophores). Molar absorptivity (ε) is defined as:

Molar (where *A*= absorbance, c = sample concentration in moles/litre and l
Absorptivity, ε = length of light path through the sample in cm.)
A = *A*/ c l

If the isoprene spectrum on the right was obtained from a dilute hexane solution ($c = 4 * 10^{-5}$ moles per litre) in a 1 cm sample cuvette, a simple calculation using the above formula indicates a molar absorptivity of 20,000 at the maximum absorption wavelength.

Indeed the entire vertical absorbance scale may be changed to a molar absorptivity scale once this information about the sample is in hand.

Chart

Chromophore	Example	Excitation	λ_{max}, nm	ε	Solvent
C=C	Ethene	$\pi \rightarrow \pi^*$	171	15,000	hexane
C≡C	1-Hexyne	$\pi \rightarrow \pi^*$	180	10,000	hexane
C=O	Ethanal	$n \rightarrow \pi^*$	290	15	hexane
		$\pi \rightarrow \pi^*$	180	10.000	hexane
N=O	Nitromethane	$n \rightarrow \pi^*$	275	17	ethanol
		$\pi \rightarrow \pi^*$	200	5,000	ethanol
C-X X=Br	Methyl bromide	$n \rightarrow \sigma^*$	205	200	hexane
X=I	Methyl Iodide	$n \rightarrow \sigma^*$	255	360	hexane

From the chart above it should be clear that the only molecular moieties likely to absorb light in the 200 to 800 nm region are pi-electron functions and hetero atoms having non-bonding valence-shell electron pairs. Such light absorbing groups are referred to as chromophores.

A list of some simple chromophores and their light absorption characteristics is provided on the left above. The oxygen non-bonding electrons in alcohols and ethers do not give rise to absorption above 160 nm. Consequently, pure alcohol and ether solvents may be used for spectroscopic studies.

The presence of chromophores in a molecule is best documented by UV-Visible spectroscopy, but the failure of most instruments to provide absorption data for wavelengths below 200 nm makes the detection of isolated chromophores problematic. Fortunately, conjugation generally moves the absorption maxima to longer wavelengths, as in the case of isoprene, so conjugation becomes the major structural feature identified by this technique.

Molar absorptivities may be very large for strongly absorbing chromophores (>10,000) and very small if absorption is weak (10 to 100). The magnitude ofε reflects both the size of the chromophore and the probability that light of a given wavelength will be absorbed when it strikes the chromophore.

THE IMPORTANCE OF CONJUGATION

The molar absorptivity (ε) roughly doubles with each new conjugated double bond. Spectroscopists use the terms defined in the table on the right when describing shifts in absorption.

Thus, extending conjugation generally results in bathochromic and hyperchromic shifts in absorption. The appearance of several absorption peaks or shoulders for a given chromophore is common for highly conjugated systems, and is often solvent dependent.

This fine structure reflects not only the different conformations such systems may assume, but also electronic transitions between the different vibrational energy levels possible for each electronic state. Vibrational fine structure of this kind is most pronounced in vapor phase spectra, and is increasingly broadened and obscured in solution as the solvent is changed from hexane to methanol.

Terminology for Absorption Shifts

Nature of Shift	Descriptive Term
To Longer Wavelength	Bathochromic
To Shorter Wavelength	Hypsochromic
To Greater Absorbance	Hyperchromic
To Lower Absorbance	Hypochromic

To understand why conjugation should cause bathochromic shifts in the absorption maxima of chromophores, we need to look at the relative energy levels of the pi-orbitals. When two double bonds are conjugated, the four p-atomic orbitals combine to generate four pi-molecular orbitals (two are bonding and two are antibonding). In a similar manner, the three double bonds of a conjugated triene create six pi-molecular orbitals, half bonding and half antibonding.

The energetically most favourable $\pi \rightarrow \pi^*$ excitation occurs from the highest energy bonding pi-orbital (HOMO) to the lowest energy antibonding pi-orbital (LUMO). The following diagram illustrates this excitation for an isolated double bond (only two pi-orbitals) and, on clicking the diagram, for a conjugated diene and triene.

In each case the HOMO is coloured blue and the LUMO is coloured magenta. Increased conjugation brings the HOMO and LUMO orbitals closer together. The energy (ΔE) required to effect the electron promotion is therefore less, and the wavelength that provides this energy is increased correspondingly (remember $\lambda = h \bullet c/\Delta E$).

Many other kinds of conjugated pi-electron systems act as chromophores and absorb light in the 200 to 800 nm region. These include unsaturated aldehydes and ketones and aromatic ring compounds. The spectrum of the unsaturated ketone (on the left) illustrates the advantage of a logarithmic display of molar absorptivity. The $\pi \rightarrow \pi^*$ absorption located at 242 nm is very strong, with an $\varepsilon = 18{,}000$. The weak $n \rightarrow \pi^*$ absorption near 300 nm has an $\varepsilon = 100$.

Benzene exhibits very strong light absorption near 180 nm ($\varepsilon > 65{,}000$), weaker absorption at 200 nm ($\varepsilon = 8{,}000$) and a group of much weaker bands at 254 nm ($\varepsilon = 240$). Only the last group of absorptions are completely displayed because of the 200 nm cut-off characteristic of most spectrophotometers. The added conjugation in naphthalene, anthracene and tetracene causes bathochromic shifts of these absorption bands.

A DOUBLE BEAM UV-VISIBLE ABSORPTION SPECTROMETER

This page describes a double beam UV-visible absorption

spectrometer in enough detail to meet the requirements of UK-based chemistry courses for 16-18 year olds.

THE OVERALL DESIGN

If you pass white light through a coloured substance, some of the light gets absorbed. A solution containing hydrated copper(II) ions, for example, looks pale blue because the solution absorbs light from the red end of the spectrum. The remaining wavelengths in the light combine in the eye and brain to give the appearance of cyan (pale blue).

Some colourless substances also absorb light- but in the ultra-violet region. Since we can't see UV light, we don't notice this absorption. Different substances absorb different wavelengths of light, and this can be used to help to identify the substance- the presence of particular metal ions, for example, or of particular functional groups in organic compounds.

The amount of absorption is also dependent on the concentration of the substance if it is in solution. Measurement of the amount of absorption can be used to find concentrations of very dilute solutions. An absorption spectrometer measures the way that the light absorbed by a compound varies across the UV and visible spectrum.

A Simple Double Beam Spectrometer

We'll start with the full diagram, and then explain exactly what is going on at each stage.

The Light Source

You need a light source which gives the entire visible spectrum plus the near ultra-violet so that you are covering the range from about 200 nm to about 800 nm. (This extends slightly into the near infra-red as well.)

You can't get this range of wavelengths from a single lamp, and so a combination of two is used- a deuterium lamp for the UV part of the spectrum, and a tungsten/ halogen lamp for the visible part. The combined output of these two bulbs is focussed on to a diffraction grating.

The Diffraction Grating and the Slit

You are probably familiar with the way that a prism splits light into its component colours. A diffraction grating does the same job, but more efficiently.

The slit only allows light of a very narrow range of wavelengths through into the rest of the spectrometer. By gradually rotating the diffraction grating, you can allow light from the whole spectrum (a tiny part of the range at a time) through into the rest of the instrument.

The Rotating Discs

This is the clever bit! Each disc is made up of a number of different segments. Those in the machine we are describing have three different sections - other designs may have a different number.

The light coming from the diffraction grating and slit will hit the rotating disc and one of three things can happen.

1. If it hits the transparent section, it will go straight through and pass through the cell containing the sample. It is then bounced by a mirror onto a second rotating disc.

   This disc is rotating such that when the light arrives from the first disc, it meets the mirrored section of the second disc. That bounces it onto the detector.
2. If the original beam of light from the slit hits the mirrored section of the first rotating disc, it is bounced down along the green path. After the mirror, it passes through a reference cell (more about that later).

   Finally the light gets to the second disc which is rotating in such a way that it meets the transparent section. It goes straight through to the detector.
3. If the light meets the first disc at the black section, it is blocked- and for a very short while no light passes through the spectrometer. This just allows the computer to make allowance for any current generated by the detector in the absence of any light.

The Sample and Reference Cells

These are small rectangular glass or quartz containers. They are often designed so that the light beam travels a distance of 1 cm through the contents.

The sample cell contains a solution of the substance you are testing- usually very dilute. The solvent is chosen so that it doesn't absorb any significant amount of light in the wavelength range we are interested in (200- 800 nm).

The reference cell just contains the pure solvent.

The Detector and Computer

The detector converts the incoming light into a current. The higher the current, the greater the intensity of the light.

For each wavelength of light passing through the spectrometer, the intensity of the light passing through the reference cell is measured. This is usually referred to as I_o - that's I for Intensity. The intensity of the light passing through the sample cell is also measured for that wavelength- given the symbol, I.

If I is less than I_o, then obviously the sample has absorbed some of the light. A simple bit of maths is then done in the computer to convert this into something called the *absorbance* of the sample- given the symbol, A. For reasons which will become clearer when we do a bit of theory on another page, the relationship between A and the two intensities is given by:

$$A = \text{Log}_{10} \frac{I_o}{I}$$

On most of the diagrams you will come across, the absorbance ranges from 0 to 1, but it can go higher than that.

An absorbance of 0 at some wavelength means that no light of that particular wavelength has been absorbed. The intensities of the sample and reference beam are both the same, so the ratio I_o/I is 1. Log_{10} of 1 is zero.

An absorbance of 1 happens when 90 per cent of the light at that wavelength has been absorbed- which means that the intensity is 10 per cent of what it would otherwise be.

In that case, I_o/I is 100/I0 (=10) and $\log_{10}$ of 10 is 1.

The Chart Recorder

Chart recorders usually plot absorbance against wavelength. The output might look like this:

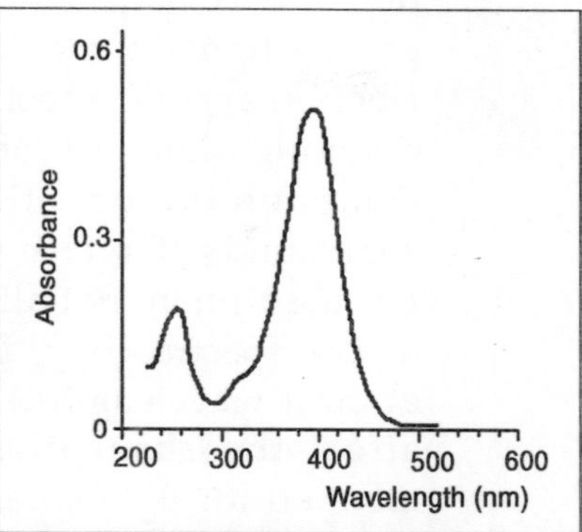

This particular substance has what are known as *absorbance peaks* at 255 and 395 nm.

PRINCIPLE OF ULTRAVIOLET-VISIBLE ABSORPTION

Molecules containing π-electrons or non-bonding electrons (n-electrons) can absorb the energy in the form of ultraviolet or visible light to excite these electrons to higher anti-bonding molecular orbitals. The more easily excited the electrons (*i.e.,* lower energy gap between the HOMO and the LUMO), the longer the wavelength of light it can absorb.

APPLICATIONS

UV/Vis spectroscopy is routinely used in analytical chemistry for the quantitative determination of different analytes, such as transition metal ions, highly conjugated organic compounds, and biological macromolecules.

Spectroscopic analysis is commonly carried out in solutions but solids and gases may also be studied.

- Solutions of transition metal ions can be coloured (*i.e.,* absorb visible light) because d electrons within the metal atoms can be excited from one electronic state to another. The colour of metal ion solutions is strongly affected by the presence of other species, such as certain anions or ligands. For instance, the colour of a dilute solution of copper sulfate is a very light blue; adding ammonia intensifies the colour and changes the wavelength of maximum absorption (λ_{max}).

- Organic compounds, especially those with a high degree of conjugation (*e.g.*, DNA, RNA, protein), also absorb light in the UV or visible regions of the electromagnetic spectrum. The solvents for these determinations are often water for water-soluble compounds, or ethanol for organic-soluble compounds. (Organic solvents may have significant UV absorption; not all solvents are suitable for use in UV spectroscopy. Ethanol absorbs very weakly at most wavelengths.) Solvent polarity and pH can affect the absorption spectrum of an organic compound. Tyrosine, for example, increases in absorption maxima and molar extinction coefficient when pH increases from 6 to 13 or when solvent polarity decreases.
- While charge transfer complexes also give rise to colours, the colours are often too intense to be used for quantitative measurement.

The Beer-Lambert law states that the absorbance of a solution is directly proportional to the concentration of the absorbing species in the solution and the path length. Thus, for a fixed path length, UV/Vis spectroscopy can be used to determine the concentration of the absorber in a solution. It is necessary to know how quickly the absorbance changes with concentration. This can be taken from references (tables of molar extinction coefficients), or more accurately, determined from a calibration curve.

A UV/Vis spectrophotometer may be used as a detector for HPLC. The presence of an analyte gives a response assumed to be proportional to the concentration. For accurate results, the instrument's response to the analyte in the unknown should be compared with the response to a standard; this is very similar to the use of calibration curves. The response (*e.g.*, peak height) for a particular concentration is known as the response factor.

The wavelengths of absorption peaks can be correlated with the types of bonds in a given molecule and are valuable in determining the functional groups within a molecule. The

Woodward-Fieser rules, for instance, are a set of empirical observations used to predict λ_{max}, the wavelength of the most intense UV/Vis absorption, for conjugated organic compounds such as dienes and ketones. The spectrum alone is not, however, a specific test for any given sample. The nature of the solvent, the pH of the solution, temperature, high electrolyte concentrations, and the presence of interfering substances can influence the absorption spectrum. Experimental variations such as the slit width (effective bandwidth) of the spectrophotometer will also alter the spectrum. To apply UV/Vis spectroscopy to analysis, these variables must be controlled or accounted for in order to identify the substances present.

BEER-LAMBERT LAW

The method is most often used in a quantitative way to determine concentrations of an absorbing species in solution, using the Beer-Lambert law:

$$A = \text{Log}_{10}\left(I_0 / I\right) = \in .c.L,$$

where *A* is the measured absorbance, *I* is the intensity of the incident light at a given wavelength, *I* is the transmitted intensity, *L* the pathlength through the sample, and *c* the concentration of the absorbing species. For each species and wavelength, ε is a constant known as the molar absorptivity or extinction coefficient. This constant is a fundamental molecular property in a given solvent, at a particular temperature and pressure, and has units of $1/M^* \text{cm}$ or often $AU/M^* \text{cm}$.

The absorbance and extinction ε are sometimes defined in terms of the natural logarithm instead of the base-10 logarithm.

The Beer-Lambert Law is useful for characterising many compounds but does not hold as a universal relationship for the concentration and absorption of all substances. A 2nd order polynomial relationship between absorption and concentration is sometimes encountered for very large, complex molecules such as organic dyes (Xylenol Orange or Neutral Red, for example).

Practical Considerations

The Beer-Lambert law has implicit assumptions that must be met experimentally for it to apply otherwise there is a possibility of deviations from the law to be observed. For instance, the chemical makeup and physical environment of the sample can alter its extinction coefficient. The chemical and physical conditions of a test sample therefore must match reference measurements for conclusions to be valid.

Spectral Bandwidth

A given spectrometer has a spectral bandwidth that characterises how monochromatic the light is. It is important to have monochromatic source of radiation for analysis of the sample. If this bandwidth is comparable to the width of the absorption features, then the measured extinction coefficient will be altered. In most reference measurements, the instrument bandwidth is kept below the width of the spectral lines. When a new material is being measured, it may be necessary to test and verify if the bandwidth is sufficiently narrow. Reducing the spectral bandwidth will reduce the energy passed to the detector and will, therefore, require a longer measurement time to achieve the same signal to noise ratio.

Wavelength Error

In liquids, the extinction coefficient usually changes slowly with wavelength. A peak of the absorbance curve (a wavelength where the absorbance reaches a maximum) is where the rate of change in absorbance with wavelength is smallest. Measurements are usually made at a peak to minimize errors produced by errors in wavelength in the instrument, that is errors due to having a different extinction coefficient than assumed.

Stray Light

Another important factor is the purity of the light used. The most important factor affecting this is the stray light level of the monochromator

The detector used is broadband, it responds to all the light that reaches it. If a significant amount of the light passed through the sample contains wavelengths that have much lower extinction coefficients than the nominal one, the instrument will report an incorrectly low absorbance. Any instrument will reach a point where an increase in sample concentration will not result in an increase in the reported absorbance, because the detector is simply responding to the stray light. In practice the concentration of the sample or the optical path length must be adjusted to place the unknown absorbance within a range that is valid for the instrument. Sometimes an empirical calibration function is developed, using known concentrations of the sample, to allow measurements into the region where the instrument is becoming non-linear.

As a rough guide, an instrument with a single monochromator would typically have a stray light level corresponding to about 3 AU, which would make measurements above about 2 AU problematic. A more complex instrument with a double monochromator would have a stray light level corresponding to about 6 AU, which would therefore allow measuring a much wider absorbance range.

Absorption Flattening

At sufficiently high concentrations, the absorption bands will saturate and show absorption flattening. The absorption peak appears to flatten because close to 100 per cent of the light is already being absorbed. The concentration at which this occurs depends on the particular compound being measured. One test that can be used to test for this effect is to vary the path length of the measurement. In the Beer-Lambert law, varying concentration and path length has an equivalent effect—diluting a solution by a factor of 10 has the same effect as shortening the path length by a factor of 10. If cells of different path lengths are available, testing if this relationship holds true is one way to judge if absorption flattening is occurring.

Solutions that are not homogeneous can show deviations from the Beer-Lambert law because of the phenomenon of absorption flattening. This can happen, for instance, where the absorbing substance is located within suspended particles. The deviations will be most noticeable under conditions of low concentration and high absorbance. The reference describes a way to correct for this deviation.

Measurement Uncertainty Sources

The above factor contribute to the measurement uncertainty of the results obtained with UV/Vis spectrophotometry. If UV/Vis spectrophotometry is used in quantitative chemical analysis then the results are additionally affected by uncertainty sources arising from the nature of the compounds and/or solutions that are measured. These include spectral interferences caused by absorption band overlap, fading of the colour of the absorbing species (caused by decomposition or reaction) and possible composition mismatch between the sample and the calibration solution.

ULTRAVIOLET-VISIBLE SPECTROPHOTOMETER

The instrument used in ultraviolet-visible spectroscopy is called a UV/Vis spectrophotometer. It measures the intensity of light passing through a sample (*I*), and compares it to the intensity of light before it passes through the sample (I_o). The ratio *I*/*I* is called the *transmittance,* and is usually expressed as a percentage (%T). The absorbance, A, is based on the transmittance:

$$A = -\log(\%T / 100\%)$$

The UV-visible spectrophotometer can also be configured to measure reflectance. In this case, the spectrophotometer measures the intensity of light reflected from a sample (*I*), and compares it to the intensity of light reflected from a reference material (I_o) (such as a white tile). The ratio *I*/*I* is called the *reflectance,* and is usually expressed as a percentage (%R).

The basic parts of a spectrophotometer are a light source, a holder for the sample, a diffraction grating in a monochromator or a prism to separate the different wavelengths of light, and a detector. The radiation source is often a Tungsten filament (300-2500 nm), a deuterium arc lamp, which is continuous over the ultraviolet region (190-400 nm), Xenon arc lamp, which is continuous from 160-2,000 nm; or more recently, light emitting diodes (LED) for the visible wavelengths. The detector is typically a photomultiplier tube, a photodiode, a photodiode array or a charge-coupled device (CCD).

Single photodiode detectors and photomultiplier tubes are used with scanning monochromators, which filter the light so that only light of a single wavelength reaches the detector at one time. The scanning monochromator moves the diffraction grating to "step-through" each wavelength so that its intensity may be measured as a function of wavelength. Fixed monochromators are used with CCDs and photodiode arrays. As both of these devices consist of many detectors grouped into one or two dimensional arrays, they are able to collect light of different wavelengths on different pixels or groups of pixels simultaneously.

A spectrophotometer can be either *single beam* or *double beam*. In a single beam instrument (such as the Spectronic 20), all of the light passes through the sample cell. *Io* must be measured by removing the sample. This was the earliest design and is still in common use in both teaching and industrial labs.

In a double-beam instrument, the light is split into two beams before it reaches the sample. One beam is used as the reference; the other beam passes through the sample. The reference beam intensity is taken as 100 per cent Transmission (or 0 Absorbance), and the measurement displayed is the ratio of the two beam intensities. Some double-beam instruments have two detectors (photodiodes), and the sample and reference beam are measured at the same time. In other instruments, the two beams pass through a beam chopper, which blocks one beam at a time. The detector alternates between measuring the sample beam and the reference beam in synchronism with the chopper. There may also be one or more dark intervals in the chopper cycle. In this case, the measured beam intensities may be corrected by subtracting the intensity measured in the dark interval before the ratio is taken.

Samples for UV/Vis spectrophotometry are most often liquids, although the absorbance of gases and even of solids can also be measured. Samples are typically placed in a transparent cell, known as a cuvette. Cuvettes are typically rectangular in shape, commonly with an internal width of 1 cm. (This width becomes the path length, L, in the Beer-Lambert law.) Test tubes can also be used as cuvettes in some instruments. The type of sample container used must allow radiation to pass over the spectral region of interest. The most widely applicable cuvettes are made of high quality fused silica or quartz glass because these are transparent throughout the UV, visible and near infrared regions. Glass and plastic cuvettes are also common, although glass and most plastics absorb in the UV, which limits their usefulness to visible wavelengths.

Specialised instruments have also been made. These include attaching spectrophotometers to telescopes to measure the spectra of astronomical features. UV-visible microspectrophotometers consist of a UV-visible microscope integrated with a UV-visible spectrophotometer.

A complete spectrum of the absorption at all wavelengths of interest can often be produced directly by a more sophisticated spectrophotometer. In simpler instruments the absorption is determined one wavelength at a time and then compiled into a spectrum by the operator. By removing the concentration dependence, the extinction coefficient (ε) can be determined as a function of wavelength.

MICROSPECTROPHOTOMETRY

UV-visible spectroscopy of microscopic samples is done by integrating an optical microscope with UV-visible optics, white light sources, a monochromator, and a sensitive detector such as a charge-coupled device (CCD) or photomultiplier tube (PMT). As only a single optical path is available, these are single beam instruments. Modern instruments are capable of measuring UV-visible spectra in both reflectance and transmission of micron-scale sampling areas. The advantages of using such instruments is that they are able to measure microscopic samples but are also able to measure the spectra of larger samples with high spatial resolution.

As such, they are used in the forensic laboratory to analyse the dyes and pigments in individual textile fibres, microscopic paint chips and the colour of glass fragments. They are also used in materials science and biological research and for determining the energy content of coal and petroleum source rock by measuring the vitrinite reflectance. Microspectrophotometers are used in the semiconductor and micro-optics industries for monitoring the thickness of thin films after they have been deposited. In the semiconductor industry, they are used because the critical dimensions of circuitry is microscopic.

A typical test of a semiconductor wafer would entail the acquisition of spectra from many points on a patterned or unpatterned wafer. The thickness of the deposited films may be calculated from the interference pattern of the spectra. A map of the film thickness across the entire wafer can then be generated and used for quality control purposes.

6

Microwave Spectroscopy

The study of the interaction of matter and electromagnetic radiation in the microwave region of the spectrum.

The interaction of microwaves with matter can be detected by observing the attenuation or phase shift of a microwave field as it passes through matter. These are determined by the imaginary or real parts of the microwave susceptibility (the index of refraction). The absorption of microwaves may also trigger a much more easily observed event like the emission of an optical photon in an optical double-resonance experiment or the deflection of a radioactive atom in an atomic beam.

At room temperature, the relative population difference between the states involved in a microwave transition is a few percent or less. The population difference can be close to 100 per cent at liquid helium temperatures, and microwave spectroscopic experiments are often performed at low temperatures to enhance population differences and to eliminate certain line-broadening mechanisms. The population differences between the states involved in a microwave transition can also be enhanced by artificial means. When the molecules or atoms with inverted populations are placed in an appropriate microwave cavity, the cavity will oscillate spontaneously as a maser (microwave amplification by stimulated emission of radiation).

The magnetic dipole and electric quadrupole interactions between the nuclei and electrons in atoms and molecules can lead to energy splittings in the microwave region of the spectrum. Thus, microwave spectroscopy has been used extensively for precision determinations of spins and moments of nuclei. The rotational frequencies of molecules often fall within the microwave range, and microwave spectroscopy has contributed a great deal of information about the moments of inertia, the spin-rotation coupling mechanisms, and other physical properties of rotating molecules.

The magnetic resonance frequencies of electrons in fields of a few thousand gauss (a few tenths of a tesla) lie in the microwave region. Thus, microwave spectroscopy is used in the study of electron-spin resonance or paramagnetic resonance.

The cyclotron resonance frequencies of electrons in solids at magnetic fields of a few thousand gauss (a few tenths of a tesla) lie within the microwave region of the spectrum. Microwave spectroscopy has been used to map out the dependence of the effective mass on the electron momentum.

TYPES OF MICROWAVE SPECTROMETER

There are two types of microwave spectrometer in use. In the conventional Stark-modulated spectrometer, the sample is contained in a long (1- to 3-metre, or 3.3- to 9.8-foot) section of a rectangular waveguide, sealed at each end with a microwave transmitting window (*e.g.*, mica or Mylar), and connected to a vacuum line for evacuation and sample introduction.

The radiation from the source passes through a gaseous sample and is detected by a crystal diode detector that is followed by an amplifier and display system (chart recorder). In order to increase the sensitivity of the instrument, signal modulation by application of a high-voltage square wave across the sample is used. The second type is the Fourier-transform spectrometer, in which the radiation is confined in an evacuated cavity between a pair of spherical mirrors and the sample is introduced by a pulsed nozzle that lowers the temperature of the sample to less than 10 K.

The sample is subjected to rotational energy excitation by application of a pulsed microwave signal, and the resulting emission signal is detected and Fourier-transformed to an absorption versus frequency spectrum. In both instruments the energy absorbed or emitted as the molecules undergo transitions from one quantised rotational state to another is observed. The Fourier-transform instrument has the advantage of providing higher resolution (1 kilohertz [kHz] relative to 30 kHz) and of exhibiting a much simpler spectrum due to the low sample temperature that insures that the majority of the molecules are in the few lowest energy states.

For observation of its rotational spectrum, a molecule must possess a permanent electric dipole moment and have a vapour pressure such that it can be introduced into a sample cell at extremely low pressures (5–50 millitorr; one millitorr equals 1×10^{-3} millimetre of mercury or 1.93×10^{-5} pound per square inch). The spectra of molecules with structures containing up to 15 atoms can be routinely analysed, but the density and overlapping of spectral lines in the spectra of larger molecules severely restricts analysis.

MOLECULAR APPLICATIONS

The relationship between the observed microwave transition frequency and the rotational constant of a diatomic molecule can provide a value for the internuclear distance. The quantitative geometric structures of molecules can also be obtained from the measured transitions in its microwave spectrum. In addition to geometric structures, other properties related to molecular structure can be investigated, including electric dipole moments, energy barriers to internal rotation, centrifugal distortion parameters, magnetic moments, nuclear electric quadrupole moments, vibration-rotation interaction parameters, low-frequency vibrational transitions, molecular electric quadrupole moments, and information relative to electron distribution and bonding. Microwave spectroscopy has provided the detailed structure and associated parameters for several thousand molecules.

The use of Fourier-transform spectrometers has provided a method for studying many short-lived species such as free radicals (*i.e.*, OH, CN, NO, CF, CCH), molecular ions (*i.e.*, CO^+, HCO^+, HCS^+), and Van der Waals complexes (*i.e.*, C_6H_6–HCl, H_2O–H_2O, Kr″HF, SO_2″SO_2).

There is a special relationship between microwave spectroscopy and radio astronomy. Much of the impetus for the investigation of the microwave spectra of radical and molecular ions stems from the need for identifying the microwave emission signals emanating from extraterrestrial sources. This collaboration has resulted in the identification in outer space of several dozen species, including the hydroxyl radical, methanol, formaldehyde, ammonia, and methyl cyanide.

For a polyatomic molecule, which is characterised by three moments of inertia, the microwave spectrum of a single molecular species provides insufficient information for making a complete structure assignment and calculating the magnitude of all bond angles and interatomic distances in the molecule.

For example, the values of the three moments of inertia of the $^{12}CH_2{}^{81}Br^{12}C^{14}N$ molecule will depend on eight bond parameters (four angles and four distances), hence it is not possible to obtain discrete values of these eight unknowns from three moments. This problem can be circumvented by introducing the assumption that the structure of the molecule will not significantly change if one or more atoms are substituted with a different isotopic species. The three moments of an isotopically substituted molecule are then derived from its microwave spectrum and, since they depend on the same set of molecular parameters, provide three additional pieces of data from which to obtain the eight bond parameters.

By determining the moments of inertia of a sufficient number of isotopically substituted species, it is possible to obtain sufficient data from which to completely determine the structure. The best structural information is obtained when an isotopic species resulting from substitution at each atom site in the molecule can be studied.

INFRARED SPECTROSCOPY

This technique covers the region of the electromagnetic spectrum between the visible (wavelength of 800 nanometres) and the short-wavelength microwave (0.3 millimetre). The spectra observed in this region are primarily associated with the internal vibrational motion of molecules, but a few light molecules will have rotational transitions lying in the region. For the infrared region, the wavenumber (ν, the reciprocal of the wavelength) is commonly used to measure energy. Infrared spectroscopy historically has been divided into three regions, the near infrared (4,000–12,500 inverse centimetres [cm^{-1}]), the mid-infrared (400–4,000 cm^{-1}) and the far infrared (10–400 cm^{-1}). With the development of Fourier-transform spectrometers, this distinction of areas has blurred and the more sophisticated instruments can cover from 10 to 25,000 cm^{-1} by an interchange of source, beam splitter, detector, and sample cell.

INTERFACE OF RADIATION WITH MATTER

We are now in a position to consider what happens when this radiation interacts with matter. Our main reason for doing this is to find out what happens to the radiation as it passes through matter and also to set ourselves up for considering how it interacts with living tissue and how to detect radiation. Since all radiation detectors are made from some form of matter it is useful to first of all know how radiation interacts so that we can exploit the effects in the design of such detectors.

Before we do this let us first remind ourselves of the physical characteristics of the major types of radiation. We have covered this information in some detail earlier and it is summarised in the table below for convenience.

We will now consider the passage of each type of radiation through matter with most attention given to gamma-rays because they are the most common type used in nuclear medicine. One of the main effects that you will notice irrespective of the type of radiation is that ions are produced when radiation interacts with matter. It is for this reason that it is called ionising radiation.

Table 6.1

Radiation	Mass	Electric Charge	Velocity
Alpha Particles	Relatively heavy	Double positive	Relatively slow
Beta Particles	about 8,000 times lighter	negative	less than the velocity of light
Gamma Rays	None	None	3×10^8 m/s in free space

Before we start though you might find an analogy useful to help you with your thinking. This analogy works on the basis of thinking about matter as an enormous mass of atoms (that is nuclei with orbiting electrons) and that the radiation is a particle/photon passing through this type of environment. So the analogy to think about is a spaceship passing through a meteor storm like you might see in a science-fiction movie where the spaceship represents the radiation and the meteors represent the atoms of the material through which the radiation is passing. One added feature to bring on board however is that our spaceship sometimes has an electric charge depending on the type of radiation it represents.

ALPHA PARTICLES

We can see from the table above that alpha-particles have a double positive charge and we can therefore easily appreciate that they will exert considerable electrostatic attraction on the outer orbital electrons of atoms near which they pass. The result is that some electrons will be attracted away from their parent atoms and that ions will be produced. In other words ionisations occur.

We can also appreciate from the table that alpha-particles are quite massive relative to the other types of radiation and also to the electrons of atoms of the material through which they are passing. As a result they travel in straight lines through matter except for rare direct collisions with nuclei of atoms along their path.

A third feature of relevance here is the energy with which they are emitted. This energy in the case of alpha-particles is always distinct. For example ^{221}Ra emits an alpha-particle with an energy of 6.71 MeV. Every alpha-particle emitted from this radionuclide has this energy. Another example is ^{230}U which emits three alpha-particles with energies of 5.66, 5.82, 5.89 MeV.

Finally it is useful to note that alpha-particles are very damaging biologically and this is one reason why they are not used for in-vivo diagnostic studies.

BETA PARTICLES

We can see from the table that beta-particles have a negative electric charge. Beta-minus particles last considerably longer and are therefore the focus of our attention here.

Because of their negative charge they are attracted by nuclei and repelled by electron clouds as they pass through matter. The result once again without going into great detail is ionisation.

The path of beta-particles in matter is often described as being tortuous, since they tend to ricochet from atom to atom.

A final and important point to note is that the energy of beta-particles is never found to be distinct in contrast to the alpha-particles above. The energies of the beta-particles from a radioactive source forms a spectrum up to a maximum energy. Notice from the figure that a range of energies is present and features such as the mean energy, E_{mean}, or the maximum energy, E_{max}, are quoted.

The question we will consider here is: why should a spectrum of energies be seen? Surely if a beta-particle is produced inside a nucleus when a neutron is converted into a proton, a single distinct energy should result. The answer lies in the fact that two particles are actually produced in beta-decay. We did not cover this in our treatment for fear of complicating things too much at that stage of this wikibook. But we will cover it here briefly for the sake of completeness.

The second particle produced in beta-decay is called a neutrino and was named by Enrico Fermi. It is quite a mysterious particle possessing virtually no mass and carrying no charge, though we are still researching its properties today. The difficulty with them is that they are very hard to detect and this has greatly limited our knowledge about them so far.

The beta-particle energy spectrum can be explained by considering that the energy produced when a neutron is converted to a proton is shared between the beta-particle and the anti-neutrino. Sometimes all the energy is given to the beta-particle and it receives the maximum energy, E_{max}. But more often the energy is shared between them so that for example the beta-particle has the mean energy, E_{mean} and the neutrino has the remainder of the energy. Finally it is useful to note that beta-particles are quite damaging biologically and this is one reason why they are not used for *in-vivo* diagnostic studies.

GAMMA RAYS

Since we have been talking about energies above, let us first note that the energies of gamma-rays emitted from a radioactive source are always distinct. For example ^{99m}Tc emits gamma-rays which all have an energy of 140 keV and ^{51}Cr emits gamma-rays which have an energy of 320 keV.

Gamma-rays have many modes of interaction with matter.

Those which have little or no relevance to nuclear medicine imaging are:

- Mössbauer Effect.
- Coherent Scattering.
- Pair Production.

Those which are very important to nuclear medicine imaging, are the Photoelectric Effect and the Compton Effect. We will consider each of these in turn below. Note that the effects described here are also of relevance to the interaction of X-rays with matter since as we have noted before X-rays and gamma-rays are essentially the same entities. So the treatment below is also of relevance to radiography.

Photoelectric Effect

When a gamma-ray collides with an orbital electron of an atom of the material through which it is passing it can transfer all its energy to the electron and cease to exist. On the basis of the Principle of Conservation of Energy we can deduce that the electron will leave the atom with a kinetic energy equal to the energy of the gamma-ray less that of the orbital binding energy. This electron is called a photoelectron.

Note that an ion results when the photoelectron leaves the atom. Also note that the gamma-ray energy is totally absorbed in the process.

Two subsequent points should also be noted. Firstly the photoelectron can cause ionisations along its track in a similar manner to a beta-particle. Secondly X-ray emission can occur when the vacancy left by the photoelectron is filled by an electron from an outer shell of the atom.

Compton Effect

This type of effect is somewhat akin to a cue ball hitting a coloured ball on a pool table. Here a gamma-ray transfers only part of its energy to a valance electron which is essentially free. Notice that the electron leaves the atom and may act like a beta-particle and that the gamma-ray deflects off in a different direction to that with which it approached the atom. This deflected or scattered gamma-ray can undergo further Compton Effects within the material.

Note that this effect is sometimes called Compton Scattering.

The two effects we have just described give rise to both absorption and scattering of the radiation beam. The overall effect is referred to as attenuation of gamma-rays. We will investigate this feature from an analytical perspective. Before we do so, we'll briefly consider the interaction of radiation with living matter.

RADIATION BIOLOGY

It is well known that exposure to ionising radiation can result in damage to living tissue. We've already described the initial atomic interactions. What's important in radiation biology is that these interactions may trigger complex chains of biomolecular events and consequent biological damage.

The primary means by which ionising radiations lose their energy in matter is by ejection of orbital electrons. The loss of orbital electrons from the atom leaves it positively charged. Other interaction processes lead to excitation of the atom rather than ionisation.

Here, an outer valence electron receives sufficient energy to overcome the binding energy of its shell and moves further away from the nucleus to an orbit that is not normally occupied. This type of effect alters the chemical force that binds atoms into molecules and a regrouping of the affected atoms into different molecular structures can result. That is, excitation is an indirect method of inducing chemical change through the modification of individual atomic bonds.

Ionisations and excitations can give rise to unstable chemical species called free radicals. These are atoms and molecules in which there are unpaired electrons. They are chemically very reactive and seek stability by bonding with other atoms and molecules. Changes to nearby molecules can arise because of their production.

In the case of X- and gamma-ray interactions, the energy of the photons is usually transferred by collisions with orbital electrons, *e.g.*, via photoelectric and Compton effects. These radiations are capable of penetrating deeply into tissue since their interactions depend on chance collisions with electrons. Indeed, nuclear medicine imaging is only possible when the energy of the gamma-rays is sufficient for complete emission from the body, but low enough to be detected.

The interaction of charged particles (*e.g.*, alpha and beta particles), on the other hand, can be by collisions with atomic electrons and also via attractive and repulsive electrostatic forces. The rate at which energy is lost along the track of a charged particle depends therefore on the square of the charge on that particle.

That is, the greater the particle charge, the greater the probability of it generating ion pairs along its track. In addition, a longer period of time is available for electrostatic forces to act when a charged particle is moving slowly and the ionisation probability is therefore increased as a result.

The situation is illustrated in the Figure 6.1 where tracks of charged particles in water are depicted. Notice that the track of the relatively massive α-particle is a straight line, with a large number of interactions (indicated by the asterisks) per unit length.

Notice also that the tracks for electrons are tortuous, and that the number of interactions per unit length is considerably less.

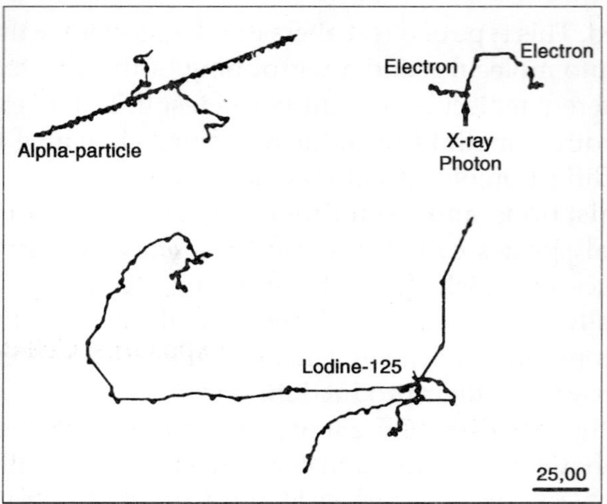

Fig. 6.1

Ionisations and excitations along particle tracks in water, for a 5.4 MeV α-particle (top left), for electrons generated following the absorption of a 1.5 keV X-ray photon (top right) and electrons generated during the decay of iodine-125.

The Linear Energy Transfer (LET) is defined as the energy released per unit length of the track of an ionising particle. A slowly moving, highly charged particle therefore has a substantially higher LET than a fast, singly charged particle. An alpha particle of 5 MeV energy and an electron of 1 MeV energy have LETs, for instance, of 95 and 0.25 keV/μm, respectively.

The ionisation density and hence the energy deposition pattern associated with the heavier charged particle is very much greater than that arising from electrons.

The energy transferred along the track of a charged particle will vary because the velocity of the particle is likely to be continuously decreasing. Each interaction removes a small amount of energy from the particle so that the LET gradually increases along a particle track with a dramatic increase (called the Bragg Peak) occurring just before the particle comes to rest.

The International Commission on Radiation Units and Measurements (ICRU) suggest that lineal energy is a better indicator of relative biological effectiveness (RBE). Although lineal energy has the same units as LET (*e.g.*, keV/μm), it is defined as the: ratio of the energy deposited in a volume of tissue to the average diameter of that volume.

Since the microscopic deposition of energy may be quite anisotropic, lineal energy should be a more appropriate measure of potential damage than that of LET. The ICRU and the ICRP have accordingly recommended that the radiation effectiveness of a particular radiation type should be based on lineal energy in a 1 μm diameter sphere of tissue. The lineal energy can be calculated for any given radiation type and energy and a Radiation Weighting Factor, (w_R) can then be determined based on the integrated values of lineal energy along the radiation track.

All living things on this planet have been exposed to ionising radiation since the dawn of time. The current situation for humans is summarised in the Table 6.2:

Table 6.2 Adapted with Permission from Applied Imaging Technology

Source	Effective Dose (mSv/year)	Comment
Cosmic radiation	~0.4	About 100,000 cosmic ray neutrons and 400,000 secondary cosmic rays penetrate our bodies every hour - and it increases with altitude!
Terrestrial radiation	~0.5	Over 200 million gamma-rays pass through our body every hour from sources such as soil and building materials
Internal radiation	~0.3	About 15 million ^{40}K atoms and about 7,000 natural uranium atoms disintegrate inside our bodies every hour, primarily from our diet
Radon and other gases	~1.3	About 30,000 atoms disintegrate inside our lungs every hour as a result of breathing

The sum total of this *Natural* Background Radiation is about 2.5 mSv per year, with large variations depending on altitude and dietary intake as well as geological and geographical location.

Its generally considered that repair mechanisms exist in living matter and that these can be invoked following radiation damage at the biomolecular level. These mechanisms are likely to have an evolutionary basis arising as a response to radiation fluxes generated by natural background sources over the aeons. Its also known that quite considerable damage to tissues can arise at quite higher radiation fluxes, even at medical exposures. Cell death and transformations to malignant states can result leading to latent periods of many years before clinical signs of cancer or leukemia, for instance, become manifest. Further treatment of this vast field of radiation biology however is beyond our scope here.

PRACTICAL RADIATION SAFETY

Since nuclear medicine involves handling substantial quantities of radioactive materials a radiation hazard arises for the user. Although this risk may be small, it remains important to keep occupational exposures as low as reasonably achievable (*i.e.,* the ALARA principle). There are a number of practices that can be adopted to aid in achieving this aim, which include:

- Maintaining a comprehensive record of all radioactive source purchases, usage, movement and storage.
- Storage of radioactive sources in a secure shielded environment. Specially dedicated facilities are required for the storage, safe handling, manipulation and dispensing of unsealed radioactive sources. Storage areas should be designed for both bulk radioisotope and radioactive waste. Furthermore, radioactive patients should be regarded as unsealed sources.
- Adequate ventilation of any work area. This is particularly important to minimize the inhalation of Technigas and potentially volatile radioisotopes such as I–125 and I–131. It is preferable to use fume hoods when working with volatile materials.

- Ensuring that any Codes of Safe Practice are adhered to and develop sensible written protocols and working rules for handling radioisotopes.
- Benches should be manufactured with smooth, hard impervious surfaces with appropriate splash-backs to allow ready decontamination following any spillage of radioisotopes. Laboratory work should be performed in stainless steel trays lined with absorbent paper.
- Protocols for dealing with minor contamination incidents of the environment or of staff members must be established. Remember that no matter how good work practices are, minor accidents or incidents involving spillage of radioisotopes can take place.
- Excretion of radioactive materials by patients may be via faeces, urine, saliva, blood, exhaled breath or the skin. Provision to deal with any or all of these potential pathways for contamination must be made.
- Provision for collection and possible storage of both liquid and solid radioactive waste may be necessary in some circumstances. Most short-lived, water soluble liquid waste can be flushed into the sewers but longer lived isotopes such as I-131 may have to be stored for decay. Such waste must be adequately contained and labelled during storage.
- Ensure that appropriate survey monitors are available to determine if any contamination has occurred and to assist in decontamination procedures. Routine monitoring of potentially contaminated areas must be performed.
- Ensure that all potentially exposed staff are issued with individual personnel monitors.
- Protective clothing such as gowns, smocks, overboots and gloves should be provided and worn to prevent contamination of the personnel handling the radioactivity. In particular, gloves must be worn when administering radioactive materials orally or

intravenously to patients. It should be noted that penetration of gloves may occur when handling some iodine compounds so that wearing a second pair of gloves is recommended. In any event, gloves should be changed frequently and discarded ones treated as radioactive waste.

- Eating and drinking of food, smoking, and the application of cosmetics is prohibited in laboratories in which unsealed sources are utilised.
- Mouth pipetting of any radioactive substance is totally prohibited.
- Precautions should be taken to avoid punctures, cuts, abrasions and any other open skin wounds which otherwise might allow egress of radiopharmaceuticals into the blood stream.
- Always ensure that there is a net benefit resulting from the patient procedure. Can the diagnosis or treatment be made by recourse to an alternative means using non- ionising radiation?
- A useful administrative practice is to implement a programme of routine and or random laboratory audits, to establish that safe work practices are being adhered to.
- Ensure that all staff, including physicians, technologists, nurses and interns and other students, who are involved in the practice of nuclear medicine receive the relevant level of training and education appropriate to their assigned tasks. The training programme could be in the form of seminars, refresher courses and informal tutorials.
- A substantive Quality Assurance (QA) programme should be implemented to ensure that the function of the Dose Calibrator, Gamma Camera, computer and other ancillary equipment is optimised.
- Finally, it is worth reiterating, that attempts should be made to minimize the activity used in all procedures. Remember that the more activity you use the more radiation exposure you will receive.

The potential hazards to staff in nuclear medicine include:

- Milking the $^{99m}T_c/^{99}M_o$ generator, drawing up and measuring the amount of radioisotope prior to administration.
- Delivering the activity to the patient by injection or other means and positioning the now radioactive patient in the imaging device.
- Removing the patients from the imaging device and returning them to the ward where they may continue to represent a radiation hazard for some time. For Tc-99m, a short-lived radionuclide the hazard period will be only a few hours but for therapeutic isotopes the hazardous period may be several days.
- Disposal of radioactive waste including body fluids, such as blood and urine, but also swabs, syringes, needles, paper towels, etc.
- Cleaning up the imaging area after the procedure.
- Contamination.

The table below lists the dose rates from patients having nuclear medicine examinations. In general, the hazards from handling or dealing with radioactive patients arise in two parts:

- *External hazard*: This will be the case when the radioisotope emits penetrating γ-rays. Usually, this hazard can be minimised by employing shielding and sensible work practices.
- *Radioactive contamination*: This is potentially of more concern as it may lead to the inhalation or ingestion of radioactive material by staff. Possible sources of contamination are radioactive blood, urine and saliva, emanating from a patient, or airborne radioactive vapour. Again, sensible work practices, which involve high levels of personal hygiene, should ensure that contamination is not a major issue.

One of the most common nuclear medicine diagnostic procedures is the bone scan using the isotope Tc-99m. The exposure rate at 1 metre from a typical patient will peak at approximately 3 μSv per hour immediately after injection dropping steadily because of radioactivity decay and through excretion so that after 2 hours it will be about 1.5 μSv per hour. Neglecting any further excretion, the total exposure received by an individual, should that person stand one meter from the patient for the whole of the first 24 hours, would be ~17 μSv. For a person at 3 meters from the patient this number would reduce to 1.7 μSv and for a distance of 5 metres it would be ~0.7 μSv. These values have been estimated on the basis of the inverse square law.

One point to make is that these figures assume no reduction in exposure caused by intervening attenuation such as building materials. Also note that excretion is in fact quite important in terms of patients clearing radioactivity from their body. Patients should be encouraged to drink substantial quantities of liquid following their scan, as this will improve excretion and aid in minimizing not only their radiation dose but also that of nursing staff.

It is informative to digress and address the issue as to whether or not it is safe to radiograph a patient if the latter has just been injected for a bone scan. Whilst this practice is not recommended in view of the ALARA principle, there are situations when such an eventuality may occur through no fault of any particular person. Two quite separate concerns are frequently raised.

Firstly, claims are made that the λ-rays emanating from the radioactive patient will degrade image quality and, secondly, that these same λ-rays represent a substantial risk to the radiographer. From a consideration of the numbers above, these concerns are not warranted, as in the few minutes that the patient may be close to the imaging device and/or the radiographer, the total absorbed dose received by either is going to be a fraction of a μGy. Even, in the potentially more serious scenario, where a sonographer may be required to perform an occasional abdominal ultrasound examination on a radioactive patient, the radiation dose received by the sonographer is still negligible in the context of the natural background dose he or she receives.

Contamination is one of the more insidious sources of accidental exposure as it can arise from innocuous events such as handling a tap, the telephone or power switch with contaminated gloves. However, the major source of hazard in nuclear medicine or laboratory departments relates to the potential for the ingestion or inhalation of radionuclides such as I-131 that will target specific organs. Any ingested or inhaled iodine will readily accumulate in the thyroid leading to an unnecessary and avoidable thyroid absorbed dose.

Although the immediate administration of stable iodine or equivalent (KI, $KClO_4$ or Lugols solution) may help minimize this uptake after a suspected uptake or misadventure, the real concern in those instances is when there is no awareness or knowledge of the uptake. Accordingly, high levels of personal hygiene must be practised in radioisotope laboratories.

The latter means wearing gloves, aprons or smocks and masks when handling radionuclides. Hands should be washed thoroughly and often. Eating of food or drinking in clinical areas and laboratory areas is strictly forbidden.

Decontamination facilities such as an emergency shower facility must be available and bench top and personal monitoring for contamination is also indicated. Decontamination usually involves little more than thorough washing of the skin surface with an appropriate soap or detergent. Care must be taken to avoid abrading the skin as this may allow direct entry of radioactivity into the blood stream.

Invariably, the radioisotopes used are highly penetrating so that it is rarely practicable in nuclear medicine departments for workers to protect themselves by continuously wearing very thick lead aprons for hours on end. When milking the generator, handling high specific activity sources or conducting some patient examinations it may be practicable to do so, but this would not be the normal situation. Note that the HVL for the 140 keV γ-ray of Tc-99m is ~0.25 mm of lead so that the commercially available lead aprons are of limited usefulness.

Nevertheless, a number of safety measures based on shielding can be implemented, such as:

- Some dose reduction, most particularly to the fingers, can be achieved by using lead syringe shields during the drawing up and injection phase.
- Radioisotopes should be stored in lead pots (except β emitters). Specifically, high activity sources such as $^{99m}Tc/^{99}Mo$ generators, should be located behind lead brick walls or stored in lead safes. Known beta emitters should be shielded in the first instance by low atomic number materials such as perspex to minimize the production of bremsstrahlung radiation. Bremsstrahlung radiation arises when highly energetic charged particles are stopped in high atomic number materials. They are in fact X-rays and as such are relatively penetrating but a thin outer shield of lead will protect against the minimal levels of bremsstrahlung produced in the perspex.

Access to areas where such sources are stored should be restricted.

INTERACTION BETWEEN PENETRATING RADIATION AND MATTER

When x-rays or gamma rays are directed into an object, some of the photons interact with the particles of the matter and their energy can be absorbed or scattered. This absorption and scattering is called attenuation. Other photons travel completely through the object without interacting with any of the material's particles. The number of photons transmitted through a material depends on the thickness, density and atomic number of the material, and the energy of the individual photons.

Even when they have the same energy, photons travel different distances within a material simply based on the probability of their encounter with one or more of the particles of the matter and the type of encounter that occurs. Since the probability of an encounter increases with the distance traveled, the number of photons reaching a specific point within the matter decreases exponentially with distance traveled. As shown in the graphic to the right, if 1000 photons are aimed at ten 1 cm layers of a material and there is a 10 per cent chance of a photon being attenuated in this layer, then there will be 100 photons attenuated. This leave 900 photos to travel into the next layer where 10 per cent of these photos will be attenuated. By continuing this progression, the exponential shape of the curve becomes apparent.

The formula that describes this curve is:

$$I = I_0 e^{-\mu x}$$

The factor that indicates how much attenuation will take place per cm (10 per cent in this example) is known as the linear attenuation coefficient, m. The above equation and the linear attenuation coefficient.

ALBERT EINSTEIN AND THE THEORY OF RELATIVITY

Newton's theory of gravitation was soon accepted without question, and it remained unquestioned until the beginning of this century. Then Albert Einstein shook the foundations of physics with the introduction of his Special Theory of Relativity in 1905, and his General Theory of Relativity in 1915 (Here is an example of a thought experiment in special relativity). The first showed that Newton's Three Laws of Motion were only approximately correct, breaking down when velocities approached that of light. The second showed that Newton's Law of Gravitation was also only approximately correct, breaking down in the presence of very strong gravitational fields.

NEWTON VS. EINSTEIN: ALBERT'S TURN TO KICK BUTT

We only summarize the differences between Newton's theory of gravitation and the theory of gravitation implied by the General Theory of Relativity. They make essentially identical predictions as long as the strength of the gravitational field is weak, which is our usual experience. However, there are three crucial predictions where the two theories diverge, and thus can be tested with careful experiments.

- The orientation of Mercury's orbit is found to precess in space over time. This is commonly called the "precession of the perihelion", because it causes the position of the perihelion to move. Only part of this can be accounted for by perturbations in Newton's theory. There is an extra 43 seconds of arc per century in this precession that is predicted by the Theory of General Relativity and observed to occur (a second of arc is 1/3600 of an angular degree). This effect is extremely small, but the measurements are very precise and can detect such small effects very well.
- Einstein's theory predicts that the direction of light propagation should be changed in a gravitational field, contrary to the Newtonian predictions. Precise observations indicate that Einstein is right, both about the effect and its magnitude. A striking consequence is gravitational lensing.
- The General Theory of Relativity predicts that light coming from a strong gravitational field should have its wavelength shifted to larger values (what astronomers call a "red shift"), again contary to Newton's theory. Once again, detailed observations indicate such a red shift, and that its magnitude is correctly given by Einstein's theory.
- The electromagnetic field can have waves in it that carry energy and that we call light. Likewise, the gravitational field can have waves that carry energy and are called gravitational waves. These may be thought of as ripples in the curvature of spacetime that travel at the speed of light.

  Just as accelerating charges can emit electromagnetic waves, accelerating masses can emit gravitational waves. However gravitational waves are difficult to detect because they are very weak and no conclusive evidence has yet been reported for their direct observation. They have been observed *indirectly* in the binary pulsar. Because the arrival time of pulses from the pulsar can be measured very precisely, it can be determined that the period of the binary system is gradually decreasing. It is found that the rate of period change (about 75 millionths of a second each year) is what would be expected for energy being lost to gravitational radiation, as predicted by the Theory of General Relativity.

THE MODERN THEORY OF GRAVITATION

And there is stands to the present day. Our best current theory of gravitation is the General Theory of Relativity. However, only if velocities are comparable to that of light, or gravitational fields are much larger than those encountered on the Earth, do the Relativity theory and Newton's theories differ in their predictions. Under most conditions Newton's three laws and his theory of gravitation are adequate.

ROTATIONAL SPECTROSCOPY

The rotational spectrum of trifluoroiodomethane, CF_3I, between 6 and 18 gigahertz in frequency. The spectrum was measured over a couple of hours while using a chirped-pulse Fourier transform microwave spectrometer at the University of Bristol. The rotational transitions are labelled to indicate the rotational levels involved in the transition. Each rotational transition is extensively split by the effects of nuclear quadrupole coupling with the ^{127}I nucleus.

Rotational spectroscopy measures the absorption or emission of light by molecules in order to understand changes in their rotational energy. Microwave frequencies are most often used by experiments but rotational spectroscopy and microwave spectroscopy are not exactly the same. The earliest experiments in microwave spectroscopy involved studies of a vibrational mode of ammonia. Rotational spectroscopy is sometimes referred to as pure rotational spectroscopy and is distinct from ro-vibrational and ro-vibronic spectroscopies where changes in vibrational and/or electronic energies accompany those in rotations. Rotational spectroscopy is practical only in the gas phase where it is possible to distinguish transitions between individual quantum states known as rotational energy levels.

Molecular rotational motions are rapidly quenched and converted into other forms of energy in solids and liquids. Rotational spectra can be observed for molecules that have a permanent electric dipole moment. The electric field of the radiation exerts a torque on the molecule through its dipole moment causing the molecule to rotate more quickly (in excitation) or slowly (in relaxation). Homonuclear diatomic molecules such as dioxygen (O_2), dihydrogen (H_2), etc., do not have a dipole moment and, hence, no pure rotational spectrum. On rare occasions, the effects of centrifugal distortion allow spectra to be observed of molecules that do not have a permanent electric dipole moment. Likewise, electronic excitations can occasionally lead to asymmetric charge distributions and a net dipole moment.

Among the diatomic molecules, carbon monoxide (CO) has one of the simplest rotational spectra. As for tri-atomic molecules, hydrogen cyanide (HCa ≡ N) has a simple rotational spectrum for a linear molecule and hydrogen isocyanide (HN=C:) for a non-linear molecule. The difficulty involved in the interpretation of rotational spectra increases with the size and conformational flexibility of a molecule.

APPLICATIONS

Unlike NMR, Infrared and UV-Visible spectroscopies, microwave spectroscopy has not yet found widespread application in analytical chemistry. However, it is a powerful technique that continues to be used for contemporary research around the world. It is a uniquely precise tool for the determination of molecular structure in gas phase molecules.

It can be used to establish barriers to internal rotation such as that associated with the rotation of the CH_3 group relative to C_6H_5Cl in chlorotoluene (C_7H_8Cl), for example. When hyperfine structure can be observed, the technique can also provide information on the electronic structures of molecules. Much of current understanding of the nature of weak molecular interactions such as van der Waals, hydrogen and halogen bonds has been established through rotational spectroscopy. When connected with radio astronomy, the technique has had a key role in establishing the chemical composition of the interstellar medium.

HISTORICAL ACHIEVEMENTS

The microwave spectrum of a molecule (NH_3) was performed by Cleeton and Williams in 1934. Subsequent experiments exploited powerful sources of microwaves such as the klystron, many of which were developed for radio detection and ranging (RADAR) during the Second World War. Early RADAR tests illustrated starkly the significance of molecular absorption at microwave frequencies.

Charles Hard Townes recalls how atmospheric water vapour absorbed the microwave radiation from one source limiting the range to eight miles in RADAR applications. The number of experiments in microwave spectroscopy surged immediately after the war. By 1948, Gordy was able to prepare a review of the results contained in approximately 100 research papers.

Microwave spectroscopy became established as a uniquely powerful tool for the precise determination of structural details such as bond lengths and angles in gas phase molecules.

The invention of an instrument that achieved microwave amplification by stimulated emission of radiation (MASER) was reported by Townes *et al.* in 1955. The invention of the MASER ultimately stimulated the development of modern lasers which are used in applications as diverse as compact disc players, surgery and barcode readers.

The identification of molecules in the interstellar medium was a highlight of the 1960s. Microwave transitions were measured in the laboratory and matched to emissions from the interstellar medium using a radio telescope. NH_3 was the first stable polyatomic molecule to be identified in the interstellar medium. Many molecules of varying size and complexity have since been identified through radio astronomy. The combination of rotational spectroscopy and radio astronomy remains important in modern astrophysical chemistry.

A collaboration between Jim Heath, Sean O'Brien, Robert Curl, Harry Kroto and Richard Smalley aimed to measure the microwave spectra of unsaturated carbon chain molecules that Kroto hoped to identify around carbon-rich stars. Instead, the group identified the buckminsterfullerene molecule, C_{60}, and characterised its structure in a landmark paper in *Nature* in 1985. This work and subsequent developments led to the current interest in carbon nanotubes and a Nobel prize for Kroto, Smalley and Curl in 1996.

UNDERSTANDING THE ROTATIONAL SPECTRUM

In quantum mechanics the free rotation of a molecule is quantised, that is the rotational energy and the angular momentum can take only certain fixed values; what these values are is related simply to the moment of inertia, *I*, of the molecule.

In general, for any molecule, there are three moments of inertia: $I_A I$, and *Ic* about three mutually orthogonal axes *A*, *B*, and C with the origin at the center of mass of the system. Linear molecules are a special case because one of the moments of inertia (I_A, the moment of inertia along molecular axis) is negligible (*i.e.*, IA <<IB= Ic).

The general convention is to define the axes such that the axis A has the smallest moment of inertia, the axis B axis is the next smallest and so on such that $I_A \leq I_B \leq$ Ic. (A rarely used convention defines the A axis along a symmetric axis of the molecule, if one exists.

To avoid confusion, this article uses the prior convention.) The particular pattern of energy levels (and, hence, of transitions in the rotational spectrum) for a molecule is determined by its symmetry. A convenient way to look at the molecules is to divide them into four different classes (based on the symmetry of their structure). These are linear molecules, symmetric tops, spherical tops, and asymmetric tops. (Equivalently, many authors use the word "rotor" instead of "top".)

Linear Molecules

For a linear molecule the moments of inertia are related by $I_A << I_B$ = Ic. For most of the purposes, *I* is taken to be zero. For a linear molecule, the separation of lines in the rotational spectrum can be related directly to the moment of inertia of the molecule, and, for a molecule of known atomic masses, can be used to determine the bond lengths (structure) directly. For diatomic molecules, this process is trivial, and can be made from a single measurement of the rotational spectrum. For linear molecules with more atoms, rather more work is required, and it is necessary to measure molecules in which more than one isotope of each atom have been substituted (effectively this gives rise to a set of simultaneous equations that can be solved for the bond lengths).

Symmetric Tops

A symmetric top is a molecule in which two moments of inertia are the same. As a matter of historical convenience, spectroscopists divide molecules into two classes of symmetric tops, Oblate symmetric tops (saucer or disc shaped) with $I_A = I_B < I$ and Prolate symmetric tops (rugby football, or cigar shaped) with $I_A < I_B$ = Ic. The spectra look rather different, and are instantly recognisable. As with linear molecules, the structure of symmetric tops (bond lengths and bond angles) can be deduced from their spectra.

Spherical Tops

A spherical top molecule can be considered as a special case of *symmetric tops* with equal moment of inertia about all three axes ($I_A = I_B + I_G$).

Asymmetric Tops

An asymmetric top occurs if all three moments of inertia are different. Most large molecules are asymmetric tops, even when they have a high degree of symmetry. In general, for such molecules, a simple interpretation of the spectrum is not normally possible. However, molecules have spectra similar to those of a linear molecule or a symmetric top, in which case the molecular structure may also be similar to that of a linear molecule or a symmetric top.

For the most general case, however, all that can be done is to fit the spectra to three different moments of inertia. If the molecular formula is known, then educated guesses can be made of the possible structure, and, from this guessed structure, the moments of inertia can be calculated. If the calculated moments of inertia agree well with the measured moments of inertia, then the structure can be said to have been determined. For this approach to determining molecular structure, isotopic substitution is invaluable.

SPECTRAL LINES, WIDTH OF

Spectral lines in optical spectra of atoms, molecules, and other quantum systems are characterised by a range of frequencies v or a range of wavelengths $\lambda = c/\nu$, where c is the speed of light. Such a frequency or wavelength range is called the width of spectral lines.

A certain range $\Delta\nu_{ki}$ of frequencies near the frequency ν_{ki} of a radiative transition between discrete energy levels ε_k and ε_i corresponds to every such transition; the transition frequency

$$\nu M_{ki} = (\varepsilon_k - \varepsilon_i)lh = (\varepsilon_k - \varepsilon_j)/2\pi h\hbar, \text{ where } h = 2\pi\hbar$$

is Planck constant. The value of $\Delta\nu_{ki}$ gives the width of a spectral line, that is, the extent to which a given spectral line is non-monochromatic. A spectral-line profile $\phi(\nu)$—that is, the frequency dependence of the intensity of emission or absorption—usually has a maximum at or near the transition frequency ν_{ki}. The frequency range between points where the intensity falls to half the maximum intensity is taken as the width of a spectral line. Hence, the width of a spectral line is often referred to as the half-width of a spectral line. If the Doppler effect is not taken into account, the width $\Delta\nu_{ki}$ of a spectral line is given by the sum of the widths of the energy levels ε_k and ε_i:

$$\Delta\nu_{ki} = (\Delta\varepsilon_k - \Delta\varepsilon_i)\backslash h \approx (1/\tau_k + 1/\tau_i)/2\pi.$$

In other words, the shorter the lifetimes $\hat{o}_k$ and $\hat{o}_i$ at the energy levels, the greater the value of $\Delta\nu_{ki}$.

The natural width of a spectral line is given by the expression $(\Delta v_{ki})_{nat} = (A_k + A_i)/2\pi$, where A_k and A_i are the total probabilities of spontaneous transitions from the levels ε_k and ε_i to all lower-lying levels. The natural width is very small.

For atoms and molecules, the width of spectral lines is governed mainly by the broadening of the energy levels of the atoms or molecules during interactions with surrounding particles and by the broadening of the spectral lines as a result of the Doppler effect. In a gas or a plasma, the energy levels of the particles are broadened during collisions. Depending on the type of broadening, a symmetrical or an asymmetrical spectral-line profile is produced. A symmetrical profile, which is characteristic of radiation broadening.

LINES SEARCH FORM

The ASD Lines Search Form, referred to as the "Lines Form," provides access to transition data for atoms and ions. The Lines Form prompts the user for the following pieces of information:

MAIN PARAMETERS

- Spectra of interest (*e.g.*, Na I, Na II, Mg I–III, Mn–Co Ar-like).
- Lower and upper limits of the wavelength range
- Wavelength units.
  Wavelengths may be displayed in ångströms, nanometers, or micrometers. Wavelength units are selected by using the pulldown menu on the Lines Form.

For searches, a variety of output options, optional search criteria, and additional search criteria are available.

Lines searches are either wavelength ordered or multiplet ordered.

Dynamic Plots

This option allows graphical display of two types of dynamically created plots, *i.e.*, line identification plots and Saha-LTE (local thermodynamic equilibrium) plasma emission plots. The plots are created as PDF files and require appropriate software (*e.g.*, Adobe Acrobat Reader or xpdf) for graph display.

- *Line Identification Plot:* Selecting this option would produce a PDF file showing positions of all spectral lines within the chosen wavelength range.
- *Saha-LTE Spectrum:* Selecting this option would produce a PDF file showing line emission from an optically thin plasma having the chosen values of electron temperature and electron density. The plasma emission is generated in arbitrary units. If only one ion is chosen for plot generation, then the populations of the energy levels are calculated according to the Boltzmann formula $N_i = N_0/g_0{}^*g_i{}^*\exp(-E_i/T_e)$ where N_i is the level population, N_0 is the population of the ground state level, g_i and g_0 are the statistical weights of the levels, E_i is the energy of the level with respect to the ground state in eV, and T_e is the electron temperature in eV to be entered in the text field. In this case the electron density N_e is not required to be entered.

If several ions are chosen for plot generation (*e.g.*, "C I–V" is entered in the "Spectra" text field), then first the ionisation distribution between different ions is calculated according to the Saha formula, and then within each ion, the populations are calculated using the Boltzmann distribution formula. In this case both electron temperature and electron density are mandatory parameters.

The spectrum may be convoluted with the Doppler (Gaussian) line profile for each of the spectral lines. The number of data points for the spectrum is to be less or equal than 20 000. By default, the entered electron temperature T_e is used for calculation of the line width parameter. An ion temperature T_i may be entered if $T_i \neq T_e$.

JAVA GROTRIAN DIAGRAMS

Options on the Lines Form Page

- *Java subwindow size:* A user can choose the size of the subwindow which shows the Grotrian diagram

(GD). There are four sizes available (in pixels): 640×640, 800×640, 1024×768, and 1280×1024.

- *Grouping by configuration:* Normally the levels are grouped into series according to their core so that, for instance, in O I the levels belonging to configurations $2p^3(^4S^\circ)nl$ and $2p^3(^2D^\circ)nl$ would be assigned to different series. For ions with multiple cores, it may be more convenient to have such levels grouped according to configuration only, and if such an option is selected by clicking the corresponding checkbox, then for the OI case mentioned above those levels would belong to the same series of $2p^3nl$.
- *Term multiplicity*
  This option allows display of the levels belonging only to a particular term subsystem of the ion. The text entered in the text field should be a valid beginning of an atomic term designation. For example, entering "3" would result in display of only triplet levels and transitions between them, while entering "1P" would produce GD only for levels belonging to the ^1P terms and corresponding transitions.
- *Show only radiative linked levels*
  By default, all levels belonging to the chosen ion are displayed in the GD. Selecting this option would result in display of only those levels which are connected by radiative transitions.
- *Make Grotrian Diagram*
  Pressing the "Make Grotrian Diagram" button creates a Java Grotrian diagram on the new page.

Output Options

The following options apply to all lines and levels searches and are collectively referred to as output options.

- choice of display using an HTML table or an ASCII table.
- choice of removing Javascript tags in the output (may be convenient for ASCII table when saving the output into a file)

- level units. The user may choose between cm^{-1}, eV, or Rydberg.
- choice of viewing the (scrollable) data all at once, or one page at a time.
- choice of page size. The number of lines displayed on each page of output may be modified so that for each user's screen, the maximum number of lines may be viewed per screen-full.
- output ordering. The output can be sorted according to either wavelength or multiplet order. The multiplet order is available for *one* ion only.

Wavelength Ordering

All spectra are intermingled according to wavelength ordering. A spectrum must be provided if no wavelength range is indicated.

Multiplet Ordering

Multiplets are transitions that share the same term and configuration. Multiplets have been ordered in the transition probability compilations according to energies and *g* values of the lower and upper levels, and have been assigned arbitrary multiplet numbers that reflect this order.

To view multiplet ordered data, the user must select the "multiplet ordering" radio box.

In some cases, a multiplet is missing from the numbered list. In general, this is because some property of a compiled wavelength or level involved is not consistent with other more recent compilations, such as the NIST energy level data.

Only the lines with energy level classification are displayed in the multiplet-ordered output, and therefore the total number of lines shown at the top of the page may be different for wavelength and multiplet orderings.

The default is to display output in its entirety as an HTML formatted table. By default, levels are displayed in cm^{-1}.

Optional Search Criteria

The following search criteria may be specified:

- Maximum lower level energy.
- Maximum upper level energy.
- Preference of whether the transition strength bounds will apply to A_{ki} (default), f_{ik}, S, or log(gf) values.
- Minimum transition strength.
- Maximum transition strength.
- Accuracy minimum for A_{ki} (default), f_{ik}, S, and log(gf).
- Relative intensity minimum.

Additional Search Criteria

There are numerous options that apply for lines searches. The following options apply to all lines searches and are collectively referred to as additional search criteria options.

- Interest in displaying either:
  - All lines of data meeting the search criteria,
  - Only lines with transition probability data,
  - Only lines with energy level classifications, or
  - Only lines with observed wavelengths.

The default is to display all lines of data meeting the search criteria, regardless of whether the lines contain transition probability data or energy level classifications.

- Choice of bibliographic information output

If the corresponding radio box is selected, the bibliographic references for transition probabilities (TP) and spectral lines will be shown in two separate columns.

- Choice of display of wavelength data:
  - Observed wavelength
  - Ritz wavelength
  - The default is to suppress the display of the "observed-Ritz" column of data. Checking the "observed-Ritz" option will cause that column of data to be generated in the output.
- Choice of wavelength units.

The default is to display wavelengths in: Vacuum (< 2,000 Å), Air (2,000 Å to 20,000 Å), Vacuum (> 20,000 Å).

For wavelength ordered output, the table headings for the wavelength columns change as needed to reflect the change in units.

For multiplet ordered output, the units of wavelength in different ranges are specified at the top of the output page.

Alternative choices are:

- Vacuum (< 2,000 Å), Air (2,000 Å to 10,000 Å), Wavenumber (> 10,000 Å)
- Vacuum (< 10,000 Å), Wavenumber (> 10,000 Å)
- Vacuum (< 2,000 Å), Air (2,000 Å to 20,000 Å), Vacuum (> 20,000 Å)
- Vacuum (all wavelengths)
- Air (all wavelengths)
- Wavenumber (all wavelengths)

To change the default, the user simply needs to click on one of the radio buttons. The user will also need to check appropriate checkboxes if individual columns of wavelength information are desired

- Choice of display of transition strength information. The default is to display the following columns of data:
  - A_{ki}
  - Accuracy
  - Relative intensity.

  By default, A_{ki} (or $g_k A_{ki}$) are displayed in units of s^{-1}. They can be displayed in units of 10^8 s^{-1} if a proper checkbox is checked.

  To suppress display of the Relative Intensity data column, the corresponding checkbox can be unchecked.

  Although f_{ik}, S, and $\log(gf)$ values are not displayed by default, if the corresponding checkboxes are clicked, then those data values will be displayed.
- Choice of transition type

  By default, both electric dipole-allowed (E1) and forbidden (M1, E2, M2...) transitions are displyed in the output. To diplay only allowed or only forbidden transitions, a user must uncheck the checkbox corresponding to the unwanted type of transitions
- Choice of levels information: For lines output, the default is to display:

— Configurations,
— Terms,
— Energies, and
— *J* values.

To suppress display of the information listed above, the corresponding checkbox can be unchecked.

SELECTING SPECTRA FOR LINE SEARCHES

On the Lines Form, to specify an element, simply enter the element symbol (*e.g.*, Fe). Element symbols and Roman numerals need not be capitalised. Multiple elements are separated by a semicolon.

To indicate the spectrum of a given element, enter either a Roman numeral or an Arabic numeral after the element name. (Note: Fe 0 = Fe I, Fe 1 = Fe II, etc.). Alternatively, the spectrum may be specified by the name of its isoelectronic sequence (*e.g.*, Li-like, Ni-like). The absence of a Roman or Arabic numeral or an isoelectronic sequence name after an element symbol indicates all stages of ionisation. Spectra of the same element are separated by a comma, while spectra of different elements are separated by a semicolon. A range of spectra is indicated by using a hyphen between stages of ionisation or between names of isoelectronic sequences.

If the user has not provided enough information to specify spectra, an error message will be displayed.

Table 6.3 Examples of Spectral Notation (Case Insensitive)

Na I	Neutral Sodium
Na 0	Neutral sodium
Na I; Fe I	Neutral sodium and neutral iron
Fe I-III	Fe, ionisation stages one, two, and three
Fe I-III,V	Fe, ionisation stages one, two, three, and five
Fe	All ionisation stages of iron
he	All ionisation stages of helium
C I; N II; O III	List of spectra specifying neutral carbon, nitrogen II, and oxygen III.
C-O C-like	List of carbon-like spectra of all elements between carbon and oxygen (produces the same results as the previous example).

Contd...

C-O I-III	List of spectra of neutral, singly-ionised, and doubly-ionised elements between carbon and oxygen.
C-N I-II; Ne IV-V	List of spectra specifying C I, C II, N I, N II, Ne IV, and Ne V.
Mg He-like-Li-like; Al Li-like	List of spectra specifying Mg X, Mg XI, and Al XI.

PLOTTING JAVA GROTRIAN DIAGRAMS

Working with the Grotrian Diagram Plot

Basically, only a computer mouse and a space bar are used for interaction with this plot.

- *Default view:* Initially all levels and transitions are shown on the plot. Each energy level is shown by a horisontal bar. The colours (black and blue) have no meaning and are used simply to help with visualisation of the plot. The X-axis corresponds to different level series, and the Y-axis shows the level energy in cm^{-1}. The radiative transitions between the levels are shown as slanted gray lines. The ionisation limits are shown as magenta horisontal lines. At the top of the plot, the total number of levels, lines and ionisation limits is displayed. These parameters are automatically updated when zooming in or out. In the bottom right part of the plot, the maximum and minimum values of the transition probability for the displayed lines are given in the input text fields. The "Submit" and "Reset" buttons are used for setting the limits for transition probabilities, while the "Isolate" button is used to single out one level and all relevant transitions. The green field ("zoom field" below) next to the Y-axis is used for zooming in and out.

Selecting, Deselecting and Cycling over Objects

Mouse:

- Clicking on any level colours it and all relevant transitions in red. In addition, the basic data on this level, *e.g.*, energy, configuration, etc., are displayed in the info field.

- Clicking on any line colours the line and the lower and upper level in red. In addition, the basic data on the levels and line (wavelength, transition probability, etc.) are shown in the info field.
- Consecutive clicking on two levels is equivalent to clicking on the corresponding spectral line. If there is no line connecting the levels, no Line information is shown in the info field although the data on both levels is displayed.
- Clicking anywhere in the white background of the GD subwindow deselects the already selected object(s).

Space bar:

- If no objects have been selected, pressing a space bar selects a first spectral line in the following order: the levels are assumed to be arranged first according to the X-axis label (from left to right) and then according to the level energy. Since the ground state always has a zero energy, pressing the bar would normally highlight a line originating from the ground state.
- If a line has been selected, pressing a space bar cycles over all spectral lines on the plot in the order described above, that is, (i) for the same lower level, the upper level is updated, and (ii) after all lines for a particular lower level have been cycled through, the lower level is updated, and so on.
- If a level has been selected, pressing a space bar cycles over all energy levels within the levels series.
- The data shown in the info field is the same as for the mouse selection.
- *Zooming in and out:* The green field to the right of the Y-axis is used for zooming in. The upper and lower limits for the energy levels are set up by clicking the mouse in the zoom field. The upper and lower limits are shown by horizontal blue lines. When both limits are selected, the "Zoom" button

above the Y-axis becomes highlighted and clicking on it with the mouse results in updating the subwindow. This procedure can be repeated infinitely. After zooming in, the "Reset" button on the above the Y-axis becomes highlighted, and clicking on it restores the *original* plot.

- *Filtering A-values:* To choose the limits for the radiative transition probabilities, a user must enter new values in the "minA" and "maxA" text fields in the bottom right part of the plot and press the "Submit" button. By default, the minimum and maximum values of transition probabilities for all lines shown on the plot are displayed in those fields. The "Reset" button restores the default limits.
- *Isolating a Level:* In order to isolate one energy level with all radiatively connected levels, one has first to select a level by a mouse click. Then, the "Isolate" button in the bottom right part of the plot becomes highlighted, and pressing it would result in displaying the red group of levels and lines only. If necessary, a user can then perform zoom or transition probability limiting procedures on this subset of levels. After isolating a level, the "Isolate" button changes its label to "Show All", and pressing this new button would show all available levels and transitions.

OUTPUT FOR LINES

The output on the screen is HTML-formatted by default, but a significantly faster ASCII format may also be selected.

Help Popup Windows

The output may contain some symbols or combinations thereof coloured in red. This means that moving a mouse over such symbols would result in appearance of a small popup window showing some explanatory text provided the Javascript language is enabled in the browser options or preferences. Moving the mouse out would remove the popup window unless a user clicked on the red symbols. In that case, the popup window remains visible until the next mouse click on the same symbols. For the Ritz wavelengths, such popup windows appear also for the brown asterisk and pink plus symbols.

ION

This column contains the spectrum name containing an element symbol and a Roman numeral denoting the spectrum number (I for neutral atom, II for singly ionised, etc.). This column appears only if multiple spectra have been specified in the Lines Form input.

Observed Wavelength, Ritz Wavelength, and Obs.-Ritz Wavelength

The "Ritz" wavelengths are the wavelengths derived from the lower and upper levels of the transitions.They are available only if both levels of the. transition are known. If they are available, they usually are more accurate than the observed wavelengths, especially in the vacuum ultraviolet spectral region. The accuracy of the Ritz wavelengths depends on the quality of the energy level values. In some cases, the observed wavelength may be more accurate than the Ritz one, which is indicated by the number of given significant figures. The quality of the Ritz wavelengths can also be assessed by estimating the average deviation "Obs.-Ritz" for the given spectral region. Sometimes, the uncertainties of both observed and Ritz wavelengths can be retrieved from the bibliographic references provided for each line or from the Primary Source references at the top of the output page. The user can always choose the best available wavelength from the ASD output.

The user may choose to display both Ritz and observed wavelengths. The Obs-Ritz value may also be displayed. By default, wavelengths are given for vacuum wavelengths below 2000 Å and above 20000 Å, with standard-air wavelengths in between.

Indexes of refraction of air are derived from the five-parameter formula given by E.R. Peck and K. Reeder. These authors fitted data between 1850 Å and 17000 Å. The conversion between air and vacuum wavelength entails an ambiguity near the boundary of the air region. For example, a wavelength of 2000.648 Å in vacuum corresponds to 2000.000 Å in "standard air" (*i.e.*, 15 °C, 101 325 Pa pressure, with 0.033 per cent CO_2). Conversely, an air wavelength of 1999.352 Å corresponds to 2000.000 Å in vacuum. In this database, as the default, the following convention is adopted in terms of the energy difference or wavenumber, $\sigma = E_k - E_i$:

For $\sigma \geq 50{,}000$ cm^{-1}	→ vacuum wavelengths,
For 5000 cm^{-1} $< \sigma <$ 50,000 cm^{-1}	→ air wavelengths,
For $\sigma \leq 5000$ cm^{-1}	→ vacuum wavelengths.

Thus, if the tabulated wavelength lies within 2000 ± 0.648 Å, one must check the energy difference to ascertain whether it is for vacuum or air.

An explanation of the number of decimal places in each wavelength is provided in the section on significant figures.

Significant Figures

Ritz Wavelengths:

"Ritz" wavelengths are derived from level energies via the Ritz principle: The wavelength in vacuum is equal to the inverse of the difference in energies, σ, between the upper and lower energy levels of the transition:

$$\lambda = 1/\sigma,$$

where the wavenumber $\sigma = E_k - E_i$. The energies E_k and E_i are of the upper and lower levels of the transition, respectively. The units of this derived wavelength are the inverse of the energy units. For example, if the energy units are in inverse centimeters (cm^{-1}), the Ritz wavelength, derived by taking the inverse of $E_k - E_i$, is in cm. One multiplies a wavelength in cm by 10^7 to obtain nanometer units, or 10^8 to obtain ångströms.

The problem addressed here is to express the Ritz wavelength with a precision comparable to that of the energy difference from which it is derived. Because the wavelength and difference in energies are inversely related, a given number of significant figures does not always correspond to the comparable precision for both. For example, if the energy difference σ is 0.99, an extra significant figure is required to express the Ritz wavelength of comparable precision: 1.01.

The number of significant figures of any number, X, is equal to $[\log_{10}(X)] + dp + 1$, where dp indicates the number of decimal places and the square brackets indicate the integer value without roundoff, *e.g.*, [5.6] = 5. Using this, we set the significant figures equal to one another, except for a "shift" between them to account for the fact that they are inversely related:

$$[\log_{10}(\lambda)] + dp_{\lambda} = [\log_{10}(\sigma) + \Delta] + dp\sigma.$$

Here Δ indicates a shift between the two quantities to account for the fact that they are inversely related. The units of λ are physically reasonable for values of this shift range from 0 to 1, and the chosen value depends on the criteria one applies. The number of decimal places in the energy difference, dp_{σ}, is set to the smaller of the dp's for the lower and upper level energies of the transition. Applying the relation between λ and ό to the above expression, one obtains:

$$dp_{\lambda}(\text{cm}) = [2\log_{10}(\sigma) + D] + dp_{ό}.$$

If $\Delta = 0$, dp_{λ} will yield a sufficient number of significant figures such that when the derived wavelength is inverted, in all cases the resulting σ will be no less precise than the original σ from which the wavelength was derived. Unfortunately, this choice often yields an overly optimistic precision for the derived wavelength. We have chosen $\Delta = 0.5$ as a compromise between the full inversion precision and a realistic precision in the derived wavelength. In the large majority of cases, the error in σ upon inverting the derived wavelength is at most 1 in the last decimal place. This factor of 0.5 corresponds to a shift of half a decade, which is intuitively reasonable for two quantities that are inversely related. Thus the expression we use in determining the number of decimal places in the derived Ritz wavelength is:

$$dp_{\lambda}(\text{A}) = [2\log_{10}(\sigma) - 7.5] + dp_{\sigma}.$$

If dp_λ is negative, we set the actual number of decimal places to zero and replace the final dp_λ digits in the integer part of the wavelength with zeros.

In general, the uncertainty of the least significant figure can be as large as 25.

When the wavelengths are calculated online from the available energies of the lower and upper levels, either an asterisk "*" or a plus "+" is appended to the wavelength value. The former simply indicates that this value was calculated online, while the latter points out that a number of trailing zeros in the energies were not accounted for in the wavelengths calculation and therefore the actual accuracy of this particular wavelength may be higher.

Wavenumbers Derived from Wavelengths

When the user requests transition wavenumbers, σ, (in place of or in addition to wavelengths), these quantities are calculated from the level energy differences when they are available for both the lower and upper level. When either the lower or upper energy is not available, the transition wavenumber is calculated from the observed wavelength. The most common cases in ASD of transitions without available energy level information occur for elements with $Z > 28$. Because these wavelengths are typically truncated, the uncertainty in the least significant figure is negligible. Thus we set Δ in the above expressions to zero, and use the following expression:

$$dp_\sigma = [2\log_{10}(\lambda)] + dp_\lambda.$$

Relative Intensity

Relative intensities are source dependent and typically are useful only as guidelines for low density sources. These are values intended to represent the strengths of the lines of a spectrum as they would appear in emission. The values in the Database are taken from the cited publications. Usually, they are not normalised in any way. In some cases the intensity values were derived from observed photometric signals. This would be true for spectra measured by Fourier transform spectroscopy or in special cases where spectra were recorded photometrically. However, in most cases the values represent blackening of photographic emulsions used to record an observed spectrum.

These values can be semi-quantitative in that the transmission of the blackened emulsion was quantitatively measured and used to determine the intensity values. In other cases, the blackening was estimated visually and the estimates were used for the intensity values. Thus, the values can range from being approximately quantitative to only qualitative. Since the Database does not contain information on the origin of the relative intensities, the relative intensities should be considered as qualitative values that describe the appearance of a particular spectrum in emission.

The following points should be kept in mind when using the relative intensities:

- There is no common scale for relative intensities. The values in the database are taken from the values given by the authors of the cited publications. Since different authors use different scales, the relative intensities have meaning only within a given spectrum; that is, within the spectrum of a given element in a given stage of ionisation.
- The relative intensities are most useful in comparing strengths of spectral lines that are not separated widely. This results from the fact that most relative intensities are not corrected for spectral sensitivity of the measuring instruments (spectrometers, photomultipliers, photographic emulsions).
- The relative intensities for a spectrum depend on the light source used for the excitation. These values can change from source to source, and this is another reason to regard the values as being only qualitative.

TRANSITION STRENGTHS

Either transition probability "A_{ki}" weighted transition probability "$g_k A_{ki}$" (s^{-1} or $10^8\ s^{-1}$), absorption oscillator strength or f value ("f_{ik}"), line strength "S", or "log(gf)" can be displayed. Note that f_{ik}, S, and log(gf) are not displayed by default. Also note that log(gf) is shorthand for $\log_{10}(g_i f_{ik})$.

A_{ki} represents the emission transition probability. In the following formulas, it is assumed to be in units of 10^8 sec^{-1}.

f_{ik} is the absorption oscillator strength or f-value.

$f_{ik} = A_{ki} \cdot 1.49919 \cdot 10^{-16}\, g_k/g_i\, \lambda^2$, for all multipole types, where λ is the wavelength in ångströms,

log(gf) is the $\log_{10}(g_i f_{ik})$, where $g_i = 2J_i + 1$.

S is the line strength. It is the electric dipole matrix element squared and is independent of the transition wavelength.

Accuracy

An estimated accuracy is listed for each transition strength, indicated by a code letter as given in the table below:

AAA	≤	0.3%
AA	≤	1%
A+	≤	2%
A	≤	3%
B+	≤	7%
B	≤	10%
C+	≤	18%
C	≤	25%
D+	≤	40%
D	≤	50%
E	>	50%.

The uncertainties are obtained from critical assessments, and in general, reflect estimates of predominately systematic effects discussed in the NIST critical compilations. If the accuracy is followed by a prime (′), then a multiplet in the original compilation has been separated into its component lines and the transition probability was derived from the compiled value assuming spin-orbit coupling. This may decrease the listed accuracy, especially for weaker transitions.

Transition multipole: Multiply A_{ki} by listed factor to get S:

E1	Electric dipole	$4.935525 \cdot 10^{-19}$	g_k	λ^3
M1	Magnetic dipole	$3.707342 \cdot 10^{-14}$	g_k	λ^3
E2	Electric quadrupole	$8.928970 \cdot 10^{-19}$	g_k	λ^5

M2	Magnetic quadrupole	$6.707037 \cdot 10^{-14}\ g_k$	λ^5
E3	Electric octupole	$3.180240 \cdot 10^{-18}\ g_k$	λ^7
M3	Magnetic octupole	$2.38885 \cdot 10^{-13}\ g_k$	λ^7

where λ is the wavelength in angstroms and g_k is the statistical weight of the upper level. The numerical factor for the electric quadrupole conversion from A_{ki} to S follows a more modern convention than that used in the original publications, which will be used in future NIST publications.

$$E_i - E_k$$

Lower level and upper level energies of the transition are displayed in the units specified.

Configurations

Configurations of the lower and upper levels are displayed. For ASCII output, periods are inserted in the configuration labels whenever necessary to avoid ambiguity due to the lack of superscripts, and angular brackets enclose J values of the parent term.

ROTATIONAL ENERGY LEVELS AND ROTATIONAL SPECTRA

This is an introduction to various aspects of quantised rotation and most particularly to methods of studying rotational energy levels, *i.e.*, rotational spectroscopy using the Raman effect, microwave spectroscopy, far infrared spectroscopy and infrared vibration-rotation spectroscopy. The problems cover aspects of each of these. Once you have done this you will find it helpful to use the infrared spectroscopy and the Raman spectroscopy applets (interactive calculations) to look in more detail at vibration-rotation spectra (topic (v)) and pure rotation spectra (topic (iii)) respectfully.

The basic topics to cover are:

(i) The rotational energy levels of molecules in the gas phase. The quantitative treatment of the rigid rotor model for linear molecules. The extra complications in the rotational energy levels of symmetric top molecules. A qualitative understanding of the effects of centrifugal distortion on the energy levels.

(ii) The population of rotational levels as determined by the competition between Boltzmann factor and degeneracy of the level. Special effects arising from Bose-Einstein or Fermi-Dirac statistics both in spectroscopy and in heat capacities (you may find it useful to refer ahead to the rotational heat capacity applet in statistical mechanics.). Consider especially the examples H_2, D_2, CO_2, and C_2H_2.

(iii) Selection rules for pure rotational spectra in microwave, infrared, and Raman spectroscopy. The intensities of the lines and the overall appearance of the pure rotational spectrum in the infrared and Raman. Determination of the rotational constants from the spectrum.

(iv) The quantitative use of rotational spectra to determine bondlengths. Consider what type of molecules can be studied in this way. The use of isotopic substitution to gain extra information.

(v) The rotational fine structure in a vibration rotation band. P, Q and R branches and the general appearance of the band. Combination sum and difference plots for determining the rotational constants.

FAR INFRARED PURE ROTATION SPECTRUM OF A DIPOLAR MOLECULE

Infrared rotational spectra are excited by electromagnetic radiation in the far-infrared region of the spectrum, 10–200 cm^{-1} and are always observed in absorption. Thus, only increases in the rotational quantum number are observed. Normally, for a molecule to absorb in the far infrared it must have a permanent dipole moment (this is alos true for the closely related microwave spectrum). Molecules with permanent dipole moments do not show any spin statistics in their rotational spectrum because they do not have any symmetry at right angles to the main axis of symmetry of the molecule (if there is one).

Suggested "experiments" are:

(i) The B slider controls the value of B. You will be able to observe that the spacing of the lines is approximately 2B. You should write out the formula for the lines to see why this is.

(ii) With the value of B fixed vary the temperature and note how the maximum moves further from the band origin as the temperature increases. The reason for the maximum is that as J increases the increasing degeneracy $(2J + 1)$ favours a higher population but the decreasing Boltzmann factor favours a lower one. The different rate at which these factors change generates the maximum. The actual population of the levels and the number of transitions occurring between levels is shown on the right hand side of the diagram.

(iii) Note the effect of varying the distortion constant D. This covers a realistic range in this diagram but only has a relatively small effect, and then only on the highest frequency lines. Why are only the highest frequency lines affected?

RAMAN PURE ROTATIONAL SPECTRUM OF A LINEAR MOLECULE

A Raman spectrum is excited by electromagnetic radiation in the visible region of the spectrum, 15000-20000 cm^{-1}, 700-400 nm, a long way from energies associated with rotational transitions (far infrared). To emphasise this difference the spectrum is shown as it might actually appear in the upper half of the diagram and is plotted as a function of wavelength. The unchanged Rayleigh line always appears very strongly (more strongly than shown) at the centre of the spectrum. Since this is a pure rotation spectrum only the ground state value of B affects the spectrum. A slider to vary the centrifugal distortion constant is included with values in the range typical of these types of molecules, but the effect, which is just visible, only really shows up in quantitative calculations.

Suggested "experiments" are:

(i) The B (lower) slider controls the value of B. You will be able to observe that the spacing of the lines is approximately 4B. You should write out the formula for the lines to see why this is.

(ii) With the value of B fixed vary the temperature and note how the maxima in the O and S branches move further from the band origin as the temperature increases. The reason for the maximum is that as J increases the increasing degeneracy (2J + 1) favours a higher population but the decreasing Boltzmann factor favours a lower one. The different rate at which these factors change generates the maximum.

(iii) The spin statistics are controlled by the right hand slider and all the common cases are included. Note that, when one set of lines is completely missing (slider moved to zero) the pattern of line spacings is different from that when odd and even J are equally weighted. The first S line, S(0), is present but the first O line, O(1), is absent.

INFRARED VIBRATION-ROTATION SPECTRUM (TRANSITION MOMENT PARALLEL TO MOLECULAR AXIS)

The calculation of the infrared spectrum is complete and includes the effects of centrifugal distortion, although these cannot be adjusted. If you download the programmes the parameters of the control programme can be changed to calculate any chosen spectrum for stretching of a linear molecule. Just set the parameter "control" to 1 and the remaining parameters are obvious.

The following are suggested "experiments" for the infrared spectrum.

(i) The B (lower) slider controls the value of B in the lower state and the B (upper) slider controls the value of the upper state B *relative to B (lower).* Leaving the other sliders at their initial setting vary these two sliders. You should be able to observe that the spacing of the lines is approximately 2B and that a difference between the upper and lower state Bs leads to a convergence of the lines in one branch and a divergence in the other. You should write out the formula for the lines to see why this is. The most common difference in the two B values leads to a the convergence being in the R branch. Note that the maxima in the P and R branches occur at a similar distance in cm^{-1} from the band origin (2000 cm^{-1}) regardless of the value of B.

(ii) With the values of B lower and upper fixed vary the temperature and note how the maxima in the P and R branches move further from the band origin as the temperature increases. The reason for the maximum is that as J increases the increasing degeneracy (2J + 1) favours a higher population but the decreasing Boltzmann factor favours a lower one. The different rate at which these factors change generates the maximum. This gives a very useful means of estimating temperatures, especially in inaccessible situations such as in planetary atmospheres. If you keep the temperature fixed and increase B (lower) to a moderately high value you will realise that the discreteness of the lines makes it less and less accurate to determine temperature from the line of maximum intensity.

7

Mössbauer Spectroscopy

INTRODUCTION

Mössbauer spectroscopy is a versatile technique that can be used to provide information in many areas of science such as Physics, Chemistry, Biology and Metallurgy. It can give very precise information about the chemical, structural, magnetic and time-dependent properties of a material. Key to the success of the technique is the discovery of recoilless gamma ray emission and absorption, now referred to as the 'Mössbauer Effect', after its discoverer Rudolph Mössbauer, who first observed the effect in 1957 and received the Nobel Prize in Physics in 1961 for his work.

This introduction to the theory and applications of Mössbauer spectroscopy is composed of four sections. First the theory behind the Mössbauer effect is explained. Next how the effect can be used to probe atoms within a system is shown. Then the principal factors of a Mössbauer spectrum are illustrated with spectra taken from research work.

The Mössbauer Effect

Nuclei in atoms undergo a variety of energy level transitions, often associated with the emission or absorption of a gamma ray. These energy levels are influenced by their surrounding environment, both electronic and magnetic, which can change or split these energy levels.

These changes in the energy levels can provide information about the atom's local environment within a system and ought to be observed using resonance-fluorescence. There are, however, two major obstacles in obtaining this information: the 'hyperfine' interactions between the nucleus and its environment are extremely small, and the recoil of the nucleus as the gamma-ray is emitted or absorbed prevents resonance.

In a free nucleus during emission or absorption of a gamma ray it recoils due to conservation of momentum, just like a gun recoils when firing a bullet, with a recoil energy E_R. The emitted gamma ray has E_R less energy than the nuclear transition but to be resonantly absorbed it must be E_R *greater* than the transition energy due to the recoil of the absorbing nucleus. To achieve resonance the loss of the recoil energy must be overcome in some way.

As the atoms will be moving due to random thermal motion the gamma-ray energy has a spread of values E_D caused by the Doppler effect. This produces a gamma-ray energy profile. To produce a resonant signal the two energies need to overlap and this is shown in the red-shaded area. This area is shown exaggerated as in reality it is extremely small, a millionth or less of the gamma-rays are in this region, and impractical as a technique.

What Mössbauer discovered is that when the atoms are within a solid matrix the effective mass of the nucleus is very much greater.

The recoiling mass is now effectively the mass of the whole system, making E_R and E_D very small. If the gamma-ray energy is small enough the recoil of the nucleus is too low to be transmitted as a phonon (vibration in the crystal lattice) and so the whole system recoils, making the recoil energy practically zero: a recoil-free event.

In this situation, if the emitting and absorbing nuclei are in a solid matrix the emitted and absorbed gamma-ray is the same energy: resonance!

If emitting and absorbing nuclei are in identical, cubic environments then the transition energies are identical and this produces a spectrum: a single absorption line.

Now that we can achieve resonant emission and absorption can we use it to probe the tiny hyperfine interactions between an atom's nucleus and its environment? The limiting resolution now that recoil and doppler broadening have been eliminated is the natural linewidth of the excited nuclear state. This is related to the average lifetime of the excited state before it decays by emitting the gamma-ray.

For the most common Mössbauer isotope, ^{57}Fe, this linewidth is 5×10^{-9}ev. Compared to the Mössbauer gamma-ray energy of 14.4keV this gives a resolution of 1 in 10^{12}, or the equivalent of a small speck of dust on the back of an elephant or one sheet of paper in the distance between the Sun and the Earth. This exceptional resolution is of the order necessary to detect the hyperfine interactions in the nucleus.

As resonance only occurs when the transition energy of the emitting and absorbing nucleus match exactly the effect is isotope specific. The relative number of recoil-free events (and hence the strength of the signal) is strongly dependent upon the gamma-ray energy and so the Mössbauer effect is only detected in isotopes with very low lying excited states. Similarly the resolution is dependent upon the lifetime of the excited state.

These two factors limit the number of isotopes that can be used successfully for Mössbauer spectroscopy. The most used is ^{57}Fe, which has both a very low energy gamma-ray and long-lived excited state, matching both requirements well. The isotopes in which the Mössbauer effect has been detected.

So far we have seen one Mössbauer spectrum: a single line corresponding to the emitting and absorbing nuclei being in identical environments. As the environment of the nuclei in a system we want to study will almost certainly be different to our source the hyperfine interactions between the nucleus and the its environment will change the energy of the nuclear transition. To detect this we need to change the energy of our probing gamma-rays.

The technique of Mössbauer spectroscopy is widely used in mineralogy to examine the valence state of iron, which is found in nature as Fe^0 (metal), Fe^{2+}, and Fe^{3+}, as well as the type of coordination polyhedron occupied by iron atoms (trigonal, tetrahedral, octahedral, etc.). It is sometimes used to determine redox ratios in glasses and (less successfully) in rocks. Mössbauer spectroscopy is also used to assist in the identification of Fe oxide phases on the basis of their magnetic properties.

The Mössbauer effect as generally applied to the study of minerals relies on the fact that ^{57}Fe, which is a decay product of ^{57}Co, is unstable. ^{57}Fe decays by giving off a gamma ray (λray), along with other types of energy. The nuclear decay scheme for $^{57}Co \rightarrow ^{57}Fe$ and various backscattering processes for ^{57}Fe that can follow resonant absorption of an incident gamma photon. If a nucleus gives off radiation or any other form of energy (in this case, in the form of a γ-ray), the nucleus must recoil (or move) with an equal and opposite momentum to preserve its energy (E), in the same way that a gun (by analogy, the nucleus) recoils when a bullet (the γ–ray) is fired out of it. We describe this general case in terms of energy by saying that:

$$E_{g\text{–ray emission}} = E_{transition} - E_{R'}$$

where

$E_{\gamma\text{-ray emission}}$ = the energy of the emitted x-ray
$E_{transition}$ = the energy of the nuclear transition
E_R = the energy of the recoil.

A schematic (fig.) of the vibrational energy levels in a solid. On the left, the recoil energy E_R of an emitted gamma photon is less than what is needed to reach the next higher energy level, so that excitation of a vibrational mode has low probability. The probability that no excitation will occur is given the symbol *f*, which represents the fraction of recoil-free events.

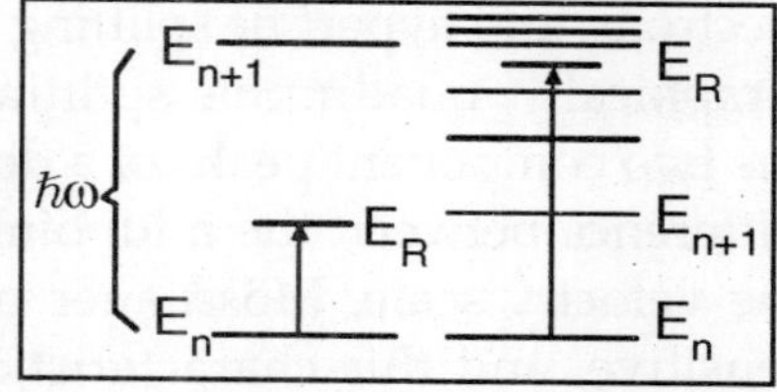

A gamma ray would be emitted without losing energy to the solid, in what is called a zero-phonon transition. In other words, sometimes the nucleus absorbs the energy of the γ-ray and it doesn't recoil (instead, the entire structure, rather than just the nucleus, absorbs the energy). The variable *f* indicates the probability of this happening. This process of recoil-less emission forms the basis for Mössbauer spectroscopy. On the right, E_R is significantly greater in energy than the lowest excitation energy of the solid, which is E_{n+1}- E_n. Absorption of the recoil energy, E_R, by the solid thus becomes probable, and the photon emerges with energy reduced by E_R and with Doppler broadening. Ωε represents frequency, and $\hbar$ is Planck's constant divided by 2π.

The Mössbauer effect occurs because in solids, the value of *f* is high enough that recoil-free absorption is possible. Thus an atom of ^{57}Co can decay to ^{57}Fe, which gives off a γ–ray, and may be absorbed without recoil by a nearby ^{57}Fe, which happens to have just the right splitting between the energy levels in its nucleus to absorb it. This scenario will only happen if the decaying Co atom is surrounded by the same atoms as the absorbing Fe. If the receiving Fe atoms are in a different matrix (say, in a mineral) than in the emitter, then no absorption can occur.

Mössbauer spectra are described using three parameters: isomer shift (δ), which arises from the difference in *s* electron density between the source and the absorber, quadrupole splitting (Δ which is a shift in nuclear energy levels that is induced by an electric field gradient caused by nearby electrons, and hyperfine splitting (for magnetic materials only). Graphically, quadrupole splitting is the separation between the two component peaks of a doublet, and isomer shift is the difference between the midpoint of the doublet and zero on the velocity scale. Mössbauer parameters are temperature-sensitive, and this characteristic is sometimes exploited by using lower temperatures to improve peak resolution and induce interesting magnetic phenomena.

If the electrons around the Fe atom create a magnetic field, as in the case of magnetite, then the energy levels in the Fe nucleus will split to allow six possible nuclear transitions, and a sextet (six-peak) spectrum results. The positions of the peaks in the sextet defines what is called the hyperfine splitting (Hint or BHf, depending on the units used) of the nuclear energy levels.

Iron atoms in different local environments and those having different oxidation states absorb at different, diagnostic energies. A typical Mössbauer spectrum thus consists of sets of peaks (usually doublets and sextets), with each set corresponding to an iron nucleus in a specific environment in the sample (an Fe nuclear site). Different sets of peaks appear depending on what the Fe nucleus "sees" in its environment. The nuclear environment depends on a number of factors including the number of electrons (Fe^0, Fe^{2+}, Fe^{3+}), the number of coordinating anions, the symmetry of the site, and the presence/absence of magnetic ordering (which may be temperature-dependent). Thus the spectrum of a given mineral may consist of a superposition of doublets and sextets.

The combination of isomer shift and quadrupole splitting parameters (along with the hyperfine field, in the case of magnetically ordered phases) is usually sufficient to identify the valence state and site occupancy of Fe in a given site and individual mineral. In minerals, these ranges have largely been determined empirically from Mössbauer spectra measured with use of spectrum-fitting routines commonly available to the geological community. Exact values of Mössbauer parameters are difficult to predict from theory because long-range interactions in complicated mineral structures are difficult to anticipate.

The Fe atoms in minerals are predictably found in coordination polyhedra of appropriate size based on radius ratios. The isomer shift and quadrupole splitting of several minerals whose iron valence state and coordination number are independently known (usually from single crystal X-ray diffraction). Fe^{3+} occurs primarily in 4– or 6–coordination with oxygen, while Fe^{2+} may be rarely 4–or 5– coordinated, commonly 6-coordinated, and occasionally 8-coordinated with oxygen. Fe in 4-fold coordination with sulfur has subtly different parameters due to the effects of covalent bonding. Variations in Mössbauer parameters that are characteristic of each type of coordination polyhedron can be related to polyhedral site distortion.

MÖSSBAUER SPECTROSCOPY INSTRUMENTATION

The basic elements of a Mössbauer spectrometer are a source, sample, detector, and a drive to move the source or absorber. Most commonly, this is done by moving the source towards and away from the sample, while varying velocity linearly with time. For example, for ^{57}Fe, moving the source at a velocity of 1 mm/sec towards the sample increases the energy of the emitted photons by about ten natural linewidths. For simplicity, "mm/sec" is the conventional "energy" unit in Mössbauer spectroscopy. It is also possible to leave the source stationary and oscillate the sample, as is done with synchrotron Mössbauer.

The location of the detector relative to the source and the sample defines the geometry of the experiment; most commonly, either transmission or backscatter modes are used.

Applications

The combination of isomer shift and quadrupole splitting (along with the hyperfine field, in the case of magnetic phases) is used to identify the valence state and site occupancy of Fe in a given site and individual mineral. If the phase is magnetically ordered, additional information in the form of a value for the magnetic field (usually given in Teslas) can help with identification of some phases.

In some cases, Mössbauer spectrometers are also used to identify minerals. This application is limited, however, by the fact that many different minerals can have site geometries that are the same, such that their Mössbauer spectra and the resultant peak parameters will also be the same. For example, the spectra of amphibole and pyroxene group minerals are all very similar, so you could not tell these minerals apart by their Mössbauer spectra alone!

STRENGTHS AND LIMITATIONS OF MÖSSBAUER SPECTROSCOPY

Strengths

Along with wet chemistry, Mössbauer spectroscopy remains the "gold standard" for quantitative determination of the valence state of iron in minerals and identification of various iron oxides. It is also well-suited for determination of the coordination number of Fe atoms.

Limitations

The biggest limitation of the Mössbauer is that it is inherently a bulk technique; it uses powders spread thinly across an absorber to get optimal experimental conditions. In recent years, improvements in electronics and detectors have made it possible to run very small samples (1–5 mg). Another approach to this problem is the Mössbauer milliprobe developed by Catherine McCammon at Bayreuth.

This modification, which uses a lead plate to restrict gamma rays to a small diameter (~100 μm), can be used to study single grains in thin sections or single crystals.

The vast majority of rock-forming minerals on Earth contain Fe^{2+} in octahedral coordination, and thus have very similar Mössbauer parameters. For example, pyroxene, amphibole, and mica spectra are all nearly indistinguishable. Furthermore, most minerals exhibit a range of Mössbauer parameters as a function of cation substitution. Finally, the parameters vary as a function of temperature, and the magnitude of that variation is distinctive to each mineral composition.

For these reasons, Mössbauer spectroscopy is not ideally suited to mineral identification (except for iron oxides, where magnetic properties can be extremely diagnostic) and is typically not used for this purpose (though it has been pressed into such service in extraterrestrial applications).

Sample Collection and Preparation

Sample preparation for Mössbauer spectroscopy is relatively simple. The sample to be analysed is powdered and spread across a sample holder with a diameter equal to that of the window in the detector.

The amount of sample used affects the resultant spectrum. If too little sample is used, then some γ-rays will never encounter an Fe atom, and therefore have no chance to experience recoil-less emission. Use of too much sample can affect the area, intensity, width, and detailed shape of the Mössbauer lines. If the chemical composition of the material is known before the experiment, then the optimal amount of sample for any given experimental geometry can be calculated. In most laboratories, samples are mixed with some inert material such as sucrose of graphite to assist in spreading the sample evenly across the diameter of the sample holder. The sample is them held in place with something thin and non-absorbant to γ–rays such as cellophane or kapton tape.

DATA COLLECTION, RESULTS AND PRESENTATION

Techniques for processing Mössbauer data are complex and variable. There are many Mössbauer spectral analysis programmes used to interpret the spectra of geologic (and other) materials.

Mössbauer spectra of minerals frequently exhibit highly overlapping peaks, and under these conditions the particular fitting techniques and model assumptions used can make a difference in how the spectra are interpreted. Typically, members of a research group will use only one of these spectral analysis programmes, and differences in interpretation that might arise from the use of different programmes are therefore virtually unknown. In addition, there are many physical models that have been applied to interpret Mössbauer spectra, and there have been very few published comparisons of any of these models.

Software for analysis of Mössbauer spectra uses a variety of different physical models to generate model spectra with which to compare the measured spectra, and different fitting algorithms to analyse the data.

It is important to assume a theoretically reasonable model when fitting Mössbauer spectra because it is possible, based on the data alone, to fit spectra to an unphysical model and still get superficially reasonable chi-squared values. Three different line shapes are commonly employed in modeling of Mössbauer spectra.

- Lorentzian (Cauchy) line shapes, used to describe spectral lines resulting from broadened resonance and other phenomena, have been used since the technique was first developed. This line shape gives a good approximation of line shapes in spectra of paramagnetic materials where all of the Fe nuclei are in identical electronic environments. It is less useful when variations in the geometry of the coordination polyhedra and variable distance between the Fe atom and nearest oxygens and next nearest cations occur—as is the case in most minerals.
- Beginning in the 1970's, many Mössbauer routines began to address the variations in coordination polyhedra around the Fe nucleus by adding a Gaussian component to the Lorentzian line shape. The resultant hybrid line shape, which is a Gaussian distribution of Lorentzian line shapes, is called a Voigt line shape, and is generally approximated by a linear combination of the two line shapes that is called a pseudo-Voigt function.
- Quadrupole splitting distributions (QSDs) are a further evolution in modeling Mossbauer spectra of minerals in which there are poorly-resolved quadrupole pairs, as is certainly the case in phyllosilicate spectra. The QSDs model the local distortions and atomic disorder surrounding the Fe atoms, rather than simply reflecting the ideal point symmetries of the relevant sites. The QSD method performs better than Lorentzian fits in a number of ways. Fits with Lorentzian doublets tend to overestimate the spectral backgrounds, put large wings or tails on the main absorption peaks, and give unreasonably large linewidths.

Error analysis varies from laboratory to laboratory. In general, areas of doublets are quoted to no better than one significant figure after the decimal. Values of isomer shift and quadrupole splitting are usually ±0.02 mm/s, and hyperfine fields are highly variable. Mössbauer spectroscopy can generally detect features down to roughly 1 per cent of the total Fe. The technique usually is not used for samples containing less than 0.1 wt% FeO.

One final and fundamental constraint on geological applications of Mössbauer results must be mentioned because it is frequently misunderstood. ^{57}Fe Mössbauer spectroscopy can determine only the relative amounts of iron in various types of sites and valence states. It cannot determine the total number of Fe atoms that are present in a material (*i.e.*, relative to the other atoms present) because the presence of other elements has no effect on the Mössbauer spectrum except as they alter the Fe environment and reduce the overall intensity of the spectrum, but not its dependence on velocity. It should be emphasised, therefore, that Mössbauer spectroscopy is a tool to investigate the nature and relative contents of Fe-bearing minerals in a sample. It provides no information on minerals that do not contain Fe in their structures.

FUNDAMENTALS OF MÖSSBAUER SPECTROSCOPY

Such miniscule variations of the original gamma-ray are quite easy to achieve by the use of the doppler effect. In the same way that when an ambulance's siren is raised in pitch when it's moving towards you and lowered when moving away from you, our gamma-ray source can be moved towards and away from our absorber. This is most often achieved by oscillating a radioactive source with a velocity of a few mm/s and recording the spectrum in discrete velocity steps.

Fractions of mm/s compared to the speed of light (3×10^{11}mm/s) gives the minute energy shifts necessary to observe the hyperfine interactions. For convenience the energy scale of a Mössbauer spectrum is thus quoted in terms of the source velocity.

With an oscillating source we can now modulate the energy of the gamma-ray in very small increments. Where the modulated gamma-ray energy matches precisely the energy of a nuclear transition in the absorber the gamma-rays are resonantly absorbed and we see a peak.

As we're seeing this in the transmitted gamma-rays the sample must be sufficiently thin to allow the gamma-rays to pass through, the relatively low energy gamma-rays are easily attenuated.

The absorption peak occurs at 0mm/s, where source and absorber are identical. The energy levels in the absorbing nuclei can be modified by their environment in three main ways: by the Isomer Shift, Quadrupole Splitting and Magnetic Splitting.

Isomer Shift

The isomer shift arises due to the non-zero volume of the nucleus and the electron charge density due to s-electrons within it. This leads to a monopole (Coulomb) interaction, altering the nuclear energy levels.

Any difference in the s-electron environment between the source and absorber thus produces a shift in the resonance energy of the transition. This shifts the whole spectrum positively or negatively depending upon the s-electron density, and sets the centroid of the spectrum.

As the shift cannot be measured directly it is quoted relative to a known absorber. For example ^{57}Fe Mössbauer spectra will often be quoted relative to alpha-iron at room temperature. The isomer shift is useful for determining valency states, ligand bonding states, electron shielding and the electron-drawing power of electronegative groups.

For example, the electron configurations for Fe^{2+} and Fe^{3+} are $(3d)^6$ and $(3d)^5$ respectively. The ferrous ions have less s-electrons at the nucleus due to the greater screening of the d-electrons. Thus ferrous ions have larger positive isomer shifts than ferric ions.

Quadrupole Splitting

Nuclei in states with an angular momentum quantum number $I>1/2$ have a non-spherical charge distribution. This produces a nuclear quadrupole moment. In the presence of an asymmetrical electric field (produced by an asymmetric electronic charge distribution or ligand arrangement) this splits the nuclear energy levels. The charge distribution is characterised by a single quantity called the Electric Field Gradient (EFG).

In the case of an isotope with a I=3/2 excited state, such as ^{57}Fe or ^{119}Sn, the excited state is split into two substates $m_I=\pm 1/2$ and $m_I=\pm 3/2$.

The magnitude of splitting, Delta, is related to the nuclear quadrupole moment, Q, and the principle component of the EFG, V_{zz}, by the relation Delta=$eQV_{zz}/2$.

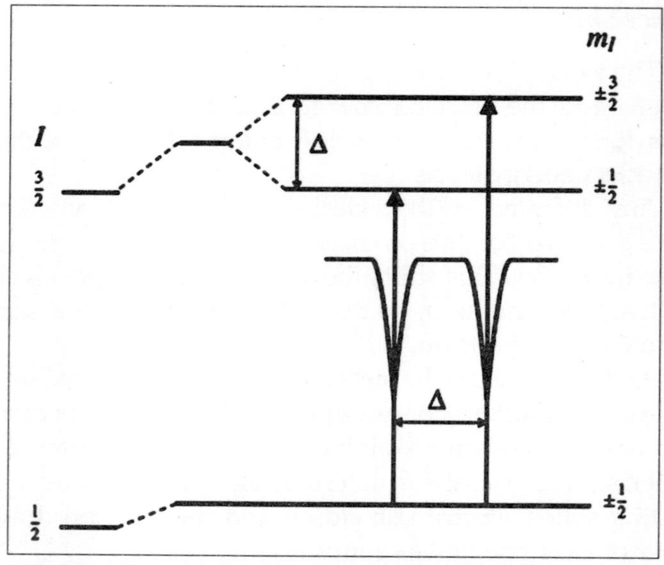

Quadrupole Splitting for a 3/2 to 1/2 Transition. The Magnitude of Quadrupole Splitting, Delta, is Shown

Magnetic Splitting

In the presence of a magnetic field the nuclear spin moment experiences a dipolar interaction with the magnetic field ie Zeeman splitting. There are many sources of magnetic fields that can be experienced by the nucleus. The total effective magnetic field at the nucleus, B_{eff} is given by:

$$B_{eff} = (B_{contact} + B_{orbital} + B_{dipolar}) + B_{applied}$$

the first three terms being due to the atom's own partially filled electron shells. $B_{contact}$ is due to the spin on those electrons polarising the spin density at the nucleus, $B_{orbital}$ is due to the orbital moment on those electrons, and $B_{dipolar}$ is the dipolar field due to the spin of those electrons.

This magnetic field splits nuclear levels with a spin of I into (2I+1) substates. Transitions between the excited state and ground state can only occur where m_I changes by 0 or 1. This gives six possible transitions for a 3/2 to 1/2 transition, giving a sextet, with the line spacing being proportional to B_{eff}.

The line positions are related to the splitting of the energy levels, but the line *intensities* are related to the angle between the Mössbauer gamma-ray and the nuclear spin moment. The outer, middle and inner line intensities are related by:

$$3: (4\sin^2 theta)/(1+\cos^2 theta): 1$$

meaning the outer and inner lines are always in the same proportion but the middle lines can vary in relative intensity between 0 and 4 depending upon the angle the nuclear spin moments make to the gamma-ray. In polycrystalline samples with no applied field this value averages to 2 but in single crystals or under applied fields the relative line intensities can give information about moment orientation and magnetic ordering.

These interactions, Isomer Shift, Quadrupole Splitting and Magnetic Splitting, alone or in combination are the primary characteristics of many Mössbauer spectra. Some recorded spectra which illustrate how measuring these hyperfine interactions can provide valuable information about a system.

Hyperfine Interactions at Work

Mössbauer spectroscopy can be a useful analytical tool for studying a variety of systems and phenomena. The spectra have been taken from active research projects and chosen to visually represent the hyperfine interactions.

Tin Dioxide Assisted Antimony Oxidation

Antimony-containing tin dioxide is an important catalyst for selective oxidation of olefins. Of particular importance in studying these systems to is to know the relative concentrations of the antimony charge states (3+ and 5+) during the catalytic process.

Three ^{121}Sb spectra taken at various stages during the catalytic process: (1) fresh Sb_2O_3, (2) Sb_2O_3 calcined at 1000C and (3) the calcined material after catalysis. Firstly the isotope-specificity of Mössbauer spectroscopy picks out only the antimony atoms from the Sn-Sb-O composite. Readily apparent from spectrum 1 is that practically all of the antimony is in a single state (the red component). Comparison with previous experiments shows that the isomer shift for this majority component matches that of Sb3+. The asymmetric shape is due to the quadrupole splitting in this isotope, which has 8 lines (it is a 7/2 to 5/2 transition).

Firstly the isotope-specificity of Mössbauer spectroscopy picks out only the antimony atoms from the Sn-Sb-O composite. Readily apparent from spectrum 1 is that practically all of the antimony is in a single state (the red component). Comparison with previous experiments shows that the isomer shift for this majority component matches that of Sb3+. The asymmetric shape is due to the quadrupole splitting in this isotope, which has 8 lines (it is a 7/2 to 5/2 transition).

After calcining the spectrum is now composed of two components of equal area. The second (green) component corresponds to the Sb5+ ion. The component areas give the relative proportion of each site within the compound, in this case 1:1 indicating either Sb_2O_4 or Sb_6O_{13}. After the catalysis in spectrum 3 we can see that the antimony is now all in the 3+ charge state again.

Tin spectra were also recorded, showing a single line spectrum of identical isomer shift during all parts of the process, indicating no change in the tin charge state.

In cases like this basic deductions can be made even without computer analysis: one can simply see one component appear and disappear and the differences in isomer shift are readily apparent. Unfortunately it isn't always quite this obvious!

Off-center Tin Atoms in PbSnTeSe

Off-center impurities are those which can be displaced from their regular positions in a crystal lattice. They can be considered as existing in an asymmetric double potential well. Such atoms can change their position as the temperature changes. Unfortunately there are often many other phenomena in such systems that can mask the off-centering effect.

Mössbauer spectroscopy provides a good tool for observing this effect. Firstly the movement of the off-center atom within the lattice will change the symmetry of the electric field it is in: hence changing the quadrupole splitting. Mössbauer spectroscopy is also isotope and site specific, meaning we can observe the off-center single component without any masking from other elements or effects.

A compound which was thought to exhibit off-centering is $Pb_{0.8}Sn_{0.2}Te_{0.8}Se_{0.2}$, with tin as an off-center atom. Spectra are sample at 200K and 20K. There are two components: one from an off-center site and one from a normal single-potential site. It can be seen in the highlighted region that the small green component develops from a single line to a (broad) doublet. The quadrupole splitting is increasing, indicating the electric field environment around these particular atoms is become more asymmetrical. This is consistent with an atom moving within an asymmetric potential well.

The other component shows no variation in quadrupole splitting. A series of spectra were taken in a temperature cycle and a hysteresis was observed in the values of quadrupole splitting. These results show that tin is an off-center atom in this compound and that there are two tin sites within it: one normal and one off-center.

Uranium/Iron Multilayers

Magnetic multilayers are very important in today's technology, particularly in the areas of data storage and retrieval. A recent development is the use of actinides, such as uranium. Uranium in the right environment displays very large orbital magnetic moments, crucial to engineering systems with strong magnetic anisotropy and for magneto-optical applications. As part of this research sputtered Uranium/Iron multilayers have been produced and Mössbauer spectroscopy has been used to investigate the state of the iron within them.

As these samples are sputtered onto a thick substrate we cannot use conventional Mössbauer spectroscopy in Transmission Mode (TM) as the substrate would block the gamma-rays and we would receive no signal at all. There is a technique known as Conversion Electron Mössbauer Spectroscopy or CEMS which records the conversion electrons emitted by the resonantly excited nuclei in the absorber. In TM mode we record the absorption peaks as the gamma-rays are resonantly absorbed and so see dips, whilst in CEMS we record the electrons emitted from those excited nuclei and so see emission peaks. As the electrons are strongly attenuated by the sample as they pass through it most of the signal only comes from the uppermost 1000Angstroms.

The ^{57}Fe CEMS spectra from three Uranium/Iron multilayers of varying layer thicknesses. They are composed of three components: two sextets and one doublet. The hyperfine parameters of the two sextets correspond to alpha-iron, the red component being fully crystalline and the green component being from diffuse and poorly crystalline alpha-iron. The magnetic splitting shows that the iron in these two components is magnetically ordered.

The third component has an isomer shift and quadrupole splitting consistent with previous work on the UFe_2 intermetallic. This is paramagnetic at room temperature, as shown by the doublet. It is a doublet and not a sextet even though the intermetallic has a magnetic moment as the moment direction changes much faster in the paramagnetic state than the time it takes Mössbauer spectroscopy to record it and thus the experienced hyperfine field averages to zero.

As the iron layer thickness is increased to 43Angstroms the relative proportion of alpha-iron to UFe_2 increases and also the proportion of fully crystalline iron increases. As the iron layer is increased further to 180Angstroms this proportion becomes even greater. We can deduce from this that the thicker the iron layer the greater the *proportion* of crystalline iron, but more detailed analysis of the component areas compared to the layer thickness shows that the absolute thicknesses of the poorly crystalline iron and UFe_2 stay roughly constant.

Mössbauer spectroscopy has easily shown the existence of the three different iron sites within the sample and how their proportion has varied with layer thickness.

Superspin glass transition in $Al_{49}Fe_{30}Cu_{21}$

The magnetic properties of granular alloys and heterogeneous nanostructures built by ferromagnetic and non-magnetic components attract much attention due both to the fundamental interest of their rich phenomenology and to their potential applications, for instance in magnetoresistive devices and magnetic recording. Of particular interest are superspin glasses but their study is made difficult by the different possible sources for non-equilibrium magnetic behaviour and the mixtures of particle phases within the samples.

Mössbauer spectroscopy, as seen in the previous examples, is very good at distinguishing particular sites or phases within a sample. And as seen in the previous example can show the difference between magnetically ordered and paramagnetic sites. As the superspin glass phase reaches its freesing temperature the atoms become magnetically ordered and this will show up in the spectra as a sextet appearing.

A series of ^{57}Fe spectra were recorded from a ball-milled sample of $Al_{49}Fe_{30}Cu_{21}$ with decreasing temperature. At 40K, above the freesing temperature, there are two components of unequal proportion, both doublets. As the temperature is reduced the smaller component starts to spread outwards into a magnetic sextet. The peaks are broad and diffuse due to there being a distribution of grain sizes within the sample and hence a distribution of magnetic hyperfine fields. Plotting the recorded hyperfine field against temperature can then give the superspin glass transition temperature for this compound.

Mössbauer spectroscopy showed quite readily the onset of the superspin glass 'freesing' and the proportion of the magnetic particles and their surrounding non-magnetic matrix. Analysis of the hyperfine field distribution also proved consistent with that expected for a superspin glass. How Mössbauer spectroscopy can be a useful analytical tool for studying a variety of systems and phenomena. The spectra have been taken from active research projects and chosen to visually represent the hyperfine interactions.

HYPERFINE INTERACTIONS

Isomer Shift

The nucleus and its electrons interact in several ways, the most obvious being the electrostatic attraction. If the Fe57 nuclear charge distribution were the same for the I = 1/2 ground state and the I = 3/2 excited state, then the electrostatic energy of the system of electrons plus nucleus would be the same for both states. In fact the excited Fe57 nucleus is 0.1 per cent smaller in radius than the ground state nucleus, which causes the Mössbauer transition energy to depend on the electron density at the nucleus. This effect produces the so-called isomer shift of the Mössbauer spectrum, which may be written as,

$$\delta = K \{ Ss \; |y(0)|2 - Sa \; |y(0)|2 \}$$

where δ is the isomer shift, K is a positive constant depending on the change in the nuclear radius, $\Sigma s \; |\psi(0)|2$ is the electron density at the source nucleus, and $\Sigma a \; |\psi(0)|2$ is the electron density at the absorber nucleus.

To allow isomer shifts to be measured independently of the nature of the source, the centroid of the room temperature spectrum of metallic iron has been adopted as the zero of energy and all shifts are measured relative to it. This convention yields,

$$\delta = K0 - K \; Sa \; |y(0)|2$$

where K_0 is a constant. Calculations of δ are difficult to perform, hence its most valuable application is classifying various compounds according to oxidation state, degree of covalency, and coordination number. The 1s and 2s electron density at the nucleus is independent of the chemical environment of the Fe ion.

However, the 3d electrons shield the 3s electrons and cause a decrease in the electron density at the nucleus. The more delocalised the 3d electrons, the smaller the isomer shift. However, this picture is complicated by the presence of Fe 4s character in the bonding orbitals.

The 4s character also reduces the isomer shift, and it is not always clear which of the two effects is dominant. The electronic contribution to the isomer shift is essentially temperature independent and the observed decrease at high temperatures is due to the relativistic second order Doppler shift. This effect decreases the isomer shift approximately 6 * 10 –4 mm/sec for a 1 K increase in T when the temperature is above the Debye temperature.

ELECTRIC QUADRUPOLE INTERACTION

The excited (I = 3/2) state of the Fe57 nucleus possesses an electric quadrupole moment, and the presence of a low symmetry electric field will tend to orient the nuclear spin. The interaction may be written as,

$$HQ = -(Q/6)\,\underline{I}\,\underline{V}\,\underline{I}$$

where Q is the nuclear quadrupole moment, I is the nuclear spin, and $\underline{V}$ is the electric field gradient (efg) tensor. The elements of the efg tensor are,

$$Vij = d2V/\,dXi\,dXj$$

$$i,j = x,y,z$$

where V is the potential due to all charges outside the nucleus and the derivatives are evaluated at the nuclear site. The V_{ij} are the coefficients of the quadratic terms of a power series expansion of the potential about the nuclear site and are given in their principal axis system by,

$$Vzz = \{r(r)\,(3z2-r2)\,r-5\,\}\,d\underline{r}$$

and similar expressions. ρ(r) is the total charge density and the integral is taken over all space outside the nucleus. Also, $\underline{V}$ is real, symmetric, and traceless. Hence in the frame in which V is diagonal,

$$HQ = (Q/4)Vzz[Iz2 - 5/4 + (h/3)(I\times 2 - Iy2)]$$

$$h = (Vxx - Vyy)/Vzz$$

where x, y, and $\underline{z}$ denote the principal axes of the efg and h is called the asymmetry parameter. By convention, x, y, and z are chosen so that $|Vzz| \geq |Vyy| \geq |Vxx|$, which forces $0 \leq h$

≤ 1. Note, V has five independent elements. Two of these are Vzz and h and the other three are the Euler angles locating the efg principal axis system relative to some experimental frame. Reversal of the sign of the nuclear spin will not change the nuclear charge distribution; therefore the efg will not completely lift the fourfold degeneracy of the I = 3/2 states. The quartet will be split into two doublets, while the I = 1/2 states will remain degenerate. Since two transition energies are now possible, two absorption peaks will appear in the Mössbauer spectrum. Diagonalising HQ, we find that the difference in energy of the two peaks to be,

$$DE = (Q/2)\ Vzz\ (1+h2/3)1/2$$

If the recoil-free fraction does not depend on the orientation of the γ–beam relative to the Fe site, a sample with randomly oriented sites in zero applied field will produce a symmetric quadrupole pair. Since the sign of ΔE can not be determined from such a spectrum, the absolute value of ΔE is usually called "the quadrupole splitting." The sign of ΔE is usually referred to as "the sign of Vzz" and is more difficult to measure than the quadrupole splitting.

MAGNETIC HYPERFINE INTERACTION

The Fe57 nucleus possesses a magnetic moment and its energy levels will be perturbed by the local magnetic field. In the presence of a field $\underline{H}$, the interaction is,

$$\mathit{H}M = \text{--}gN\ bN\ I\ H$$

where βN is the nuclear magneton and gN is the nuclear gyromagnetic ratio. gN has the values 0.1806 ± 0.0014 and -0.1033 ± 0.0008 in the ground and excited states, respectively (Lang, 1970).

H will be the sum of an applied field with the internal field of the unpaired electrons. Depending on the magnetic properties of the sample, the internal field may or may not equal zero in the absence of the applied field. A more explicit expression of the magnetic interaction is

$$\mathit{H}M = P\ Sk\{\underline{l}k\ \underline{I} + 3(\underline{r}k\ \underline{s}k)(\underline{r}k\ I)–(sk\ I)–k(sk\ I)\}\ –$$

$$g_N b_N I\, H_{app}$$

$$P = 2\, g_N\, b\, b_N \langle r^{-3} \rangle_{eff}$$

where the sum is over the unpaired electrons, lk is the orbital angular momentum on the kth electron and b is the electron magneton. It is convenient to think of HM in terms of an effective field acting on the nuclear moment. The effective field is,

$$H_{eff} = \underline{H}_{app} + (p/g_N\beta_N)\, \Sigma\{\, l_k + 3(\underline{r}_k\ \underline{s}_k)\underline{r}_k - \underline{s}_k - k\underline{s}_k\} = \underline{H}_{app} + \underline{H}_{int}$$

The first term of $\underline{H}_{eff}$ is the applied field. The second is the field at the nucleus due to the orbital motion of the electrons. The third and fourth describe the field due to the dipole moment of the electrons. The last term is the Fermi contact term which accounts for any net polarisation of the electronic spin at the nucleus. The polarisation of s electron spin at the nucleus stems from the exchange interaction between the 3d electrons and the s electrons. Any admixture of 4s character into the 3d wave functions would also contribute to the contact field. To a good approximation the net spin at the nucleus will be proportional to $\Sigma_k \langle s_k \rangle$, the sum being taken over 3d electrons.

P and k depend on the radial part of the wave functions and on shielding effects which are difficult to calculate. Values have been determined empirically for many complexes. Lang and Marshall (1966) quoted values of $P/g_N\beta_N = -620$ kG and $k = 0.35$ for high- and low-spin ferric heme complexes. $Pk/g_N\beta_N$ is the effective field per unit spin due to the contact term. For the ferric heme complexes it would be –220 kG. For a variety of high-spin ferrous inorganic compounds the survey of Varret(1976) shows $Pk/g_N b_N$ to be approximately –250 kG. Edwards, *et al.* (1967) found $Pk/g_N b_N$ for high-spin ferrous tetrahedral compounds to be reduced to -160 kG by covalency effects.

Experimental Setup

The Mössbauer spectra are ususally recorded in the transmission geometry using a constant acceleration spectrometer operated in connection with a multi-channel analyser in the time scale mode. The source is kept at room temperature and consists of approximately 20 mCi of Co57 diffused into rhodium or paladium foil. The spectrometer is calibrated against a metallic iron foil and zero velocity is taken as the centroid of its room temperature Mössbauer spectrum. In such calibration spectra, linewidths of about 0.23 mm/s were normally observed. The duration of a typical run is a few hours for non-biological compounds and 24 hours for proteins.

Both the source velocity and the address of the active channel of the multichannel analyser (MCA) are controlled by the master oscillator. the oscillator synchronises the source acceleration and the sweep of the memory registers, causing the active channel address to be a linear function of the velocity. In other words, the pulses counted while the source is at a particular velocity are always stored in a particular register.

The master oscillator output is a rounded sawtooth or triangular wave and is applied to one of the driver inputs. The driver is essentially a difference amplifier with its output applied to the vibrator. A pick-up coil on the vibrator supplies a voltage proportional to the velocity of the source and is connected to the second input of the driver. The driver and vibrator form a tightly coupled, electro-mechanical, negative feedback loop, forcing the source velocity to be directly proportional to the master oscillator signal. The desired velocity range is selected by scaling the master oscillator signal before it is applied to the driver.

The gas proportional counter contains primarily krypton or argon plus a small amount of methane quench gas. A 14.4 keV photon entering the chamber through the mylar window ionises some of the Ar or Kr atoms, the creation of each ion/ electron pair requiring about 30 eV. The positive ions drift to the outer wall and the electrons to the center wire. The accelerating electrons ionise more atoms, the effective gas gain being approximately 1000.

The methane suppresses the random motion of the electrons, thus shortening the travel time to the center wire and the rise time of the signal pulse. The overall efficiency of a Harwell Argon counter is 60 per cent at 14.4 keV, and a 14.4 keV photon will cause about 106 ion pairs to be created. The 122 keV and 136 keV photons entering the counter Compton scatter and produce a broad background of lower energy signals. The single channel analyser (SCA) discriminates against most of these, but about 20 per cent of the pulses falling in the 14.4 keV window of the SCA are from this Compton background.

The charge pulse from the counter is amplified and differentiated by the preamp which is mounted as close to the counter as possible. Further amplification of the pulse is provided by the main amplifier and its output is applied to a single channel analyser. The SCA is set to discriminate against the non-14.4 keV signals. The signals accepted by the SCA are added to the current channel of the MCA.

The observed linewidths are larger than the intrinsic width of 0.19 mm/s since some broadening is always introduced by inhomogeneity of the environment of the iron in the source and sample. Additional broadening arises from imperfections in the source driving mechanism. Even so, typical observed linewidths obtainable in the lab are 0.23 mm/s which is close to the minimum predicted by the uncertainty principle.

We now consider the time required to record a Mössbauer spectrum. A typical sample will have 1 mg/cm2 of iron in the gamma-ray beam. For purposes of illustration, we assume the spectrum has two absorption peaks. If the Fe57 is present in its natural 2 per cent abundance, there will be 2 × 1017 Fe57 nuclei/cm2. The peak resonant cross section is approximately 2 × 10–18 cm2 (Frauenfelder, 1963). We divide this value by 8 because of the finite source linewidth, the two absorption peaks of the spectrum, and the estimated product of the recoil free fraction of the source and absorber. The observed intensity will be 5 per cent. The spectrometer will typically divide the velocity scale into 256 channels. For a 20 mCi source the total counting rate is usually about 20,000 counts/s of which about 85 per cent will be 14.4 keV radiation. The spectrometer duty cycle is about 66 per cent and r, the 14.4 keV counting rate per channel, is typically 44 counts/s/channel. The signal-to-noise ratio, S/N, is given by,

$$S/N = ap\ [\ r\ T\ ]1/2$$

where ap is the peak absorption intensity and T is the running time. If we want a S/N of 40, then, for ap = 0.05, T will be 14,500 s or 4 hours. For a given S/N, the run time is inversely proportional to the square of the peak absorption.

Applications of Mössbauer Spectroscopy

Among the drawbacks of the technique are the limited number of gamma ray sources and the requirement that samples be solid in order to eliminate the recoil of the nucleus. Mössbauer spectroscopy is unique in its sensitivity to subtle changes in the chemical environment of the nucleus including oxidation state changes, the effect of different ligands on a particular atom, and the magnetic environment of the sample.

As an analytical tool Mössbauer spectroscopy offers detection limits in the order of billionths of an electron volt.It has been especially useful in the field of geology for identifying the composition of iron-containing specimens including meteors and moon rocks. *In situ* data collection of Mössbauer spectra has also been carried out on iron rich rocks on Mars.

Another significant application of Mössbauer spectroscopy is the study of phase transformations that occur in iron catalysts during Fischer–Tropsch synthesis. While these catalysts initially consist of hematite (Fe_2O_3), during reaction they are transformed into a mixture of magnetite (Fe_3O_4) and several iron carbides. The formation of carbides appears to improve catalytic activity, however it can also lead to the mechanical break-up and attrition of the catalyst particles. This can cause difficulties in the final separation of catalyst from reaction products.

Mössbauer spectroscopy has also been used to determine the relative concentration change in the oxidation state of antimony (Sb) during the selective oxidation of olefins. During calcination all the Sb ions in an antimony-containing tin dioxide catalyst transform into the +5 oxidation state.

Following the catalytic reaction, almost all Sb ions revert from the +5 to the +3 oxidation state. A significant change in the chemical environment surrounding the antimony nucleus occurs during the oxidation state change which can easily be monitored as an isomer shift in the Mössbauer spectrum.

This technique has also been used to observe the second-order transverse Doppler effect predicted by the theory of relativity, because of very high energy resolution.

More recently, Mössbauer spectroscopy has been instrumental in developing an understanding of the structure and function of iron containing enzymes and the model complexes synthesised to mimic the functions of these enzymes. Some examples of enzymes characterised in this way are: ribonucleotide reductase methane monooxygenase, tryptophan dioxygenase, deoxypusine hydroxylase, protocatechuate 2,3 dioxygenase, and cytochrome ba3.

Mossbauer spectroscopy has also been used very successfully to investigate the electronic structure of heterobimetallic complexes.

MÖSSBAUER SPECTROMETERS

A Mössbauer spectrometer is a device that performs Mössbauer spectroscopy, or a device that uses the Mössbauer effect to determine the chemical environment of Mössbauer nuclei present in the sample. It is formed by three main parts; a source that moves back and forth to generate a doppler effect, a collimator that filters out non-parallel gamma rays and a detector.

A miniature Mössbauer Spectrometer, named (MB) MIMOS II, was used by the two rovers in NASA's Mars Exploration Rover missions.

The Mössbauer parameters: chemical isomer shift and quadrupole splitting are generally evaluated with respect to a reference material. For example, in iron compounds, the Mössbauer parameters were evaluated using iron foil (thickness less than 40 micrometers). The centroid of the six lines spectrum from metallic iron foil is –0.1 mm/s (for Co/Rh source).

All shifts in other iron compounds are computed relative to this –0.10 mm/s (at room temperature), *i.e.*, in this case isomer shifts are relative to Co/Rh source. In other words, the centre point of the Mössbauer spectrum is zero. The shift values may also be reported relative to 0.0 mm/s, here shifts are relative to the iron foil. To calculate outer line distance from six line iron spectrum:

$$V = \frac{cH_{int}\mu_N}{E\gamma}\left(3g_n^e + g_n\right)$$

where c is the velocity of light in m/s, H_{int} is the internal magnetic field of the metallic iron (33 T), μ_N is the nuclear magneton (3.1524512326×10^{-8} eV/T), E_γ is the excitation energy (14.412497 keV), g_n is the ground state nuclear splitting factor (0.09062/(I), where Isospin I=$^1/_2$) and g^*n is the excited state splitting factor of ^{57}Fe (0.1549/(I), where $I = {}^3/_2$).

By substituting the above values one would get V = 10.62 mm/s.

Other values are sometimes used to reflect different qualities of iron foils. In all cases any change in V only affects the quadrupole splitting and not the isomer shift. As the IBAME, the authority for Mössbauer spectroscopy, does not specify a particular value, anything between 10.60 mm/s to 10.67 mm/s can be used.

Trends in Mössbauer Spectrometer Designs

The state of the art in the field of Mössbauer spectrometer design is here considered. In this paper, we do not mention the questions connected with laboratory technique (the temperature or pressure chambers, the systems creating external electrical or magnetic fields, and detection devices that use any kind of electron spectrometer) or the developing field of synchrotron Mössbauer spectrometry, where the most attractive opportunities of the Mössbauer effect and synchrotron radiation are incorporated and a special mathematics is created.

Design of the Mössbauer Spectrometer

A Mössbauer spectrometer consists of an analytical bench (or cabinet) and control, energy selection, and storage systems interfaced to a personal computer. The analytical cabinet includes vibro-damping and a carrier platform, a Doppler modulator (DM), a gamma ray detector with built-in preamplifier (D), and guard and shielding collimators (C). The electronic part consists of the Doppler modulation system, the data storage and processing system, and the control devices.

Control, energy selection, and storage systems, together with necessary equipment, consist of: a function generator (FG), modulator drivers (MD), a discriminator with built-in amplifier (single channel analyser) (SCA), storage units (SU), a low voltage power stabiliser unit (LV), a high voltage power supply (HV), and a personal computer. Energy selection and storage systems may be performed in CAMAC, NIM, or Computer Technology.

In the Mössbauer spectrometer, the radioactive source S (or absorber) is attached to the moving part of the Doppler modulator. The function generator (FG) provides start and memory (channel) advance pulses for the synchronisation of the entire system; these pulses are then fed to the storage units (SU). Modulator drivers (MD) produce the control voltage signals for the Doppler modulator (DM), thus making it vibrate according to the preset law of motion. After passing through the absorber, gamma-quanta are recorded by the detector (D). The electric output signals of the detector are received by the preamplifier. The preamplifier, which is located in the detector housing, converts the charge pulse of the detector to voltage and provides matching between detector output and SCA input.

After amplification and shaping of the detector signal, the pulses from the preamplifier are sent to the input of the SCA with built-in amplifier. The amplitude selected and normalised pulses from SCA output are fed for counting to the information input of the SU. The exact matching of the working part of the moving cycles with the channel of the SU is provided by start and channel advance pulses from the FG. High voltage for the detector is provided by the HV (bias) and the stabilised voltages for preamplifiers are supplied by the LV. The counting cycle begins with the arrival of a starting pulse and stops after channel advance pulses have passed. During accumulation, the spectrum can be forwarded to the monitor of a computer using the main programme.

The global characteristics of a Mössbauer spectrometer are velocity range, velocity mode, velocity linearity, velocity time and temperature stability, velocity reproducibility, number of channels, channel capacity, and dead time of the storage system.

The velocity range of ±100 mm/s is optimum for a serial Mössbauer spectrometer, as a greater velocity range is required for only four isotopes (^{237}Np, ^{169}Tm, ^{161}Dy, and ^{238}U), seldom applied in experiments. Linearity of a velocity scale of a spectrometer is the most important parameter, as it defines the quantitative values of parameters of the hyperfine interactions in the sample under investigation. The best spectrometer should provide non-linearity of less than 0.1 per cent.

As, depending on the requirements and tasks of the experiment, it is necessary to apply various laws of velocity – rectangular, triangular, trapezoidal, sinusoidal – it is necessary to consider as the best solution the opportunity of the assignment of a mode of velocity. Time and temperature stability of spectrometer operation is necessary because some experiments continue for a long period of time (from one day to about a month), and this quantity should not exceed an error of defined parameters. The reproducibility of velocity means that we can receive the same value of parameters of a spectrometer at each new switch.

This value usually has a quantity ±0.01 per cent. The number and capacity of channels of accumulation are determined by the complexity of the Mössbauer spectrum of the sample.

The modern spectrometer should provide a variable number of channels, for example, 128, 256, 512, 1024, and capacity within the limits of 10^{24}–1 pulses.

THE DOPPLER MODULATION SYSTEM

Because the system of Doppler modulation is a specific unit proper only in Mössbauer spectrometers. The Doppler modulation system defines the quality of an abscissa axis of a resonant spectrum.

It includes the Doppler modulator (velocity transducer) and a control system (the modulator driver). Various ways of scanning (temperature, gravitational, magnetic, ultrasonic) have been offered, but the most convenient and simple use of the linear Doppler effect has appeared. This technique was offered by R. Mössbauer, and all modern spectrometers have the same logical circuit as the one in our founder's first laboratory set-up.

Doppler Modulator (DM)

Devices for Doppler modulation using rotating disks, screws, cams, hydraulic mechanisms, etc., have been offered, but the most convenient has appeared to be electrodynamic systems.

The calculations in have been shown to lead to the most successful construction of a Doppler modulator (velocity transducer), suggested by E. Kankelait. Construction has been advanced by U. Klein. In, the precision Doppler modulator, which comprises advantages of these modulators, is described. The main advantages of the suggested transducer come from using rare earth magnets and including some irregularities in the construction of moving parts, which scatter the acoustic waves in the material of the parts.

The permanent rare earth magnets form the exterior surface of the working gap. When the permanent magnets are arranged in such a manner, the magnetic field is concentrated in the working gap (more than 0.4 T) and the dissipative magnetic field on the surface of the transducer is less than 0.002 T.

Furthermore, this construction of a magnet system led us to decrease the distance between pick-up and drive coils (70 mm) and makes the mechanical bond of the coils more rigid.

The drive tube is made of aluminum-magnesium alloy. High frequency resonances are dumped by some irregularities (holes, slots, and differences in thickness) in the geometry shape of the drive tube and other moving parts. The introduced irregularities split the acoustic wave started from one edge of the moving part, and the partial waves reach the opposite edge with different phases suppressing each other. On the ends of the drive tube the drive coil (140 turns of 0.22 mm diameter copper wire) and pick-up coil (650 turns of 0.06 mm diameter copper wire) are arranged.

The resistance of the drive coil is 11 Ohm, and the resistance of the pickup coil is 650 Ohm. Flat springs are made of beryllium bronze, 0.4 mm in thickness. Metal springs allow us to move weight up to 200 g (resonance detectors, scattering samples, etc.) and work for a long time at high velocities (more than 150 mm/s). Oscillations of metal spring elements are effectively dumped by a cover of polymer resin.

Modulator Driver (Servosystem)

The first Doppler modulation system of the electrodynamic type consisted of the reference signal generator and a power amplifier. Absence of a chain of negative feedback led to the impossibility of achieving the demanded precision of reproducibility of the given law of motion because of inertial properties of the Doppler modulator and the strong influence of exterior perturbing factors (vibrations, ultrasonic and electric noise). The non-linearity for these systems, as a rule, exceeded 1 per cent.

Later, such a system was replaced by systems with negative feedback. Thus, on drive coil L1 of the Doppler modulator an amplitude and power amplified error signal are fed, where error $x(t)$ is equal to the difference between a reference signal $g(t)$ and a signal of velocity from pick-up coil L2 of the Doppler modulator: $x(t) = g(t) - y(t)$. The maximum attainable velocity precision with a backup loop is limited by the self-excitation stability condition and, as usual, the value of non-linearity is not better than 0.1 per cent.

The velocity scale linearity may be improved by adding to the error signal the signal $x'(t)$, which is the result of action of some functional L on a reference signal $g(t)$: $x'(t) = x(t) + Lg(t)$, and the real form of functional L is defined by dynamic properties of the Doppler modulator. Such approach enhances velocity linearity. Further increase in the precision (highly desirable, for example, in selective excitation double Mössbauer effect experiments) is limited because the real Doppler modulator characteristics deviate from those of an "ideal" modulator.

This demand, involving higher derivatives of the reference signal into the drive system, is difficult to realise in practice. Furthermore, a disadvantage of the modulation system of that type is the need for amplitude adjustment of the components, which are added together with error signal any time the amount of load on the moving parts of the Doppler modulator or frequency of the reference signal are changed. The alternative approach to the problem of enhancing linearity of a velocity scale consists in the use of an additional signal synthesised by processing of an error signal. The procedure for utilisation of this method is as follows: at the zero z(t) signal, the error signal $x_0(t)$ is measured over several Doppler modulator vibration cycles. By its averaging using the formula,

$$Z(t)=\sum_{2=1}^{N} x_o(t-KT)/N$$

(where T is the DM vibration period, and N is the number of vibration cycles over which the error signal $x_0(t)$ is averaged; in practice, the N value may be assumed to be 100), the signal z(t) is determined and then used as an additional control signal which is added to the error signal x(t). As a result, the regular component of the error signal x(t) is removed.

The block diagram of a velocity transducer control system that implements the above technique. The reference signal g(t) from FG is fed into the comparator (C), which generates the error signal x(t) = g(t) – y(t), where y(t) is the velocity signal applied to the second input of comparator from pick-up coil L2 of DM. The error signal x(t) is fed to the first input of the adder (A), to whose second input the signal z(t) is delivered, which is zero for the first several cycles after instrument power switch-on.

The output from adder (A), after the amplitude amplification in amplifier SA via power amplifier PA, is fed into driving coil L1 of DM; that closes the feedback loop through a rigid shaft mechanically coupling coils L1 and L2.

On termination of transients caused by instrument switch-on, the additional control signal z(t) path starts its operation. The error signal x(t), digitised by the analog-to-digital converter (ADC), is utilised by the arithmetic unit (AU) to compute the signal z(t) digital representation array according to Equation.

This array is loaded into buffer RAM of the programmable function generator (PFG) and used to generate the analog signal z(t). Thus, the optimal adjustment procedure of the velocity transducer system is performed automatically.

As reference signal generator FG, a programmable function generator on the base of a 4KX12 RAM and a digital-to-analog converter were used. The FG allows any desired motion law to be generated, and this extends substantially the application area of the Doppler modulation system since, along with the standard modulation law in the form of a symmetrical triangle with smoothed vertices, it is possible to work in a constant velocity mode, necessary to compensate the isomer shifts of untuned pairs (source-resonance converter), in a "region of interest" mode using a trapezoidal reference signal, or in a sinusoidal reference signal mode, needed in experiments using cryostats where the mechanical link modulator's shaft-specimen is much longer, etc.

The digitised error signal from the ADC output is fed via the bus into a personal computer used as arithmetic unit (AU). The computer averages the error signal according to Equation (1) and loads the result via the bus into the buffer RAM of the programmable function generator (PFG) of the same structure as reference signal FG.

The Gamma-Ray Counters and Energy Selection System

The well-known single channel nuclear spectrometer of ionising radiation is used as a recording system of gamma rays in the Mössbauer spectrometer. It includes a detector, preamplifier, amplifier, single channel analyser, and high voltage power supply.

The choice of a particular detector depends primarily upon the gamma energy range of interest. The detector must have sufficient material to absorb a large fraction of the gamma ray energy. The higher energies are more effectively absorbed by higher Z materials. Other parameters are count rate capability, resolution, and, for timing experiment applications, pulse rise time. Registration can be spent both on full-energy peak (photo-peak) and escape peak.

The kinds of detectors used in a Mössbauer spectrometer can be categorised as gas-proportional, scintillation, semiconductor, and resonance counter.

Gas-proportional detectors are used for low energy (in the range 1-30 keV) gamma rays. As a gas admixture, Ar, Kr, Xe with CO_2, and CH_4 (about 10 per cent) are commonly employed.

Scintillation detectors may be used in low and high-energy gamma rays. It consists of a photomultiplier tube to convert the light scintillation pulse into an electric pulse. Solid crystals such as NaJ(Tl) or, when we deal with fast count rate experiments $YAlO_3$(Ce), are used.

Semiconductor detectors, consisting of large crystals of, for example, very pure germanium or silicon, in which minor crystal defects or impurities may be compensated for by lithium, have superior energy resolution and are applied in the low energy range.

The resonance detectors have a selective sensitivity to resonance gamma rays and consequently a unique resolution. The discriminating efficiency of resonance detectors is due to the fact that the resonant absorption effect is used in the detection process. Resonance absorbers, called converters, are actually placed inside the detector volume. As a registration volume, any of the above detectors are used.

The scintillation detectors have high efficiency and high-speed response, the semiconductor detectors possess the best energy resolution, and the gas proportional detectors have the most successful combination of high count rate and energy resolution. When we choose the type of the detector, we should take into consideration the energy spectrum of the parent source nuclei, the resonance radiation energy value, the source activity, and we also should know if there are some additional gamma or X-ray radiations near the resonance radiation.

We can divide the various Mössbauer isotopes into types according to the choice of the best detector. Of course, there are overlapping regions where one can use both, *e.g.*, the semiconductor and the gas proportional detectors. Then the final choice of the detector depends on financial support.

For example, when we deal with ^{57}Fe isotope experiments, we can use gas proportional (Xe or Kr filled) or scintillation detectors (thickness of crystals – 0.1 mm and 0.35 mm for NaJ(Tl) or $YAlO_3$(Ce), respectively); for ^{151}Eu and ^{197}Au we can use the semiconductor detector; and for ^{119m}Sn, the scintillation (thickness of crystal – 1 mm) or the semiconductor detector. Nevertheless, for ^{121}Sb and ^{125}Te recording on photo peak, we should use the semiconductor detector or, if we apply proportional or scintillation detectors, we should record escape peak.

Some more words about newer generation semiconductor detectors – the thermo-electrically (by single stage Peltier element) cooled silicon drift detector (SDD) and the Si-PIN diode. SDDs have excellent resolution (<160 eV for energy 5.9 keV) and count rate up to several ten thousand counts per second, but small sensitivity (typically 5 mm^2). Resolution of SDDs can already be compared to that of Si(Li) or Ge detectors requiring expensive and inconvenient liquid nitrogen cooling. The Si-PIN diode has a bigger sensitivity area (up to 20 mm^2), and for low count shape (about 20 kcpc) the resolution is about 190 eV.

Any type of detector transforms the gamma-quanta energy into the charge pulse signal. The preamplifier, commonly located in the detector housing, serves for the conversion of charge pulse to voltage, signal amplification, pulse shaping, and providing a match between the high impedance of the detector from one side and the low impedance of coaxial cables to the amplifier from the other. The amplifier provides linear amplification of the pulse signal. The single channel analyser (differential discriminator) serves for selection of electric signals by the amplitude.

The ultimate result of this chain of devices is the flux of the electric pulses of the standard amplitude and shape, corresponding to the resonance radiation intensity in the total radiation flux, reaching the detector.

However, this correspondence, as of many measurements, is subjected to systematic and statistical errors that affect the measured Mössbauer spectrum. The perfect recording system should possess maximum recording efficiency, high-energy resolution capability, low noise level, and minimum "dead" time of recording (high count rate stability). These parameters should not depend on external disturbance, entering radiation intensity and the type of the isotope under investigation.

The demand of high-count rate without a loss of resolution significantly complicates recording schemes for any detector type, not speaking of semiconductor detectors. In such cases, a linear amplifier is designed by a two-channel scheme of fast-slow amplification. At the amplifier input, pole-zero cancellation and amplitude overload recovery schemes are introduced. This arsenal of electronic engineering is used for reducing errors in the Mössbauer spectrum and for saving the measurement time.

The Data Storage and the Data Processing Systems

The process of receiving the data concerning the sample under investigation with the aid of Mössbauer spectrometry includes two parts:

1. The measurement of the distribution of the number of gamma-quanta transmitted through the sample or scattered by it as a function of the energy of gamma-quanta–it is made with the help of a spectrum storing electronic system, and
2. The mathematical treatment of this distribution, which consists of the adjustment of the parameters of the physical model to the measured spectra by the least squares technique – this adjustment is carried out on a computer.

The spectrum storing system has evolved substantially since the discovery of the Mössbauer effect. In the beginning, multichannel analysers were used as the device for storage of the incoming information.

The process of data receiving was divided into parts. The spectrum measured by the multichannel analyser was brought on the intermediate data carrier and then fed into a computer for data processing. Later on, with the appearance of rather cheap and effective mini-, micro-, and personal computers, the measurement of the experimental spectra and data processing were brought close together, and the question of the optimum function distribution between a computer and the electronic part of the spectrometer arose.

It is known that there are four main techniques of computer-aided data acquisition:

1. Polling of readiness,
2. Programme interruption,
3. Direct access to the computer memory, and
4. Using an autonomous controller with buffer memory as an accumulator.

Experimental data collection operating in the polling of readiness mode needs the minimum expenditure for design and manufacture of auxiliary equipment, but it occupies the processor 100 per cent by routine operations of the polling of readiness and data transfer.

The programme interruption mode demands more interface complexity, but frees the computer processor of external device polling of readiness and gives it the possibility of performing the data processing simultaneously with the data accumulation. It is necessary to note that when the frequency of entering external service enquiry requests increases, the computer effectiveness lowers, gradually approaching 100 per cent occupation by data transfer operations.

The next step on the way to releasing the processor from data storage operations is to use the direct access to the computer memory mode. From the point of view of the programmer, the data "themselves" are co-accumulated in some array, situated in the address space of random access memory (RAM). When compared to the above-mentioned methods of data storage, the direct memory access mode is most effective from the processor viewpoint. The shortcoming of this mode is that of fixing a RAM region for data storage, which leads to limitation of computer operation. Moreover, the processor effectiveness (fast-response) is reduced, since it has to share the channel with a direct computer memory access device.

It is shown in that the most rational way of data storage from the viewpoint of effective computer use is to employ a special-purpose accumulator controlled by the computer. The accumulator performs the functions of collecting and accumulating the information in its buffer memory, and the computer accomplishes only general control of the accumulator (switches accumulation on and off, cleans the buffer memory, transfers the data from the buffer memory to RAM after a spectrum accumulation). The use of the special-purpose accumulator frees all computer resources and provides for the minimum time of service request processing.

VELOCITY CALIBRATION

This issue is one of the most important among all the others, because the precision and adequacy of the physical information extracted from the accumulated spectrum depends on the solution of this problem.

The main part of the Mössbauer spectrometer is the Doppler modulation system. The value of the resonance effect is rather small; it means that there is no considerable change in the count rate – it doesn't exceed the dynamic range of the spectrometer. That is why the shape of the Mössbauer spectrum and mainly the energy scale are defined by the characteristics of the Doppler modulation system.

The velocity scale for constant velocity spectrometers is derived in a straightforward manner. However, for velocity scanning spectrometers the situation is very complicated. In this case, we are to know the maximum velocity, the law of its change, and also the channel of zero velocity. We also have to know the real law of the velocity change, to recognise if it deviates from the preset one.

There are different ways to solve the problem of velocity calibration:

- *Measurements of Known Hyperfine Splitting Spectra.* This method is definitely a secondary calibration method. Here we can use the magnetic hyperfine splitting spectrum of ^{57}Fe resonance in metallic iron, which is known with good accuracy. If the source ^{57}Co in a metallic iron matrix is used with metallic iron as the absorber, we obtain a spectrum consisting of 19 lines. That is displaced in the velocity range ~10 mm/s and is symmetrical with respect to the zero velocity. It allows us to obtain simultaneously the calibration constant and the position of zero velocity. Accuracy of calibration in this case may be obtained up to 0.1 *per cent.*

However, for many Mössbauer resonances the range of the velocity measured by this method is very small. With a well-fabricated spectrometer giving the linear signal of the pick-up coil at large amplitudes, the velocity calibration could be extended up to 500 mm/s simply by comparison of the peak-up coil signal voltage with the reference signal. This calibration provides accuracy up to 1 per cent.

For calibration of the velocity scale at high velocity and low temperatures in the range from 200 mm/s to 1000 mm/s, one can use the magnetic hyperfine spectrum of metallic ^{159}Tm at 4.2 K.

- *Radiofrequency (RF) Modulation Technique.* The source or the absorber is mounted on the piezoelectric crystal, which is excited by RF voltage of known frequency v. The single resonance line in this case produces side bands on resonances separated from each other by E = h v. That is, to recalculate this energy difference in the term of the velocity, it is necessary to know accurately the value of gamma-ray energy. It should be noted that for many applications the direct calibration of the spectrometer in the energy units, but not in a term of velocity, represents an important task.
- *The Optical Technique.* This technique is based on searching the interferences or the Moiré fringes. Among interferometer methods, one can choose the

Michelson interferometer with a moving mirror, which is attached on one leg of the moving part of the Doppler modulator. The fringes are recorded by photocell and their number is counted and accumulated in the storage device, like gamma ray counting in the real Mössbauer experiment. If we know the light wavelength value, the open state time of any channel (dwell time), and the number of memory scanning cycles, then we can define the velocity in each channel. However, a realisation of this method causes some hindrance when very small or large velocities are calibrated.

The device using the Moiré fringes is based upon intensity modulation produced when light is passed through two gratings moving one relative to another. The variation of intensity is recorded, similar to the fringes produced in the interferometer method.

SOME UNCONVENTIONAL SCHEMES

In all spectroscopic methods, the most important tasks are to achieve the theoretically predicted resolution and to expand the potentialities and fields of the application. If the emission and absorption lines have a natural width, the experimental line width for a very thin absorber will go to its limit $2\Gamma_0$. However, when we deal with poorly resolved or unresolved spectra, for extraction of useful information it is necessary to narrow the spectrum line width. Is it possible to observe a Mössbauer spectrum with a narrower line width?

According to the Heisenberg uncertainty relation $\Gamma_{nat} \geq h\pi\pi$; therefore, it is clear that if we count gamma-quanta in a period of time, which is far beyond the mean lifetime, then we reach the higher resolution. However, for such experiments we must know the moment of the creation of the excited state in order to tune the recording system for the necessary time period. Sometimes we are lucky to have such a possibility.

Let us consider the case of the isotope ^{57}Fe. In this case, as a source we commonly use in experiment the radioactive parent isotope ^{57}Co, which decays due to beta-capture to the isomer ^{57}Fe in the excited state. After the time $\pi = 8.7$ nsec is passed, the "Mössbauer level" with the energy 14.4 keV appears. The recording of the gamma-quanta with the energy 123 keV means the creation of the 14.4 keV level.

Now we turn our attention to two other methods of line narrowing.

Mitrofanov *et al.* have proposed a new type of detector. The substance having the resonance absorption (converter) is put into the detector volume and the recording of secondary radiation created in the converter is performed (resonance detector). The final limitations here are shown by numerical calculation $\Gamma_{exp} = 1{,}47\Gamma_0$.

There is one more advantage of the resonance detector over ordinary detectors. In the transmission mode experiment, they allow the value of the Mössbauer effect to be increased considerably. Furthermore, when we use the emission mode there is no need to use the analyser and the value of the effect attains some hundreds percent. But here we should notice that the use of a resonance detector does not give the real narrowing of the source line width, but leads to the experimentally seen narrowing of the line. What features must the converter have?

It must have the line width of absorption that does not exceed the natural one, then a high value of Lamb-Mössbauer factor, and furthermore the line position of the converter in the energy scale must coincide exactly with the center of the source line. A small discrepancy leads to distortion of the experimental line shape and to the loss of recording efficiency, but a higher discrepancy ($>>\Gamma_{nat}$) makes the resonance melt into the background.

That is why we perform a laborious and unsuccessful, as a rule, search for the source-absorber "resonance pair." In some institutes, for many years they have performed experiments to synthesise iron compounds, searching for a "resonance pair" for experiments with isotope ^{57}Fe. To date, among all Mössbauer isotopes we can find only two effective resonance detectors–those for ^{119}Sn and ^{151}Eu experiments.

Researchers have proposed another method of narrowing, consisting of filtration of the resonance line. For its realisation, we should put between the source and the absorber a substance whose transmission spectrum has a doublet structure. The substance, used as a resonance filter, must also have a large value of Lamb-Mössbauer factor. Furthermore, it is necessary that the center of this doublet should coincide exactly with the center of the source line. Moreover, the value of quadrupole splitting (the distance between doublet lines) must have the optimum value. Numerical calculation showed that the best resonance filter must have the quadrupole splitting to Γ_0 ratio in the range from 2 to 3.5, and the effective resonance filter thickness must not exceed $T_f = 2.5$, otherwise the filter will loose its narrowing effect.

Again, this method leads to searching for a filter substance. This problem is more difficult than in the case of a converter of resonance detector. To date, only the isotope ^{119m}Sn has a substance that can be used as a filter.

It should be noted that we could buy richer physical information; for example, a sign of hyperfine interactions if we deal with polarised radiation (circular or linear). In this case, we must prepare the source of polarised radiation and, for it, we must synthesise a suitable single crystal that has the radioactive nuclei, or find a filter-polariser with the required characteristics.

A universal solution to these problems is the introduction into the Mössbauer spectrometer scheme of additional systems of Doppler modulation strictly synchronised with each other. The selective excitation double Mössbauer effect spectrometer is a good example of the expansion of the potentialities of the technique. For example, Mössbauer transmission spectra of goethite, substituted by aluminum, with the composition $Fe_{(1-x)}Al_xOOH$ have a sextet with spectral lines that are often asymmetrically broadened, or with a predominant doublet. At interpretation of these spectra there are doubts as to the reason for the line broadening. Is the reason the dynamic processes caused by a paramagnetic relaxation, or is the broadening caused by distribution of static hyperfine interactions? For the solution to this problem, it is necessary to measure SEDM spectra.

Mössbauer spectra for two compositions (x = 8 mol % (a) and 2 mol % (b)), which measured in transmission mode (the upper spectra) and in geometry of the selective excitation of various sublevels of the sample under investigation. Arrows indicate which lines are excited. SEDM spectra unequivocally confirm the static, not dependent on time, distribution of hyperfine fields.

8

Mass Spectrometry

INTRODUCTION

In order to measure the characteristics of individual molecules, a mass spectrometer converts them to ions so that they can be moved about and manipulated by external electric and magnetic fields.

The three essential functions of a mass spectrometer, and the associated components, are:

- A small sample is ionised, usually to cations by loss of an electron.
- The ions are sorted and separated according to their mass and charge. The Mass Analyser
- The separated ions are then measured, and the results displayed on a chart.

Because ions are very reactive and short-lived, their formation and manipulation must be conducted in a vacuum. Atmospheric pressure is around 760 torr (mm of mercury). The pressure under which ions may be handled is roughly 10^{-5} to 10^{-8} torr (less than a billionth of an atmosphere). Each of the three tasks listed above may be accomplished in different ways. In one common procedure, ionisation is effected by a high energy beam of electrons, and ion separation is achieved by accelerating and focusing the ions in a beam, which is then bent by an external magnetic field.

The ions are then detected electronically and the resulting information is stored and analysed in a computer. A mass spectrometer operating in this fashion is outlined in the following diagram. The heart of the spectrometer is the ion source. Here molecules of the sample (black dots) are bombarded by electrons (light blue lines) issuing from a heated filament. This is called an EI (electron-impact) source. Gases and volatile liquid samples are allowed to leak into the ion source from a reservoir (as shown).

Non-volatile solids and liquids may be introduced directly. Cations formed by the electron bombardment (red dots) are pushed away by a charged repellor plate (anions are attracted to it), and accelerated towards other electrodes, having slits through which the ions pass as a beam. Some of these ions fragment into smaller cations and neutral fragments. A perpendicular magnetic field deflects the ion beam in an arc whose radius is inversely proportional to the mass of each ion. Lighter ions are deflected more than heavier ions. By varying the strength of the magnetic field, ions of different mass can be focused progressively on a detector fixed at the end of a curved tube (also under a high vacuum).

When a high energy electron collides with a molecule it often ionises it by knocking away one of the molecular electrons (either bonding or non-bonding). This leaves behind a molecular ion.

THE NATURE OF MASS SPECTRA

A mass spectrum will usually be presented as a vertical bar graph, in which each bar represents an ion having a specific mass-to-charge ratio (m/z) and the length of the bar indicates the relative abundance of the ion. The most intense ion is assigned an abundance of 100, and it is referred to as the base peak.

Most of the ions formed in a mass spectrometer have a single charge, so the m/z value is equivalent to mass itself. Modern mass spectrometers easily distinguish (resolve) ions differing by only a single atomic mass unit, and thus provide completely accurate values for the molecular mass of a compound. The highest-mass ion in a spectrum is normally considered to be the molecular ion, and lower-mass ions are fragments from the molecular ion, assuming the sample is a single pure compound.

Atomic mass is given in terms of the unified atomic mass unit (symbol: μ) or dalton (symbol: Da). In recent years there has been a gradual change towards using the dalton in preference to the unified atomic mass unit. The dalton is classified as a "non-SI unit whose values in SI units must be obtained experimentally". It is defined as one twelfth of the rest mass of an unbound atom of carbon-12 in its nuclear and electronic ground state, and has a value of $1.660538782(83) \times 10^{-27}$ kg. The following diagram displays the mass spectra of three simple gaseous compounds, carbon dioxide, propane and cyclopropane.

The molecules of these compounds are similar in size, CO_2 and C_3H_8 both have a nominal mass of 44 Da, and C_3H_6 has a mass of 42 Da. The molecular ion is the strongest ion in the spectra of CO_2 and C_3H_6, and it is moderately strong in propane. The unit mass resolution is readily apparent in these spectra (note the separation of ions having m/z = 39, 40, 41 and 42 in the cyclopropane spectrum).

Even though these compounds are very similar in size, it is a simple matter to identify them from their individual mass spectra. By clicking on each spectrum in turn, a partial fragmentation analysis and peak assignment will be displayed. Even with simple compounds like these, it should be noted that it is rarely possible to explain the origin of all the fragment ions in a spectrum. Also, the structure of most fragment ions is seldom known with certainty.

Since a molecule of carbon dioxide is composed of only three atoms, its mass spectrum is very simple. The molecular ion is also the base peak, and the only fragment ions are CO (m/z=28) and O (m/z=16). The molecular ion of propane also has m/z=44, but it is not the most abundant ion in the spectrum. Cleavage of a carbon-carbon bond gives methyl and ethyl fragments, one of which is a carbocation and the other a radical.

Both distributions are observed, but the larger ethyl cation (m/z=29) is the most abundant, possibly because its size affords greater charge dispersal. A similar bond cleavage in cyclopropane does not give two fragments, so the molecular ion is stronger than in propane, and is in fact responsible for the the base peak. Loss of a hydrogen atom, either before or after ring opening, produces the stable allyl cation (m/z=41). The third strongest ion in the spectrum has m/z=39 (C_3H_3). Its structure is uncertain, but two possibilities are shown in the diagram. The small m/z=39 ion in propane and the absence of a m/z=29 ion in cyclopropane are particularly significant in distinguishing these hydrocarbons.

Most stable organic compounds have an even number of total electrons, reflecting the fact that electrons occupy atomic and molecular orbitals in pairs. When a single electron is removed from a molecule to give an ion, the total electron count becomes an odd number, and we refer to such ions as radical cations. The molecular ion in a mass spectrum is always a radical cation, but the fragment ions may either be even-electron cations or odd-electron radical cations, depending on the neutral fragment lost. The simplest and most common fragmentations are bond cleavages producing a neutral radical (odd number of electrons) and a cation having an even number of electrons.

A less common fragmentation, in which an even-electron neutral fragment is lost, produces an odd-electron radical cation fragment ion. Fragment ions themselves may fragment further. As a rule, odd-electron ions may fragment either to odd or even-electron ions, but even-electron ions fragment only to other even-electron ions. The masses of molecular and fragment ions also reflect the electron count, depending on the number of nitrogen atoms in the species.

Ions with no nitrogen or an even # N atoms	odd-electron ions even-number mass	even-electron ions odd-number mass
Ions having an odd # N atoms	odd-electron ions odd-number mass	even-electron ions even-number mass

This distinction is illustrated nicely by the follwing two examples. The unsaturated ketone, 4-methyl-3-pentene-2-one, on the left has no nitrogen so the mass of the molecular ion (m/z = 98) is an even number. Most of the fragment ions have odd-numbered masses, and therefore are even-electron cations. Diethylmethylamine, on the other hand, has one nitrogen and its molecular mass (m/z = 87) is an odd number. A majority of the fragment ions have even-numbered masses (ions at m/z = 30, 42, 56 & 58 are not labeled), and are even-electron nitrogen cations.

The weak even -electron ions at m/z=15 and 29 are due to methyl and ethyl cations (no nitrogen atoms). The fragmentations leading to the chief fragment ions will be displayed by clicking on the appropriate spectrum. Repeated clicks will cycle the display.

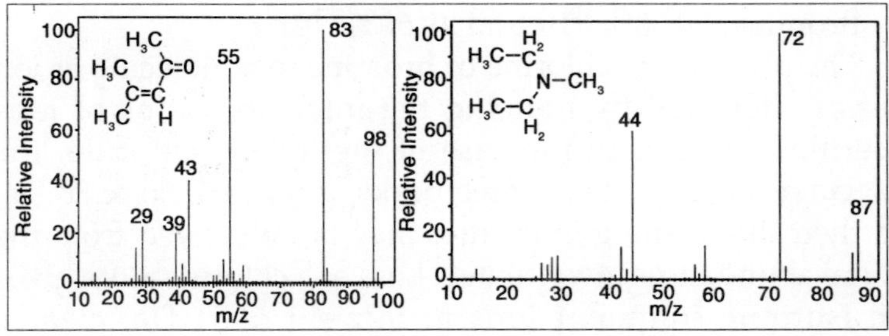

4-methyl-3-pentene-2-one N,N-diethylmethylamine

When non-bonded electron pairs are present in a molecule (*e.g.*, on N or O), fragmentation pathways may sometimes be explained by assuming the missing electron is partially localised on that atom. A few such mechanisms are shown above. Bond cleavage generates a radical and a cation, and both fragments often share these roles, albeit unequally.

ISOTOPES

Since a mass spectrometer separates and detects ions of slightly different masses, it easily distinguishes different isotopes of a given element. This is manifested most dramatically for compounds containing bromine and chlorine, as illustrated by the following examples. Since molecules of bromine have only two atoms, the spectrum on the left will come as a surprise if a single atomic mass of 80 Da is assumed for Br. The five peaks in this spectrum demonstrate clearly that natural bromine consists of a nearly 50:50 mixture of isotopes having atomic masses of 79 and 81 Da respectively. Thus, the bromine molecule may be composed of two ^{79}Br atoms (mass 158 Da), two ^{81}Br atoms (mass 162 Da) or the more probable combination of ^{79}Br–^{81}Br (mass 160 Da). Fragmentation of Br_2 to a bromine cation then gives rise to equal sized ion peaks at 79 and 81 Da.

The center and right hand spectra show that chlorine is also composed of two isotopes, the more abundant having a mass of 35 Da, and the minor isotope a mass 37 Da. The precise isotopic composition of chlorine and bromine is:

Chlorine: 75.77% ^{35}Cl and 24.23% ^{37}Cl

Bromine: 50.50% ^{79}Br and 49.50% ^{81}Br

The presence of chlorine or bromine in a molecule or ion is easily detected by noticing the intensity ratios of ions differing by 2 Da. In the case of methylene chloride, the molecular ion consists of three peaks at m/z=84, 86 & 88 Da, and their diminishing intensities may be calculated from the natural abundances given above. Loss of a chlorine atom gives two isotopic fragment ions at m/z=49 & 51 Da, clearly incorporating a single chlorine atom. Fluorine and iodine, by contrast, are monoisotopic, having masses of 19 Da and 127 Da respectively. It should be noted that the presence of halogen atoms in a molecule or fragment ion does not change the odd-even mass rules given above.

Two other common elements having useful isotope signatures are carbon, ^{13}C is 1.1 per cent natural abundance, and sulfur, ^{33}S and ^{34}S are 0.76 per cent and 4.22 per cent natural abundance respectively. For example, the small m/z=99 Da peak in the spectrum of 4-methyl-3-pentene-2-one (above) is due to the presence of a single ^{13}C atom in the molecular ion. Although less important in this respect, ^{15}N and ^{18}O also make small contributions to higher mass satellites of molecular ions incorporating these elements.

The calculator on the right may be used to calculate the isotope contributions to ion abundances 1 and 2 Da greater than the molecular ion (M). Simply enter an appropriate subscript number to the right of each symbol, leaving those elements not present blank, and press the "Calculate" button. The numbers displayed in the M+1 and M+2 boxes are relative to M being set at 100 per cent.

FRAGMENTATION PATTERNS

The fragmentation of molecular ions into an assortment of fragment ions is a mixed blessing. The nature of the fragments often provides a clue to the molecular structure, but if the molecular ion has a lifetime of less than a few microseconds it will not survive long enough to be observed. Without a molecular ion peak as a reference, the difficulty of interpreting a mass spectrum increases markedly.

Fortunately, most organic compounds give mass spectra that include a molecular ion, and those that do not often respond successfully to the use of milder ionisation conditions. Among simple organic compounds, the most stable molecular ions are those from aromatic rings, other conjugated pi-electron systems and cycloalkanes. Alcohols, ethers and highly branched alkanes generally show the greatest tendency towards fragmentation.

The mass spectrum of dodecane on the right illustrates the behavior of an unbranched alkane. Since there are no heteroatoms in this molecule, there are no non-bonding valence shell electrons. Consequently, the radical cation character of the molecular ion (m/z = 170) is delocalised over all the covalent bonds. Fragmentation of C-C bonds occurs because they are usually weaker than C-H bonds, and this produces a mixture of alkyl radicals and alkyl carbocations. The positive charge commonly resides on the smaller fragment, so we see a homologous series of hexyl (m/z = 85), pentyl (m/z = 71), butyl (m/z = 57), propyl (m/z = 43), ethyl (m/z = 29) and methyl (m/z = 15) cations. These are accompanied by a set of corresponding alkenyl carbocations (*e.g.*, m/z = 55, 41 &27) formed by loss of 2 H. All of the significant fragment ions in this spectrum are even-electron ions. In most alkane spectra the propyl and butyl ions are the most abundant.

The presence of a functional group, particularly one having a heteroatom Y with non-bonding valence electrons (Y = N, O, S, X etc.), can dramatically alter the fragmentation pattern of a compound. This influence is thought to occur because of a "localisation" of the radical cation component of the molecular ion on the heteroatom. After all, it is easier to remove (ionise) a non-bonding electron than one that is part of a covalent bond. By localising the reactive moiety, certain fragmentation processes will be favoured

The charge distributions shown above are common, but for each cleavage process the charge may sometimes be carried by the other (neutral) species, and both fragment ions are observed. Of the three cleavage reactions described here, the alpha-cleavage is generally favoured for nitrogen, oxygen and sulfur compounds.

The complexity of fragmentation patterns has led to mass spectra being used as "fingerprints" for identifying compounds. Environmental pollutants, pesticide residues on food, and controlled substance identification are but a few examples of this application. Extremely small samples of an unknown substance (a microgram or less) are sufficient for such analysis. The following mass spectrum of cocaine demonstrates how a forensic laboratory might determine the nature of an unknown street drug. Even though extensive fragmentation has occurred, many of the more abundant ions (identified by magenta numbers) can be rationalised by the three mechanisms shown above. Plausible assignments may be seen by clicking on the spectrum, and it should be noted that all are even-electron ions. The m/z = 42 ion might be any or all of the following: C_3H_6, C_2H_2O or C_2H_4N. A precise assignment could be made from a high-resolution m/z value.

Odd-electron fragment ions are often formed by characteristic rearrangements in which stable neutral fragments are lost. Mechanisms for some of these rearrangements have been identified by following the course of isotopically labeled molecular ions. A few examples of these rearrangement mechanisms may be seen by clicking the following button.

HIGH RESOLUTION MASS SPECTROMETRY

In assigning mass values to atoms and molecules, we have assumed integral values for isotopic masses. However, accurate measurements show that this is not strictly true. Because the strong nuclear forces that bind the components of an atomic nucleus together vary, the actual mass of a given isotope deviates from its nominal integer by a small but characteristic amount (remember $E = mc^2$). Thus, relative to ^{12}C at 12.0000, the isotopic mass of ^{16}O is 15.9949 Da (not 16) and ^{14}N is 14.0031 Da (not 14).

Formula	C_6H_{12}	C_5H_8O	$C_4H_8N_2$
Mass	84.0939	84.0575	84.0688

By designing mass spectrometers that can determine m/z values accurately to four decimal places, it is possible to distinguish different formulas having the same nominal mass. The table on the right illustrates this important feature, and a double-focusing high-resolution mass spectrometer easily distinguishes ions having these compositions. Mass spectrometry therefore not only provides a specific molecular mass value, but it may also establish the molecular formula of an unknown compound.

Tables of precise mass values for any molecule or ion are available in libraries; however, the mass calculator provided below serves the same purpose.

THE MASS SPECTRA OF ELEMENTS

This page looks at the information you can get from the mass spectrum of an element. It shows how you can find out the masses and relative abundances of the various isotopes of the element and use that information to calculate the relative atomic mass of the element.

It also looks at the problems thrown up by elements with diatomic molecules like chlorine, Cl_2.

MASS SPECTRUM

A mass spectrum is an intensity vs. *m/z* (mass-to-charge ratio) plot representing a chemical analysis. Hence, the mass spectrum of a sample is a pattern representing the distribution of ions by mass (more correctly: mass-to-charge ratio) in a sample. It is a histogram usually acquired using an instrument called a mass spectrometer. Not all mass spectra of a given substance are the same. For example some mass spectrometers break the analyte molecules into fragments; others observe the intact molecular masses with little fragmentation. A mass spectrum can represent many different types of information based on the type of mass spectrometer and the specific experiment applied; however, all plots of intensity vs. mass-to-charge are referred to as mass spectra. Common fragmentation processes for organic molecules are the McLafferty rearrangement and alpha cleavage.

X-AXIS: M/Z (MASS-TO-CHARGE RATIO)

The x-axis of a mass spectrum represents a relationship between the mass of a given ion and the number of elementary charges that it carries. This is written as the IUPAC standard *m/z* to denote the quantity formed by dividing the mass of an ion by the unified atomic mass unit and by its charge number (positive absolute value). This has been referred to as a mass-to-charge ratio, although in some ways it does not fit this description. The IUPAC Gold Book gives an example: "for the ion $C_7H_7^{2+}$, m/z equals 45.5".

Since a mass spectrum *x*-axis represents a relationship between the ion mass and the number of elementary charges that a given ion carries it contains mass information that may be extracted by a knowledgeable mass spectrometrist. Once this is done many mass spectrometrists use dalton (Da) as the unit of mass in order to avoid the clumsy "atomic mass units".

Alternative x-axis Notations

There are several alternatives to the standard *m/z* notation that appear in the literature; however, these are not currently accepted by standards organisations and most journals. *m/e* appears in older historical literature. A label more consistent with the IUPAC green book and ISO 31 conventions is *m/Q* or *m/q* where *m* is the symbol for mass and *Q* or *q* the symbol for charge with the units u/e or Da/e. This notation is not uncommon in the physics of mass spectrometry but is rarely used as the abscissa of a mass spectrum. It was also suggested to introduce a new unit thomson (Th) as a unit of *m/z*, where 1 Th = 1 u/e. According to this convention, mass spectra x axis could be labeled *m/z* (Th) and negative ions would have negative values. This notation is rare and not accepted by IUPAC or any other standards organisation.

History of X-axis Notation

In 1897 the mass-to-charge ratio m/e of the electron was first measured by J. J. Thomson. By doing this he showed that the electron, which was postulated before in order to explain electricity, was in fact a particle with a mass and a charge and that its mass-to-charge ratio was much smaller than the one for the hydrogen ion H^+. In 1913 he measured the mass-to-charge ratio of ions with an instrument he called a parabola spectrograph. Although this data was not represented as a modern mass spectrum, it was similar in meaning. Eventually there was a change to the notation as *m/e* giving way to the current standard of *m/z*.

Early in mass spectrometry research the resolution of mass spectrometers did not allow for accurate mass determination. Francis William Aston won the Nobel prize in Chemistry in 1922. "For his discovery, by means of his mass spectrograph, of isotopes, in a large number of non-radioactive elements, and for his enunciation of the Whole Number Rule." In which he stated that all atoms (including isotopes) follow a whole-number rule This implied that the masses of atoms were not on a scale but could be expressed as integers. (In fact multiply charged ions were rare, so for the most part the ratio was whole as well.) There have been several suggestions (*e.g.*, the unit thomson) to change the official mass spectrometry nomenclature m/z to be more internally consistent.

Y-AXIS: SIGNAL INTENSITY

The γ-axis of a mass spectrum represents signal intensity of the ions. When using counting detectors the intensity is often measured in counts per second (cps). When using analog detection electronics the intensity is typically measured in volts. In FTICR and Orbitraps the frequency domain signal (the γ–axis) is related to the power (~amplitude squared) of the signal sine wave (often reduced to an rms power); however, the axis is usually not labeled as such for many reasons. In most forms of mass spectrometry, the intensity of ion current measured by the spectrometer does not accurately represent relative abundance, but correlates loosely with it. Therefore it is common to label the γ–axis with "arbitrary units".

Y-axis and Relative Abundance

Signal intensity may be dependent on many factors, especially the nature of the molecules being analysed and how they ionise. The efficiency of ionisation varies from molecule to molecule and from ion source to ion source.

For example, in electrospray sources in positive ion mode a quaternary amine will ionise exceptionally well whereas a large hydrophobic alcohol will most likely not be seen no matter how concentrated. In an EI source these molecules will behave very differently. Additionally there may be factors that affect ion transmission disproportionally between ionisation and detection. On the detection side there are many factors that can also affect signal intensity in a non-proportional way. The size of the ion will affect the velocity of impact and with certain detectors the velocity is proportional to the signal output.

In other detection systems, such as FTICR, the number of charges on the ion are more important to signal intensity. In Fourier transform ion cyclotron resonance and Orbitrap type mass spectrometers the signal intensity (Y-axis) is related to the amplitude of the free induction decay signal. This is fundamentally a power relationship (amplitude squared) but often computed as an [rms]. For decaying signals the rms is not equal to the average amplitude. Additionally the damping constant (decay rate of the signal in the fid) is not the same for all ions. In order to make conclusions about relative intensity a great deal of knowledge and care is required.

A common way to get more quantitative information out of a mass spectrum is to create a standard curve to compare the sample to. This requires knowing what is to be quantitated ahead of time, having a standard available and designing the experiment specifically for this purpose. A more advanced variation on this the use of an internal standard which behaves very similarly to the analyte. This is often an isotopically labeled version of the analyte. There are forms of mass spectrometry, such as accelerator mass spectrometry that are designed from the bottom up to be quantitative.

BASIC PRINCIPLE OF MASS SPECTROMETER

A mass spectrometer generates multiple ions from the sample under investigation, it then separates them according to their specific mass-to-charge ratio (m/z), and then records the relative abundance of each ion type.

The first step in the mass spectrometric analysis of compounds is the production of gas phase ions of the compound, basically by electron ionisation. This molecular ion undergoes fragmentation. Each primary product ion derived from the molecular ion, in turn, undergoes fragmentation, and so on. The ions are separated in the mass spectrometer according to their mass-to-charge ratio, and are detected in proportion to their abundance. A mass spectrum of the molecule is thus produced. It displays the result in the form of a plot of ion abundance versus mass-to-charge ratio.

Ions provide information concerning the nature and the structure of their precursor molecule. In the spectrum of a pure compound, the molecular ion, if present, appears at the highest value of m/z (followed by ions containing heavier isotopes) and gives the molecular mass of the compound.

COMPONENTS

The instrument consists of three major components:

1. *Ion Source*: For producing gaseous ions from the substance being studied.
2. *Analyser*: For resolving the ions into their

characteristics mass components according to their mass-to-charge ratio.

3. *Detector system*: For detecting the ions and recording the relative abundance of each of the resolved ionic species.

In addition, a sample introduction system is necessary to admit the samples to be studied to the ion source while maintaining the high vacuum requirements (~10–6 to 10–8 mm of mercury) of the technique; and a computer is required to control the instrument, acquire and manipulate data, and compare spectra to reference libraries.

With all the above components, a mass spectrometer should always perform the following processes:

- Produce ions from the sample in the ionisation source.
- Separate these ions according to their mass-to-charge ratio in the mass analyser.
- Eventually, fragment the selected ions and analyse the fragments in a second analyser.
- Detect the ions emerging from the last analyser and measure their abundance with the detector that converts the ions into electrical signals.
- Process the signals from the detector that are transmitted to the computer and control the instrument using feedback.

ANALYSIS OF BIOMOLECULES USING MASS SPECTROMETRY

Mass spectrometry is fast becoming an indispensable field for analysing biomolecules. Till the1970s, the only analytical techniques which provided similar information were electrophoretic, chromatographic or ultracentrifugation methods. The results were not absolute as they were based on characteristics other than the molecular weight. Thus the only possibility of knowing the exact molecular weight of a macromolecule remained its calculation based on its chemical structure.

The development of desorption ionisation methods based on the emission of pre-existing ions such as plasma desorption

(PD), fast atom bombardment (FAB) or laser desorption (LD), allowed the application of mass spectrometry for analysing complex biomolecules.

Analysis of Glycans

Oligosaccharides are molecules formed by the association of several monosaccharides linked through glycosidic bonds. The determination of the complete structure of oligosaccharides is more complex than that of proteins or oligonucleotides. It involves the determination of additional components as a consequence of the isomeric nature of monosaccharides and their capacity to form linear or branched oligosaccharides. Knowing the structure of an oligosaccharide requires not only the determination of its monosaccharide sequence and its branching pattern, but also the isomer position and the anomeric configuration of each of its glycosidic bonds.

Advances in glycobiology involves a comprehensive study of structure, bio-synthesis, and biology of sugars and saccharides. Mass spectrometry (MS) is emerging as an enabling technology in the field of glycomics and glycobiology.

Analysis of Lipids

Lipids are made up of many classes of different molecules which are soluble in organic solvents. Lipidomics, a major part of metabolomics, constitutes the detailed analysis and global characterisation, both spatial and temporal, of the structure and function of lipids (the lipidome) within a living system.

Many new strategies for mass-spectrometry-based analyses of lipids have been developed. The most popular lipidomics methodologies involve electrospray ionisation (ESI) sources and triple quadrupole analysers. Using mass spectrometry, it is possible to determine the molecular weight, elemental composition, the position of branching and nature of substituents in the lipid structure.

Analysis of Proteins and Peptides

Proteins and peptides are linear polymers made up of combinations of the 20 amino acids linked by peptide bonds.

Proteins undergo several post translational modifications, extending the range of their function via such modifications.

The term Proteomics refers to the analysis of complete protein content in a living system, including co- and post-translationally modied proteins and alternatively spliced variants. Mass Spectrometry has now become a crucial technique for almost all proteomics experiments. It allows precise determination of the molecular mass of peptides as well as their sequences. This information can very well be used for protein identification, de novo sequencing, and identification of post-translational modifications.

Analysis of Oligonucleotides

Oligonucleotides (DNA or RNA), are linear polymers of nucleotides. These are composed of a nitrogenous base, a ribose sugar and a phosphate group. Oligonucleotides may undergo several natural covalent modifications which are commonly present in tRNA and rRNA, or unnatural ones resulting from reactions with exogenous compounds. Mass spectrometry plays an important role in identifying these modifications and determining their structure as well as their position in the oligonucleotide. It not only allows determination of the molecular weight of oligonucleotides, but also in a direct or indirect manner, the determination of their sequences.

SOFTWARE FOR MASS SPECTROMETRIC DATA ANALYSIS

SimGlycan® predicts the structure of glycans and glycopeptides from the MS/MS data acquired by mass spectrometry, facilitating glycosylation and post translational modification studies. SimGlycan® accepts the experimental MS profiles, of both glycopeptides and released glycans, matches them with its own database and generates a list of probable structures. The software also supports multi stage mass spectrometry data analysis which enables structural elucidation and identification of fragmentation pathways.

SimLipid is an innovative lipid characterisation tool which enables structural elucidation of unknown lipids using MS/MS data. The software analyses lipid mass spectrometric data for characterising and profiling lipids. SimLipid can also annotate mass spectra with the lipid structures identified using abbreviations.

ELECTROSPRAY IONISATION MASS SPECTROMETRY

Mass spectrometry is an analytical technique that can provide both qualitative (structure) and quantitative (molecular mass or concentration) information on analyte molecules after their conversion to ions. The molecules of interest are first introduced into the ionisation source of the mass spectrometer, where they are first ionised to acquire positive or negative charges. The ions then travel through the mass analyser and arrive at different parts of the detector according to their mass/charge (m/z) ratio. After the ions make contact with the detector, useable signals are generated and recorded by a computer system. The computer displays the signals graphically as a mass spectrum showing the relative abundance of the signals according to their m/z ratio.

Over the last decade, electrospray ionisation mass spectrometry (ESI-MS) has emerged as an important technique in clinical laboratories. It provides a sensitive, robust, and reliable tool for studying, at femto-mole quantities in micro-litre sample volumes, non-volatile and thermally labile bio-molecules that are not amenable to analysis by other conventional techniques. Coupled with a high performance liquid chromatograph (HPLC) for molecular fractionation prior to mass spectrometric analysis, HPLC/ESI-MS has become a very powerful technique capable of analysing both small and large molecules of various polarities in a complex biological sample.

With the additional separation capabilities of tandem mass spectrometry (MS in a series, commonly denoted as MS/MS), complicated sample purification and procedures for derivative formation commonly used in gas chromatography

(GC)-MS can be much simplified. Together with automated sample introduction, HPLC/ESI-MS/MS is a flow analysis technique for rapid analysis and high sample throughput. The focus of MS manufacturers in recent years has been on the development of MS analysers controlled by user-friendly computer software. Clinical biochemists and other biomedical scientists can manage this technique without an in-depth understanding of the complicated physical processes and mathematics principles.

This section aims to provide a basic understanding of the ESI process, mass analysers, data acquisition, and specific requirements for qualitative and quantitative molecular analysis. Methods for the study of inborn errors of metabolism (small molecules) and haemoglobin variants (macromolecules) will be summarised for illustration of clinical applications.

MASS SPECTROMETRY IN ELECTROMETRY

The Electrospray Ionisation Process

ESI uses electrical energy to assist the transfer of ions from solution into the gaseous phase before they are subjected to mass spectrometric analysis. Ionic species in solution can thus be analysed by ESI-MS with increased sensitivity. Neutral compounds can also be converted to ionic form in solution or in gaseous phase by protonation or cationisation (*e.g.*, metal cationisation), and hence can be studied by ESI–MS.

The transfer of ionic species from solution into the gas phase by ESI involves three steps:

1. Dispersal of a fine spray of charge droplets, followed by
2. Solvent evaporation and
3. Ion ejection from the highly charged droplets. Tube, which is maintained at a high voltage (*e.g.*, 2.5–6.0 kV) relative to the wall of the surrounding chamber. A mist of highly charged droplets with the same polarity as the capillary voltage is generated. The application of a nebulising gas (*e.g.*, nitrogen), which shears around the eluted sample solution, enhances

a higher sample flow rate. The charged droplets, generated at the exit of the electrospray tip, pass down a pressure gradient and potential gradient towards the analyser region of the mass spectrometer. With the aid of an elevated ESI-source temperature and/or another stream of nitrogen drying gas, the charged droplets are continuously reduced in size by evaporation of the solvent, leading to an increase of surface charge density and a decrease of the droplet radius. Finally, the electric field strength within the charged droplet reaches a critical point at which it is kinetically and energetically possible for ions at the surface of the droplets to be ejected into the gaseous phase. The emitted ions are sampled by a sampling skimmer cone and are then accelerated into the mass analyser for subsequent analysis of molecular mass and measurement of ion intensity.

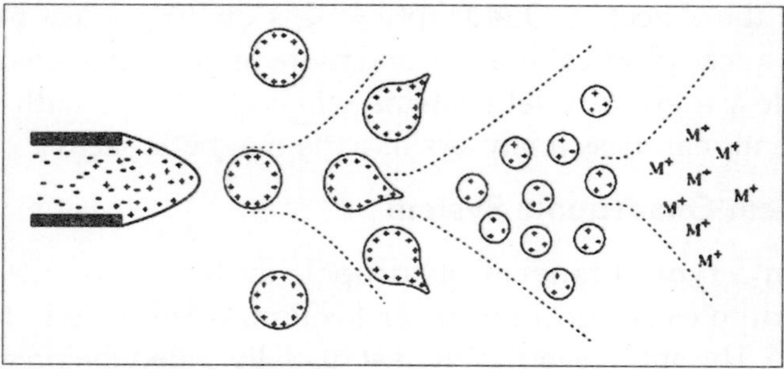

Mechanism of Electrospray Ionisation

To obtain structural information, the precursor ions of interest can be mass selected and further fragmented in a collision cell. The fragment ions can then be mass analysed by a second mass analyser of a tandem mass spectrometer system.

Mass Analysers

The Quadrupole Mass Analyser

When ions travel through a magnetic or electrical field, their movement is affected by their m/z ratio and this is the main principle of separating ions in MS. In the clinical laboratory, a quadrupole mass analyser is most commonly used. In such system, an assembly of 4 parallel metal rods is kept at equal distance. Each pair of opposite rods is connected electrically.

An equal but opposite DC voltage superimposed with a radio frequency (RF) AC voltage is applied to the diagonally placed pair of rods. The resulting electrical field causes the ions to travel forward in the z direction with oscillatory motion in the x-y plane. The amplitude of oscillation bears a unique relationship with the m/z ratio and can be controlled by changing the DC and RF voltages simultaneously in a pre-fixed ratio. These DC and RF voltages can be set so that amplitudes of oscillation for desirable m/z ratios are "stable" with the ions travelling along the z-axis without hitting the quadrupole rods, and finally reaching the detector. On the other hand, the oscillatory amplitudes of undesirable ions are large and "unstable"; they hit the metal rods, get neutralised, and fail to reach the detector. Quadrupole mass analysers are robust, economical, physically small, and more readily interfaced with a wide variety of inlet systems when compared with other conventional mass analysers like the magnetic sector.

Tandem Quadrupole System

In a typical tandem quadrupole system there are three quadrupoles set up in a linear fashion, often called "triple-quad". The analyte ion of interest (usually called the precursor ion) is mass-selected by the first quadrupole (Q1) and allowed to collide with a collision gas (usually argon) in a second RF-only quadrupole collision cell (Q2), where the precursor ions are activated by collision and undergo further fragmentation. This process is known as collision-induced dissociation (CID). The daughter ions resulting from CID are related to the molecular structure of the ions and can be monitored by a third quadrupole mass analyser (Q3) providing structural information of the molecular ions.

This tandem system is commonly denoted as MS/MS in the literature. When Q1 is set to select only one specific m/z ratio, it filters out other molecular ions having different m/z ratios. This is a "purification" step inside the MS system, eliminating complicated and time-consuming sample purification procedures prior to MS analysis.

The following modes of data acquisition are commonly used in a tandem quadrupole system:

- *Product scan (daughter scan)*: Q1 is static allowing only one ion of specific m/z ratio to pass through and Q3 scans the different CID product ions. This mode can be used for studying molecular structure; for example, amino acids sequencing of a peptide molecule.
- Precursor scan (parent scan): Q1 scans over a range of possible precursor ions and Q3 is static focusing on one unique product ion resulting from CID of a class of precursor ions. For example, m/z ratio of 85 is a common fragment ion from all the butylated acylcarnitines precursor ions (C2–C18).
- *Neutral loss*: Both Q1 and Q3 scan together at a constant difference in m/z ratio. This is used to monitor the loss of a neutral fragment for a class of molecules from CID. For example, there is a neutral loss of 102 from most of the butylated amino acids.
- *Multiple reaction monitoring*: Both Q1 and Q3 are static for a pre-determined pair of precursor and product ions. This confers the highest specificity and sensitivity and is commonly used in ESI-MS/MS quantification procedures.

The Ion Trap Mass Analyser

This system, which has become recently available, has the advantages of being smaller in size and cheaper, and being capable of performing tandem CID monitoring. It consists of three hyperbolic electrodes: the ring electrode, the entrance end cap electrode, and the exit end cap electrode. These electrodes form a cavity in which it is possible to trap (store) and analyse ions.

Both end cap electrodes have a small hole in their centres through which the ions can travel. The ring electrode is located halfway between the two end cap electrodes. Ions produced from the source enter the trap through the quadrupole and the entrance end cap electrode. Various voltages are applied to the electrodes to trap and eject ions according to their m/z ratios.

The ring electrode RF potential, an AC potential of constant frequency and variable amplitude, is applied to the ring electrode to produce a 3-dimensional quadrupolar potential field within the trapping cavity. This will trap ions in a stable oscillating trajectory confined within the trapping cell. The nature of the trajectory is dependent on the trapping potential and the m/z ratio of the ions. During detection, the electrode system potential is altered to produce instabilities in the ion trajectories and thus eject the ions in the axial direction. The ions are ejected in order of increasing m/z ratio, focused by the exit lens and detected by the ion detector system.

During tandem MS, the precursor ion is selected inside the trap where an inert gas is introduced for CID. After that, the product ions are ejected for detection. Alternatively, the product ions can be kept inside the trap and another CID reaction can be initiated and this repeat CID reaction can continue for several times (denoted as MS^n in which n is the number of CID reactions). This can help differentiate molecules with similar structures. However, ion trap analysers cannot provide precursor scan and neutral loss modes of data acquisition. For quantification, ion trap analysers are 10 times less sensitive when compared with the tandem quadrupole system operated in multiple reactions monitoring mode.

The Mass Spectrum

The mass spectrum is a graphical display of the relative a bundance of ion signals against the m/z ratios. It is a common practice that the highest signal is taken as 100 per cent abundance and all the other signals are expressed as a percentage of this. Fragmentation of the protonated or de-protonated molecular ions generated from ESI is generally limited, and the mass spectra are relatively simple.

However, multiple-protonation of proteins and peptides occurs in the ESI process, and the ESI mass spectra might become more complicated. The mass spectrum for a highly purified horse myoglobin preparation (5 μmol/L in 50 per cent acetonitrile containing 0.2 per cent formic acid). A single protein will show its characteristic cluster ions containing multiple-charged ions. The number of charges on the protein molecules will depend on the molecular weight of the protein and the number of accessible basic sites (*e.g.*, arginine, histidine, and lysine). Three basic assumptions are made in the determination of the molecular weight of a single protein.

Namely, that

- Adjacent peaks in a series only differ by one charge;
- Charging is only due to proton attachment to the molecular ions; and
- Ionisation occurs to only the intact molecule. To calculate the molecular weight of the protein, one can use 2 simultaneous equations derived from 2 adjacent ions. As an example, for the ion with a m/z ratio = 1212, it has an adjacent peak with m/z ratio = 1131. The adjacent peak must have an additional charge on the molecular ions. Therefore, 2 simultaneous equations can be set up: m/z = 1212, and m/(z+1) = 1131, solving to z = 14 and m = 16968 for the molecule.

The situation becomes more complicated if there are mixtures of different proteins present in a sample. Different MS manufacturers provide their own software for transforming complicated raw mass spectrum into the individual relative molecular masses. A mass spectrum of a mixture of purified alpha-foetal protein glycoforms. The Micromass MaxEnt programme deconvolutes the mass spectrum into the individual glycoforms. In this way, an ESI-MS system designed for measuring the m/z ratios of 4000 Da/e is capable of determining the molecular weight of large protein molecules over 100,000 Da. ESI-MS can also be applied to the study of other macromolecules, for example, oligonucleotides. The accuracy of ESI-MS for protein molecules has been documented to be ± 0.01 per cent when compared with the theoretical amino acids sequence.

Quantitative Analysis

In ESI-MS, the ion signal is proportional to analyte concentration and largely independent of flow rate and injection volume used for sample introduction. The signal is linear from the limit of detection (usually pmol/L) to around 10 mmol/L of analyte concentration. For quantitative measurement, it is important to incorporate an internal standard in the procedure to compensate for losses during sample preparation and variable detection sensitivity of the MS system.

The internal standard should have a structure similar to that of the analyte and the ideal practice is to synthesise an internal standard by incorporating stable isotopes on the molecules of interest. For example, for the quantification of free carnitine (m = 162), an internal standard containing 3 deuterium atoms to replace 3 hydrogen atoms was used (m = 165). When an ideal internal standard is not available, molecules with similar structure can also be used. For example, ascomycin has been used as an internal standard for ESI-MS/MS analysis of the immunosuppressant tacrolimus.

Another critical issue in quantitative ESI-MS is suppression of ionisation due to matrix interference. A biological sample would give significantly lower ionisation signals compared to pure standard solutions with similar analyte concentrations.

This phenomenon is the result of high concentrations of non-volatile materials from the biological sample being present in the spray with the analyte. Possible non-volatile interfering solutes are salts and lipids in the biological samples. To overcome the matrix interference, extensive sample purification processes are required; for example, liquid-liquid extraction and solid phase extraction by disposable columns. However, these elaborate procedures are time-consuming and can cause poor recovery.

A recent development is to use short LC columns (or guard columns) and apply a fast HPLC purification (*e.g.,* for 2–5 minutes) prior to MS analysis. The HPLC serves to separate the non-volatile compounds from the analyte. For HPLC systems with column-switching capability, the analyte in the biological sample can be purified and concentrated on separate columns before MS analysis. Such an automated sample purification system utilising affinity chromatography is best illustrated by a recently published rapid quantification method for transferrin isoforms in serum.

CLINICAL APPLICATIONS

SCREENING FOR INBORN ERRORS OF METABOLISM

One of the most common clinical applications of ESI-MS is in screening for inborn errors of metabolism (IEM). Patients with IEM inherit defective metabolic pathways leading to either accumulation of toxic metabolites, or deficiency in metabolites vital for homeostasis. Many of these defects have serious clinical consequences, including mild to severe mental retardation, physical handicap, and even fatality. Early diagnosis and management of some of these disorders has proven very effective in preventing clinical consequences. Among them only a small number have been successfully screened on nation-wide neo-natal screening programmes; for example, phenylketonuria (PKU) and neo-natal hypothyroi-dism.

The problems with the screening methods include laborious sample preparation, long analytical time, high false-positive rates, and the narrow disease spectrum covered by each method. The principle of the ESI-MS makes this method most suitable for measuring the same class of bio-molecules sharing similar molecular structures, and the MS/MS capability obviates complicated and tedious sample preparation procedures. Since the early 1990s, the use of ESI-MS/MS has revolutionised neo-natal screening for IEM in many developed countries.

Neo-natal Screening for Disorders of Amino Acid and Fatty acid Metabolism

Currently, nation-wide neo-natal screening programmes in North America, Europe and Australia are using automated ESI-MS/MS for metabolic profiling of amino acids and acylcarnitines from blood spots. State-of-the-art laboratories can screen several hundred samples per day. Sampling of blood spots on the Guthrie card, extraction of analytes, formation of derivatives, ESI-MS/MS analysis, and electronic data processing with computer-alert of abnormal results can all be fully automated now using micro-plate batch processing.

Amino acid profiling can detect major aminoacidopathies, such as phenylketonuria (PKU), maple syrup urine disease, homocystinuria, and galactosaemia. In the past, PKU screening required the use of blood samples collected on or after Day 5 of birth, so that sufficient phenylalanine had accumulated for detection by the insensitive Guthrie qualitative bacterial inhibition test. Utilising ESI-MS/MS measurement of the phenylalanine to tyrosine concentration ratio, screening can now be performed with high specificity and sensitivity using Day 1 blood spots.

Acylcarnitines screening is mainly for fatty acid oxidation defects. Examples of IEM being screened are: medium-chain and very-long-chain acyl-CoA dehydrogenase deficiencies; glutaric acidemia types I and II; carnitine palmitoyl transferase type II/ translocase deficiencies; primary carnitine deficiency; isovaleric acidemia/ 2-methylbutyryl-CoA dehydrogenase deficiency; and long-chain hydroxyacyl-CoA dehydrogenase/ trifunctional protein deficiencies. Recently, these cost-effective screening methods have been used to study potential IEM in sudden infant death.

Neo-natal Screening for Galactosaemia

Galactosaemia (incidence, 1: 35,000 in Denmark) is a life-threatening IEM with severe symptoms in the neo-natal period. It is most commonly caused by deficiency of the enzyme galactose-1-phosphate uridyl transferase. In this disorder, galactose derived from ingested lactose in milk and milk products accumulates in the blood and urine, leading to high intracellular concentrations of galactose-1-phosphate that is toxic to several tissues, especially the liver, brain, and renal tubules. Clinical manifestations, including vomiting, diarrhoea, jaundice and lethargy appear in neo-nates shortly after milk ingestion, progressing to coma and death from septicaemia, hepatic or renal failure. Early treatment with a galactose-free diet causes regression of signs and symptoms within 1–2 weeks.

A novel ESI-MS/MS method has been developed for the measurement of total hexose mono-phosphates on blood spots as a marker for galactose-1-phosphate. The procedure is simple and does not require sample processing for derivative formation. A retrospective study has demonstrated a diagnostic sensitivity and specificity of 100 per cent for 12 patients amongst 2055 controls.

Neo-natal Screening for Cholestatic Hepatobiliary Diseases

In prolonged neo-natal jaundice, it is important to diagnose the presence of cholestatic hepatobiliary disease such as extrahepatic biliary atresia; a condition that can result in serious morbidity and mortality. A simple and efficient ESI-MS method has been developed for measuring conjugated bile acids on blood spots, and used in the attempt to set up a neo-natal screening programme for cholestatic hepatobiliary diseases.

However, the segregation of conjugated bile acid concentrations between patients and the general population was insufficient to make mass screening for cholestatic hepatobiliary diseases a feasible option with this method alone. Low birth weight infants without the pathological conditions could also have significantly high bile acid concentrations, thereby affecting the specificity of the method. Furthermore, this screening method is also affected by the significant increases seen in bile acid concentration after feeding. Therefore, accurate sampling time might be required to improve its usefulness.

Screening for Peroxisomal Disorders

The peroxisomes are intracellular organelles responsible for the β-oxidation of very long chain and branched chain fatty acids. Peroxisomal disorders are a heterogeneous group of IEM characterised by impaired, reduced or totally absent peroxisomes. Examples of such include the Zellweger syndrome, X-linked adrenoleukodystrophy, acyl-CoA oxidase deficiency, bifunctional protein deficiency and peroxisomal thiolase deficiency.

Patients suffering from these disorders may have abnormal increases in very long chain fatty acids (VLCFA), pristanic or phytanic acids in serum. Tedious GC/MS methods have been used for the diagnosis of these conditions. A rapid ESI-MS/MS method was reported for screening peroxisomal disorders.

VLCFA ($C_{20:0}$ eicosanoic, $C_{22:0}$ docosanoic, $C_{24:0}$ tetracosanoic and $C_{26:0}$ hexacosanoic acids) in blood spots or serum need to be converted to dimethylaminoethyl esters. The sample purification, and derivative formation procedures are relatively simple compared with traditional GC/MS methods.

Since the final step in bile acid biosynthesis takes place in peroxisomes, another HPLC/ESI-MS/MS method for plasma C_{27} and C_{29} conjugated bile acids has also been proposed, to screen for peroxisomal disorders. This method does not require sample processing for derivative formation.

Screening for Disorders in Purine and Pyrimidine Metabolism

Inborn errors of purine and pyrimidine metabolism have a wide variety of clinical presentations; for example, gout, anaemia, immunodeficiency, kidney stones, convulsions, mental retardation, autism and growth retardation. Diagnosis is based on the presence of abnormal metabolites or the absence of normal metabolites in serum, urine or red blood cells.

An HPLC/ESI-MS/MS screening method has been developed for the quantification of 17 purines and pyrimidines in urine or urine-soaked filter paper strips with a turn-around-time of 15 minutes per sample.

IDENTIFICATION AND QUANTIFICATION OF HAEMOGLOBIN VARIANTS

Since the first report on the successful measurement of large bio-molecules by ESI-MS, there has been a revolution in the identification of protein molecules in biochemical research.

In the clinical laboratory, quantification of glycohaemoglobin (GHb) provides a useful tool for the monitoring of glycaemic control in diabetic patients. ESI-MS has been the recognised technology for development of the reference method. In addition, haemoglobin (Hb) variants need to be identified for the investigation of haemolytic anaemia, methaemoglobinaemia, sickle cell disease and thalassaemia. Occasionally, these variants are detected incidentally because they interfere with the measurement of GHb. ESI-MS has also become the preferred technique for a rapid systematic approach to definitive characterisation of Hb variants.

Quantification of Glycohaemoglobin

GHb is the product of irreversible non-enzymatic glycation of Hb. The percentage GHb represents an integration of the patient's average plasma glucose concentration over the life span of his/her erythrocytes (2–3 months). It has been used for monitoring diabetic control for many years. A recent review reiterated that improved glycaemic control in diabetic patients is strongly associated with decreased development and/or progression of complications.

HbA1c is the predominant species of GHb and is measured in clinical laboratories using either HPLC with ion-exchange or affinity column, or automated immunoassays. Most of these methods have acceptable analytical precision and efficiency. However, they suffer from interference by Hb variants, giving falsely high or low results. Considerable confusion on the accuracy of the methods has been reported due to the lack of international standardisation. The fundamental issue has been the lack of understanding of the specific nature of HbA1c. The use of ESI-MS eliminates this problem.

The IFCC working group on international standardisation defines HbA1c as Hb that is irreversibly glycated at one or both N-terminal valines of the β globin chains. Based on this definition, a candidate reference method was developed using HPLC/ESI-MS. It requires an overnight endoproteinase Glu-C digestion, followed by HPLC separation of the peptides. The

ESI signal intensities of the specific β N-terminal hexa-peptides of Hb0 and HbA1c are used for calculating the percentage HbA1c in the sample. This method was later adopted as the IFCC reference method. Preliminary reference values reported by IFCC, 3.36 ± 0.48 per cent (mean ± 2 SD), were significantly lower than those developed by other methods.

Subsequently, this reference method was modified for adaptation in clinical laboratories. The separation of peptides by reverse-phase HPLC method took 24 minutes. It was improved by using a different gradient mobile phase and analysis time was reduced to 8 minutes. To improve on the specificity of the measurement, multiple reactions monitoring signal acquisition was used. Precision of the method was also improved using signal intensities from both the singly- and doubly-charged peptide ions. To reduce the running cost of the method, an immobilised endoproteinase Glu-C preparation was also introduced. It has been shown that this reference method can overcome interferences by Hb variants. Despite the various improvements to the IFCC reference method, it is still too demanding for routine application.

An alternative ESI-MS method for GHb had been developed. In this method a whole blood sample is diluted 500-fold before it is analysed by ESI-MS for intact Hb globin chains. A typical ESI mass spectrum of normal Hb. The cluster ions have been deconvoluted into true molecular weights by computer softwares. Normal α and β globin chains have molecular weights of 15126.4 and 15867.2 respectively. A mass increase of 162 Da is assigned due to the addition of glucose (mass, 180 Da) and elimination of water (–18 Da). The advantages of this ESI-MS method are that it is simple and fast, with an analysis time of 3 minutes per sample, and can be easily automated. Moreover, it is not affected by Hb variants as variant globin chains and their glycated species can also be measured easily. This proposed method has also been tested for long-term performance. Over a 4-month period of routine operation, the between-assay imprecision was 1.6–5.0 per cent, with results that were correlated well with the HPLC ion-exchange method, and the β-glycated Hb percentage agreed closely with established reference values.

Identification of Haemoglobin Variants

Electrophoresis and automated HPLC are currently the major methods used in clinical laboratories for the identification of Hb variants. However, these methods do not provide definitive characterisation of the variants, especially those with amino acid substitutions not resulting in any changes to the overall charges on the Hb molecule. In the past, definitive characterisation of Hb variants involved tedious and time-consuming analytical procedures requiring days and even months for completion. Recently, a strategy for rapid definitive characterisation of Hb variants was reported using ESI-MS technique. It identified 95 per cent of the Hb variants in over 250 samples with a turn-around-time of not more than 2 days for each sample. The procedure comprises the following steps:

- Molecular weight profiling of intact α and β globin chains by direct ESI-MS on a 500-fold dilution of the whole blood sample. The cluster ion spectrum is then deconvoluted to a true molecular weight scale using computer software that is usually supplied with the MS analyser system. This step can detect Hb variants with molecular weight difference of more than 6 Da when compared with the wild type globin chains.
- Overnight trypsin digestion for investigation of the amino acid substitution on the Hb variants. ESI-MS on the tryptic digest can identify the specific peptide harbouring the substituted amino acid.
- ESI-MS/MS of the target peptide can provide the amino acid sequence of the peptide and thus the position of the substituted amino acid.

Bibliography

Andreev: *Atomic Spectroscopy*, New York , Springer, 2001.

Andrews: *An Introduction to Laser Spectroscopy*, New York, Oxford University Press, 2004.

Sathyanarayana D.N: *Introduction to Magnetic Resonance Spectroscopy: ESR, NMR, NQR*, Delhi, I.K. International, 2009.

Sharma Dinesh: *A Handbook of Spectroscopy*, Delhi, International Scientific Pub, 2007.

Fmiza Hammer, Sarup and Sons: *Inorganic Spectroscopy and Related Topics*, Banglore, New Age International, 2008.

Fritz Helmet: *Mossbauer Spectroscopy*, New York, Dorling Kindersley Publication, 2008.

Arora G D: *Electron and Neutron Diffraction Spectroscopy*, Delhi, Ivy Pub, 2008.

Whitmore G: *Encyclopaedia of Spectroscopy*, Delhi, Ivy Publishing House, 2011.

Michael Hollas J: *Modern Spectroscopy*, Banglore, Wiley Publication, 2010.

Jeanne L McHale: *Molecular Spectroscopy*, New York, Dorling Kindersley Publication, 2008.

John M. Brown: *Molecular Spectroscopy*, London, Oxford University Press, 2005.

Yadav M.S.: *Molecular Spectroscopy*, Mumbai, Arise Publication House, 2011.

Dutta Mala: *Problems in NMR Spectroscopy*, Mumbai, Arise Publication House, 2011.

Sindhu P S: *Elements of Molecular Spectroscopy*, Banglore, New Age International Publication, 2010.

Raghunathan P: *Magnetic Resonance Imaging and Spectroscopy in Medicine: Concepts and Techniques*, Delhi, Universities Press, 2007.

Bhagwan Pooja: *A Handbook of Molecular Spectroscopy*, Delhi, International Scientific Pub, 2005.

Pooja Bhagwan.: *A Handbook of Quantum Mechanics and Spectroscopy*, Delhi, International Scientific Pub, 2006.

Puneet Karnad.: *Organic Spectroscopy*, New York, RBSA Publication, 2007.

Wilfred Sugumar R: *Molecular and Atomic Spectroscopy*, Mumbai, MJP Publication House, 2008.

Tiwari R.K: *Geospectroscopy*, Delhi, Capital Publication House, 2005.

R.L. Laksh, Rajat.: *Infrared and Raman Spectroscopy*, Banglore, New Age International, 2003.

Raghavendra Reddy and Narayan Goswami.: *Applied Spectroscopy*, New York, Pacific Books International, 2012.

Sharma Ramphal: *Fundamentals of Atomic and Molecular Spectroscopy*, Delhi, Himalaya Publishing House, 2008.

Skoog, D. A.; Holler, F. J.: *Atomic and Molecular Spectroscopy*, 4e Svanberg, Springer, 2002.

Vidi Saptari.: *Fourier Transform Spectroscopy Instrumentation Engineering*, Banglore, New Age International , 2010.

Index

H

I

M

N

O

P

R

S

T

U

V